# The Intellectual Dark Web

# The Intellectual Dark Web

## A History (and Possible Future)

Jamie Q Roberts

Pitchstone Publishing
Durham, North Carolina

Pitchstone Publishing
Durham, North Carolina
www.pitchstonebooks.com



An earlier short-lived edition of this work was published by Routledge in 2024 under the title *The Way of the Intellectual Dark Web: What Joe Rogan and His Associates Can Teach Us about Political Dialogue*.

**Library of Congress Cataloging-in-Publication Data**

Names: Roberts, Jamie Q., author.
Title: The intellectual dark web : a history (and possible future) / Jamie
   Q. Roberts.
Other titles: History (and possible future)
Description: Durham, North Carolina : Pitchstone Publishing, [2025] |
   Includes bibliographical references. | Summary: "The book draws together
   and synthesizes the core ideas espoused by those associated with the
   Intellectual Dark Web and critically assesses its origins, coherence,
   and the impact it has had on politics and public discourse"— Provided
   by publisher.
Identifiers: LCCN 2024062099 (print) | LCCN 2024062100 (ebook) | ISBN
   9781634312707 (paperback) | ISBN 9781634312714 (ebook)
Subjects: LCSH: Communication in politics—United States. | Dark
   Web—History. | Intellectuals—United States. | Political
   science—Philosophy. | Freedom of speech—United States. | Mass
   media—Political aspects—United States.
Classification: LCC JA85.2.U6 R627 2025  (print) | LCC JA85.2.U6  (ebook) |
   DDC 320.97301/4—dc23/eng/20250214
LC record available at https://lccn.loc.gov/2024062099
LC ebook record available at https://lccn.loc.gov/2024062100

# Contents

*The ideal subject of totalitarian rule is not the convinced Nazi
or the convinced Communist, but people for whom the distinction between
true and false no longer exists.*

Arendt

*Of all the passions capable of enslaving man's will, none is more
incompatible with reason and liberty than religious fanaticism.*

Robespierre

*Tir'd with all these, for restful death I cry,
As, to behold desert a beggar born,
And needy nothing trimm'd in jollity,
And purest faith unhappily forsworn,
And gilded honour shamefully misplac'd,
And maiden virtue rudely strumpeted,
And right perfection wrongfully disgrac'd,
And strength by limping sway disabled,
And art made tongue-tied by authority,
And folly, doctor-like, controlling skill,
And simple truth miscall'd simplicity,
And captive good attending captain ill.
Tir'd with all these, from these would I be gone,
Save that, to die, I leave my love alone.*

Shakespeare

*Fuck you I won't do what you tell me*

Rage Against the Machine

# Preface: 'The IDW Just Won the Election!'

This book was originally published in early 2024 by an academic publisher. Two weeks after being released it was suspended from sales following a complaint or complaints. Despite asking the publisher, I never learned who complained nor the nature of the complaint(s). The publisher investigated the book and determined that the book could not return to sales in its current form. The issue, it turns out, was not the content itself – what the complaint was about – but that the book was not sufficiently scholarly; amongst other things, it needed to engage more with 'theory'.

When I decided to write a book about the Intellectual Dark Web (IDW), I knew I didn't want to write a 'scholarly' work. In the spirit of the IDW, I wanted the book to be accessible to a wide audience. But I also knew that engaging with 'scholarship' would likely weaken the book. Don't get me wrong, I admire the punctilious efforts of genuine Historians, Archaeologists, Political Scientists and so on. However, for some time, the Arts and Social Sciences have been a political monoculture. And much of what's published isn't genuine scholarship, but pseudo-intellectual guff, whose purpose is to signal group membership and allow mediocre people to build careers without doing anything genuine. This point is made by the IDW itself. If I included this pseudo-scholarship, it would be like including Astrology in a book about Psychology (well, almost). Ok, I would then spend my words debunking the dodgy scholarship, but then I'd be writing a different book – I wouldn't be providing an account of the Intellectual Dark Web. However, even if I did dedicate the book to debunking dodgy scholarship, I doubt this would have been satisfactory. When people in the academic world say they want you to 'engage with theory', they expect a degree of homage – enough so that whatever you write becomes meaningless for anyone outside the academic world. It's all part of the grooming process that allows the academia-publishing complex to continue. In Chapter 8 I quote Peter Thiel, who says that if the academic world and the heterodox world that this book is a part of 'came into contact', then 'they wouldn't both be able to exist'. This is exactly how it is.

I had, from the outset, made my intentions clear to my editor, who was a decent guy. But people move on. And the organization sniffs you out in the end.

Portentously, a week before the book was published, a friend of mine said (I have the WhatsApp voice note): 'I do hope you get in trouble. Like not too much trouble, but just enough trouble for it to be fun. That would be really interesting, and I guess that would kind of put you as a character inside your own book … You'd be able to experience firsthand what you are writing about.' So here I am, a character in my own book. Am I having fun? Sure, why not. At least it became a lot more fun when Pitchstone agreed to republish the book.

Anyway, on to the Intellectual Dark Web and this version of the book. The original manuscript was completed in mid-2023. It's now late 2024. I haven't changed the original version. However, there have been considerable developments in recent months worthy of comment.

When writing the book, my sense was that even though people didn't much refer to the Intellectual Dark Web anymore, the figures from the IDW were continuing on similar trajectories, and IDW ideas had become part of the cultural landscape – at least in the realm of independent media. But as the 2024 US election approached, several IDW figures surged into political prominence.

The story goes something like this. Given that many within the IDW were from the left, there was some hope in the mid to late teens that IDW ideas might spark a reinvigoration of the left – a Rebel Wisdom podcast featuring Helen Pluckrose and Peter Boghossian was titled 'Fighting Postmodernism from the Left'. Such ideas include the belief that open, good faith discussions are the path to truth; that people ought to be judged on their character, not the colour of their skin or their sex; and that a society that turns its back on merit and ultimately on the creative spirit will decline.

However, in recent years, not only did it become clear that the left was doubling down on its censorious and even cruel Identity Politics, but that it was the right that was starting to take up the values that were once at the core of moderate progressive politics. Vivek Ramaswamy, 2024 Republican presidential candidate, appeared on Jordan Peterson's podcast on 21 March 2023 and spoke about the emergence of the 'new left' and Wokism. A friend shared the podcast with me and I replied 'Sounds just like the IDW book!! All the same stuff. And the same ultimate message: it's all about the spirit. And everyone is crushing the spirit.'

Then, as Donald Trump's run into the 2024 election gathered pace, several IDW figures – all erstwhile Democrats – gathered around him. Elon Musk endorsed Trump following the assassination attempt on Trump on 13 July 2024, and Tulsi Gabbard became involved with Trump's campaign in August. Robert F Kennedy Jr, who had been running for president as an independent, also joined the team in August; and even though I hadn't mentioned him in this book, he has an IDW flavour – he appeared on Joe Rogan's podcast in June 2023. In the week prior to the November 5 election, Rogan hosted Trump, JD Vance – Trump's running mate – and Musk on his podcast. These conversations, each of which lasted for around 3 hours, accrued more than 50 million views on YouTube alone prior to the election. On the day before the election Rogan endorsed Trump. This was, for Rogan, a change of heart.

It makes sense that some IDW figures have aligned with Trump. Both the IDW and Trump are Populist. Populism can be understood as the virtuous people standing against the corrupt elites. 'Populism' is often a derogatory term – it construes the people not as virtuous, but as a naïve rabble that is manipulated by a demagogue. But when the elites are corrupt, and when the people are not as naïve as some might think, Populism starts to look more reasonable. I am reminded of Oliver Anthony's recent anthem: 'Rich Men North of Richmond'. He sings: 'These rich men north of Richmond, Lord knows they all just wanna have total control. Wanna know what you think, wanna know what you do, and they don't think you know, but I know that you do.'

The IDW can be understood as a broad-based (spanning the left and right) populist movement. It primarily critiqued academia and mainstream media, but also the corporate world, government and Hollywood. As Democrats increasingly became aligned with Woke corporations, and as Republicans increasingly supported values that were once associated with the left, like free speech, it became possible for erstwhile Democrats Musk, Gabbard, RFK Jr, and Rogan to get behind Trump. Yes, they could have sat this one out – lifelong Democrat and central IDW figure Eric Weinstein refused to endorse a candidate – but sometimes, especially in a binary system, people take a side.

When Trump won, I exclaimed: 'My God. The Intellectual Dark Web just won the election!' Musk, Ramaswamy, Gabbard, and RFK Jr will likely all figure prominently in Trump's new administration. The IDW is not so dark anymore.

To finish, here is a summary of my current thinking about the IDW:

1. The appearance of the IDW demonstrates yet again that 'truth will out'. Many of us have been incensed for decades about the state of academia. And once the nihilistic and pernicious ideas cooked up in the academy reached critical mass in wider society, there was sufficient demand that a collection of enterprising intellectuals and broadcasters could arise who pushed back.

2. The IDW and the podcast phenomenon more broadly is a notable instance of new technology being used to democratise knowledge. Certainly, people always grumble in private when faced with a censorious public realm or corrupt institutions. But every now and then new technology allows an explosion of dissent. Centuries ago the printing press allowed people to produce pamphlets and the like that challenged the dogmas of the Catholic Church. The internet and podcasts have performed a similar function in relation to the dogmas of academia and mainstream media.

3. The IDW is a part of a broad-based Populist movement that contends that our elite class is increasingly corrupt. These elites are found in academia, the media, government, the corporate world and entertainment.

4. For better and worse, the IDW is part of the eternal dialectic between institutionalization and freedom. In good times, institutions put in place mechanisms that keep us on the rails of the true and the good. These mechanisms span everything from education to regulation. When institutions become corrupt, the mechanisms are perverted

by people who have no special interest in the true and the good, and who use the institutions to build careers and pursue power. Not only do these people produce 'false positives' – their own bogus work – the now corrupt institutions produce 'false negatives' – they silence genuine work. Silencing is necessary because the genuine work is obviously a threat to those who produce bogus work. The IDW and the podcast phenomenon more generally has its own dynamic. It has provided a way for silenced work to be heard – the false negatives have a chance of becoming true positives. But because the world of independent media tilts much more towards freedom, it also gives a voice to bogus ideas – it produces its own false positives. It's double-edged. This is exactly how it was with the printing press: revolutionary ideas mingled with fearmongering about witches. However, I would prefer to live in a world that entertains false positives in its search for true positives, rather than one that necessarily produces false negatives to protect the false positives. In short: I'll take a few more conspiracy theories if it means that genuine ideas can have a voice. This is Joe Rogan's podcast in a nutshell.

5.  The IDW is a part of an attempt to revitalise or replace our ailing institutions. For example, the IDW has attempted to revitalise universities by criticizing them. And some within the IDW have also started new institutions: IDW figures Niall Ferguson, Bari Weiss, Bret Weinstein, Heather Heying, Ayaan Hirsi Ali, and Andrew Sullivan were behind the creation of the University of Austin. And recently, the Peterson Academy has opened its doors. But most notably, within the Trump administration, Musk will head the 'Department of Government Efficiency' whose purpose is to slash government bureaucracy.

6.  The IDW has been at the vanguard of, or at least has been metonymic of, the political realignment we are witnessing in the West. I wouldn't say that the left and right have inverted. However, several traditional left-wing values, such as championing free speech, merit, and even eccentricity, are now associated with the right.

7.  Matt Stone, one of the creators of the show *South Park*, famously said, 'I hate conservatives but I really fucking hate liberals'. Perhaps it is this that best characterises the IDW's centrist or centre-right politics.

# Acknowledgements

I'd like to thank all the people from the Intellectual Dark Web for helping me endure the mad university world. Huge thanks also to Pitchstone for publishing this book after I parted ways with my original publisher. Thanks to my family, friends, and students for talking with me about the ideas in this book and reading drafts. Amongst many others: Max Roberts, Michael Roberts, Susie Roberts, Gillian Roberts, Peter Shelling, Dale Roberts, Catherine Garruto Shelling, Peter Davis, Daniel Respall, Tim Scriven, George Aroney, Nick Hatzakos, Tom Wilkins, Stuart Rollo, James Bedford, Michael Rossiter-Thornton, John Delf, Nicholas Moll and of course, Yitzi Tuvel and Katherine. And special thanks and love to Bonnie Fisher: stay wild. May we drive onwards towards the true, the good and the beautiful and turn away from cruelty. Though God knows it ain't easy – cruelty wears many guises.

# Introduction

In the third *Alien* movie – back when there was still some hope for the franchise – Ripley is seeking the alien in a gloomy, industrial chamber on a sparsely populated prison planet. In the light of Ripley's torch, the various pipes, cables, and conduits – made all the more sinister by the Ridley Scott-style trickling water – appear like parts of the alien. It's a bit overdone, but nonetheless, the tension builds. As Ripley prepares to strike what she thinks is the alien, she says, 'You've been in my life so long, I can't remember anything else'.[1]

Thus it has been for me with the subject matter of this book. It was 2002. I was completing my honours (fourth) year dissertation within an English department. Drawing on literature I was exploring the dark side of male desire. My sense was that there are two ways for men to romantically connect with women. In the first, you fall in love with someone and commit to her; you are honest with her and care about her well-being. In the second – the dark side – you use confidence to seduce someone; you employ deception and you don't really care about her well-being. It is the distinction between, say, the good husband and the pickup artist – though I grant that it's something of a continuum. I studied Feminism, and I found that Liberal Feminism, which was dominant at the time, and perhaps still is, never mentioned the dark side, despite encouraging women to have lots of sex. Surely it makes sense, I thought, to ask: what are the types of men that women are having lots of sex with, and what are the implications of this not just for relationships, but for broader society?[2]

Turns out, these were not the kinds of questions you were meant to ask. My supervisor strongly suggested that I begin my dissertation by explaining to my readers – all three of them, including her – that I was a man and that this should be taken into account when considering my arguments. She couldn't exactly tell me that I wasn't allowed to make the arguments I was making, but she could push for me to denounce myself. I kept thinking: my arguments should stand or fall based on the reasoning and evidence I provide. And whether I begin my dissertation by outing myself as a male won't change my reasoning and evidence in any way. I also thought, it wasn't as if I ever saw an academic begin an article by saying 'I have built my career by following academic fashions, so please disregard whatever I write'. But what bothered me most was how annoyed my supervisor became when I tried to argue with her about these and other things. For her, I was just wrong. And that was the end of the story. I wasn't even allowed to get to the start line of discussion.

I refused to do what she asked. If I had acquiesced, I would have written something I didn't believe and the entire enterprise I had embarked on would have been pointless. I was so naïve that I complained. I was certain that everyone would see that my supervisor was doing it all wrong.

Needless to say, it didn't go well. And I learned fear, and for the most part, silence. Shame on me.

Back in 2002 I thought my supervisor was an anomaly. But in the subsequent years and decades I saw it all again and again, first within the university, then increasingly throughout broader society. Now Identity Politics and its epistemological forebear, Postmodernism, are everywhere. It is commonplace, for example, to find people assuming that truth is not got at through reasoning and evidence, but rather, is a property of identity, such that some people just know it and others don't – and can't. And various dubious claims are protected by aggressively policed taboos. The most famous of these from recent times are the Orwellian paradox, 'Transwomen are women' and the circular, language-disintegrating definition, 'A woman is someone who identifies as a woman'.

For a long time I thought there was no broad opposition to what I was seeing. Sure, I had come across scattered articles by dissenting academics. And I'd also encountered Steven Pinker; he had helped me feel less bad about saying 'truth' –for the first decades of the 2000s, 'truth' was the c-word of the university. But that was it. Then, in May 2018, a student of mine with whom I had argued about politics, sent me Bari Weiss's *New York Times* article 'Meet the Renegades of the Intellectual Dark Web'[3] and said that this was me.

He was right.

I began to take an interest in the IDW, and I learned that all the university guff that I had been battling – alone and badly – was being energetically opposed by a collection of charismatic academics, public intellectuals, journalists, and entertainers. And the battle was not being fought within the universities or the traditional media, but on YouTube and in particular, on podcasts.

By 2018 the scale of the IDW was staggering, and the audience of many of the central figures has only grown since then. At the heart of the IDW is Joe Rogan's hugely popular podcast: The Joe Rogan Experience – episodes regularly have over 10 million listeners. The podcast helped popularise other IDW figures, including Psychologist and academic Jordan Peterson,[4] Neuroscientist and public intellectual Sam Harris, political commentators Ben Shapiro and Dave Rubin (Harris, Shapiro and Rubin were already well known), Mathematician Eric Weinstein, and Evolutionary Biologist and academic Bret Weinstein. And beyond these are 50 or more others who have appeared on Rogan or associated with the other central IDW figures, including British public intellectuals Douglas Murray and Stephen Fry and the sometimes richest man in the world, Elon Musk. To gain a further sense of the scale of the IDW, when I enter 'Jordan Peterson' in YouTube and filter for view count, the top four videos, which include two of Peterson's Rogan appearances, have nearly 200 million views (as of October 2023). And to quote one of my younger friends who read a draft of this book: 'Especially for young people, the IDW is one of the most salient political/intellectual forces of the last decade.'

So, what does the IDW stand for – what is its way? While the IDW is not unified, the same concerns and values arise again and again. At the core of the IDW is the conviction that dodgy Progressive orthodoxies that originated within universities have spread across wider society, including the media and corporate world, and degraded our regard for truth, evidence, reasoning, free speech and civil discussion – all traditional Liberal or Enlightenment values – and imposed their own sort of intellectual tyranny. Elon Musk refers to this phenomenon as the 'Woke mind virus'.[5] Some in the IDW think that this virus is a civilisation-level threat.

There are many ways into the IDW, but the following remarks made in September 2022 on UK podcast Triggernometry (a British Joe Rogan Experience, albeit with a narrower political focus) by British satirist and IDW associate, Andrew Doyle, get us close to the heart of the matter. Doyle, who is the creator of the spoof Twitter account, Titania McGrath, is the author of *The New Puritans: How the Religion of Social Justice Captured the Western World* (2022). In the book he compares the current Social Justice movement, which is closely related to Identity Politics, with the Salem witch trials. He talks about how the mania in Salem came to an end, and what we can learn from this:

> So I think it will just take people to stand up and say no, the witches aren't real, we don't live in a country which is full of fascists, we can look at the evidence again, and make our judgement based on evidence, not based on lived experience and feelings. And if everyone just did that, if all the people in power just did that, this would end.[6]

Co-host Francis Foster points out that in Arthur Miller's *The Crucible*, which is about what occurred in Salem, the people who wouldn't submit were killed. Doyle says that the stakes are not so high these days. But he does say, 'It will be horrible for some. But it makes it easier, doesn't it, for the people to speak out later.' This is the way of the IDW. You speak up and say the witches are not real. Steven Pinker, in conversation with Jordan Peterson about the IDW, makes a similar remark:

> I think it [membership of the IDW] just comes from … not having drunk the Kool-Aid of Political Correctness, Identitarianism, Social Justice warfare, Wokeness. As long as you are not part of that tribe, as long as you haven't signed up to that, you get associated with this whimsical, humorous entity called the Intellectual Dark Web.[7]

Pinker and Peterson also talk about the fear of the Woke mob coming for them, but they remind themselves that the Woke mob is nothing compared with the hardships that IDW figure Ayaan Hirsi Ali experienced in her early years in Somalia.

But what is the meaning of the name 'The Intellectual Dark Web'? The Dark Web is a hidden part of the internet that requires special software and the like to access. It is where illicit things occur that are difficult to pull off on the normal internet – the 'Clearnet'. In coining the term, Eric Weinstein's serious joke was that the ideas discussed by IDW types stood in relation to mainstream ideas as the Dark Web stands in relation to the Clearnet.[8]

This book will provide an overview of the way of the IDW. For the most part I will present the IDW as it sees itself. I will point out problems with the IDW, but I do not have the space to thoroughly analyse each IDW claim: my aim is to reveal the IDW forest, not deliver an intimate understanding of each tree – it's a tradeoff. But also, this book is not a clever takedown of the troglodytes.

As for method. The IDW has produced and appeared in vast amounts of material. This includes ten thousand or more long-form podcasts (long conversations) and videos, as well as books, articles, and tweets. I will focus on the long-form podcasts. This is because it has been through these that so many have got to know the IDW. But also, the way of the IDW is inseparable from the podcast form itself: the medium is the message. IDW figure Lex Fridman, who has his own successful podcast, says, 'That's one of the reasons I love long-form podcasting. If you talk more than 10 minutes, it's hard to have a wall up. It all kind of crumbles away'.[9] For Fridman and others in the IDW, the message which flows from the long-form podcast is that extended open discussions are a pathway to truth. The point also is that IDW figures such as Joe Rogan established their podcasts on a shoestring budget, and they continue to run their podcasts as they see fit, without interference from producers and management – as occurs in traditional media. Though podcasts are subject to their own corruptions.

It would have been useful to survey the IDW's audience. This is important because, as David French says in an 11 May 2018 article that was part of the flurry of responses to Weiss's seminal 8 May article, the IDW is about the audience:

> Critics Miss the Point of the 'Intellectual Dark Web' … [It] isn't really about the speakers. It's about their audience … The acolytes of these free-thinkers aren't powerful. They haven't pushed through Political

Correctness. Instead, they live in fear of speaking their minds. They are growing weary of propaganda, yet many of the standard avenues for education and self-improvement now speak with one voice and permit little dissent. They fear that even asking questions could endanger their livelihoods and ruin their public reputations.[10]

However, in the absence of a larger survey, I will, as I have been doing, sometimes reflect on my own IDW-related experiences, mostly within the university. I am wary of generalising from personal experiences, yet at the same time, we dissenters do all seem to be having the same experiences – but this is not surprising given the ubiquity and one dimensionality of Identity Politics and Postmodernism.

Finally, a word about the time frame. While the IDW 'moment' was roughly between 2016 and 2020, considerable IDW material was produced before 2016. And since 2020, the same figures have remained active, continue to pursue largely unchanged agendas, still associate with one another, and importantly, reflect on earlier years. Thus, while I will concentrate on the period from 2016 to 2020, I will draw on material from before and after this.

Part 1 will introduce the main figures, outline the unifying characteristics and broad political positions within the IDW, and discuss the IDW's several origins. Part 2 will explore some additional IDW talking points. The Appendix will list the people associated with the IDW.

**Notes**

1   Movieclips 2015 June 6: 0:01:15.
2   As I will discuss later, it is interesting that this issue has been pursued by some within the IDW. Jordan Peterson and Bret Weinstein have addressed it directly, but others such as Konstantin Kisin and Francis Foster have had guests on their show that explore similar territory. The gist of the argument is that the sexual revolution hasn't been an unequivocal good for women because it has legitimized and even encouraged less desirable male behaviour.
3   Weiss 2018 May 8.
4   Peterson credits his Rogan appearances with contributing to his prominence (British GQ 2018 October 30: 0:02:40).

5 An early use of the term by Musk was when he was interviewed by The Babylon Bee (2022 December 21: 0:05:00).
6 Triggernometry 2022 September 8: 0:18:24.
7 Jordan B Peterson 2019 August 11: 57:34.
8 Sam Harris 2018 January 6 (The part where Weinstein mentions the IDW is behind a paywall. However the full video can be found on ThinkingAtheist 2018 March 22: 1:51:39). Eric Weinstein explains his thoughts about the name 'Intellectual Dark Web' in another video (see Eric Weinstein 2018 June 8).
9 Lex Fridman 2022 June 5: 1:02:52.
10 French 2018 May 11.

# Part One: An Overview of the IDW

# 1

# Who Was in the IDW?

## IDW Patient Zero

On 7 January 2015, 12 people were killed and 11 injured in the offices of the French satirical weekly newspaper *Charlie Hebdo*. The gunmen were two Muslim brothers. On 8 January 2015, an *Al Jazeera* interviewer was discussing the *Charlie Hebdo* massacre with three guests, one of whom was author and public intellectual Douglas Murray. The interviewer asks Murray: 'Do you think this attack will underscore the message of the far-right in Europe at least, of the incompatibility of Islam and the West or Western values?' Dour-faced Murray responds:

> That's a pretty atrocious question if I may say so. We are about 24 hours away from 12 people being gunned down in a newspaper office in the centre of Paris in a European city because they offended, allegedly, Islamic blasphemy laws; blasphemy laws which France, Britain and other European countries do not have and do not believe in and do not follow. And for you to turn the question immediately not on the people who've been massacred because of asserting their rights as European French citizens but on to the alleged, terrible, discrimination of the French is really quite despicable.[1]

Murray's point is that the interviewer is more concerned about preserving a certain left-wing identity than the massacre itself. In our polarised world, a portion of the left sees itself as being embattled against a racist and thus abject far-right. But if there were grounds for concern about some aspects of Islam, it would be harder to think that those who held these concerns were abject. This would be a loss for those whose identities depend upon distinguishing between their good in-group and some bad out-group.

Eric Weinstein saw the *Al Jazeera* interview and, as he says, 'fell instantly in love with him [Murray]'. He adds:

> The concept of heroism is much discussed these days in the realm of Marvel Comics, but rarely seen in the wild, as it were. This was the real thing: leadership. And my younger listeners will forgive me for saying so, but this was the best of masculinity personified.[2]

For Weinstein, the *Al Jazeera* interview is where the IDW began. In his conversation with Murray in October 2020 on what, portentously, has turned out to be the final episode of his podcast, The Portal, Weinstein reveals that Murray was 'IDW patient zero'. He says:

> [P]eople always asked me, 'Well, you named the IDW, who is in the Intellectual Dark Web?' And you were patient zero. You didn't know it. But if there was anyone in the Intellectual Dark Web, I realized after the Charlie Hebdo situation, it was you.[3]

## The Core of the IDW and the IDW Patronage System

Then there is the photo. On 3 July 2018, Joe Rogan posted a photograph on Instagram of a dinner;[4] this was not long after Bari Weiss's 8 May 2018 article in *The New York Times* that introduced the IDW to a wider audience. This photo, which includes Jordan Peterson, Eric Weinstein, Ben Shapiro, Dave Rubin, Joe Rogan, and Sam Harris, has helped to cement the pantheon – the core – of the IDW. The people missing are Eric Weinstein's brother, Bret Weinstein, and possibly also Claire Lehmann, founder of *Quillette* – although she is a unique case.

But what about patient zero Douglas Murray – ought not he to be in the core? Probably not. As much as the IDW is a way, it is also a complex patronage system – even a business model. Within this, the members of the 'core', each of whom has a podcast or media platform, reinforce one another through repeated associations with themselves – often by appearing on one another's podcasts. The core is further strengthened by a relatively stable list of associates that is an order of magnitude larger than the core, who also appear on the core's podcasts.

We see the calculus surrounding the patronage system of the IDW at work in the following remarks by Cathy Young:

> I don't know if I should consider myself a Dark Webizen. I've written for *Quillette*, mentioned in Weiss's article as part of the IDW – a smart publication committed to genuine intellectual pluralism. I've also been a guest on the IDW-identified Dave Rubin show on YouTube, of which I take a considerably dimmer view these days.[5]

Are a few *Quillette* articles and a Rubin appearance enough? Perhaps. Young made it into this book.

## Other Members of the IDW

To determine who is in the IDW, we can also consider lists produced in IDW-focused articles. Weiss's article names the following as being in the IDW: Joe Rogan, Sam Harris, Eric Weinstein, Bret Weinstein, Heather Heying, Jordan Peterson, Ben Shapiro, Dave Rubin, Douglas Murray, Claire Lehmann, Debra Soh, Michael Shermer, Maajid Nawaz, Ayaan Hirsi Ali, and Christina Hoff Sommers. Steven Pinker is also mentioned as being proximate, and it makes sense to include Weiss herself. A year and a half later, the article 'Shedding Light on the Intellectual Dark Web: A Preliminary Empirical Study'[6] added the following names: Heather Mac Donald, Niall Ferguson, Gad Saad, James Damore, Jonathan Haidt, Greg Lukianoff, Glenn Loury, John McWhorter, Peter Boghossian, James Lindsay, Helen Pluckrose, Gregg Hurwitz, Geoffrey Miller, Diane Fleischman, Coleman Hughes, Andy Ngo, Jonathan Kay, and Toby Young. I mostly agree.

But then there is billionaire entrepreneur Elon Musk, who has appeared on many IDW podcasts and who is regularly discussed and admired by IDW figures. And what ought we to do with comedians such as Bill Burr (12 Rogan appearances!), Dave Chappelle, and Ricky Gervais, who are unquestionably IDW-minded and who themselves appear on IDW podcasts; or actor, author, and public intellectual Stephen Fry who has at times associated with the core of the IDW; or Russell Brand, who has appeared on Rogan four times and whose profile is sewed into one of Jordan Petersons' jackets; or newer figures such as Lex Fridman (10 Rogan appearances) and Konstantin Kisin and Francis Foster from Triggernometry; or indeed political figures such as 2020 US Democratic Party Presidential candidates Tulsi Gabbard and Andrew Yang – Gabbard is arguably the central political figure within the IDW? All of these and many others will feature in this book.

To provide some order, I will employ four categories: core, near core, near associate, and distant associate; although I will at times simply refer to 'core' and 'associate' figures. I locate most of the people mentioned in this book in Table 1.1. After each, I include how many times he or she has appeared on Rogan (as of January 2025) and when his or her first appearance was – the Rogan appearances are so often seminal, especially for Peterson and the Weinstein brothers (listening to these 20 or so episodes gives a very strong sense of the way of the IDW). A list with individual biographies will appear in the Appendix.

**Table 1.1. IDW Figures Who Have Appeared on The Joe Rogan Experience by number of appearances on JRE**

| Name | Relationship to the IDW | Date of first appearance | Total number of appearances |
|---|---|---|---|
| Bill Burr | Distant associate | 2010 Jun | 12 |
| Gad Saad | Near associate | 2014 Jul | 11 |
| Lex Fridman | Near core | 2018 Oct | 10 |
| Sam Harris | Core | 2012 Mar | 8 |
| Jordan Peterson | Core | 2016 Nov | 8 |
| Bret Weinstein | Core | 2017 Jun | 8 |
| Tulsi Gabbard | Near associate | 2018 Sep | 7 |
| Michael Shermer | Near associate | 2016 Mar | 7 |
| Eric Weinstein | Core | 2017 Oct | 7 |
| Elon Musk | Near core | 2018 Sep | 5 |
| Russell Brand | Near associate | 2016 Jun | 4 |
| Konstantin Kisin and Francis Foster | Near associate | 2022 July | 4 |

| Name | Relationship to the IDW | Date of first appearance | Total number of appearances |
| --- | --- | --- | --- |
| James Lindsay | Near core | 2018 Oct | 4 |
| Ben Shapiro | Core | 2017 Aug | 4 |
| Matt Taibbi | Near associate | 2018 May | 4 |
| Coleman Hughes | Distant associate | 2022 Feb | 3 |
| Bill Maher | Near associate | 2020 Jan | 3 |
| Douglas Murray | Near core | 2018 Feb | 3 |
| Dave Rubin | Core | 2015 Oct | 3 |
| Debra Soh | Near assocociate | 2018 Jul | 3 |
| Peter Boghossian | Near core | 2015 Dec | 2 |
| Dave Chappelle | Distant associate | 2020 Nov | 2 |
| Erika and Nicholas Christakis | Near associate | 2019 Mar | 2 (Nicholas) |
| Jonathan Haidt | Near core | 2019 Jan | 2 |
| Heather Heying | Near core | 2018 Feb | 2 |
| Louis CK | Distant associate | 2022 Aug | 2 |
| Maajid Nawaz | Distant associate | 2018 Apr | 2 |
| Stephen Pinker | Near core | 2018 Feb | 2 |
| Abigail Shrier | Distant associate | 2020 Jul | 2 |
| Quentin Tarantino | Distant associate | 2021 Jun | 2 |
| Bari Weiss | Near core | 2019 Jan | 2 |
| James Damore | Near associate | 2017 Sep | 1 |
| Richard Dawkins | Near associate | 2019 Oct | 1 |
| Andrew Doyle | Distant associate |  | 1 |
| Ayaan Hirsi Ali | Near associate | 2021 Mar | 1 |
| Christina Hoff Sommers | Near associate | 2015 Nov | 1 |
| Geoffrey Miller | Distant associate | 2018 Sep | 1 |
| Andy Ngo | Distant associate | 2019 Jul | 1 |
| Peter Thiel | Distant associate | 2024 Aug | 1 |
| Andrew Yang | Distant associate | 2019 Feb | 1 |

| Name | Relationship to the IDW | Date of first appearance | Total number of appearances |
|---|---|---|---|
| Niall Ferguson | Distant associate | n/a | 0 |
| Diane Fleischman | Distant associate | n/a | 0 |
| David French | Distant associate | n/a | 0 |
| Stephen Fry | Distant associate | n/a | 0 |
| David Fuller | Distant associate | n/a | 0 |
| Ricky Gervais | Distant associate | n/a | 0 |
| Gregg Hurwitz | Distant associate | n/a | 0 |
| Helen Joyce | Distant associate | n/a | 0 |
| Jonathan Kay | Distant associate | n/a | 0 |
| Claire Lehmann | Core | n/a | 0 |
| Glenn Loury | Near associate | n/a | 0 |
| Greg Lukianoff | Distant associate | n/a | 0 |
| Heather Mac Donald | Distant associate | n/a | 0 |
| John McWhorter | Near associate | n/a | 0 |
| Camille Paglia | Distant associate | n/a | 0 |
| Posie Parker | Distant associate | n/a | 0 |
| Helen Pluckrose | Near core | n/a | 0 |
| Kathleen Stock | Distant associate | n/a | 0 |
| Cathy Young | Distant associate | n/a | 0 |
| Toby Young | Distant associate | n/a | 0 |

## Notes

1 HenryJacksonSoc 2015 January 9: 2:04.
2 The Portal 2020 October 24: 0:22:26.
3 The Portal 2020 October 24: 4:33:47.
4 Jjoerogan 2018 July 3.
5 Young 2018 May 20.
6 Shermer, Saide, & McCaffree 2019.

2

# What Defined the IDW?

### Good Faith Discussion as a Path to Truth

The IDW figure who has most earnestly articulated the IDW way is Bret Weinstein. Weinstein came to public attention through the Evergreen State College incident, which I will discuss in Chapter 6, and his subsequent appearance on Rogan. In June 2020, on Rebel Wisdom, Weinstein gives the following account of what characterises the IDW:

> IDW space is an environment in which the priority is put on stating what one actually believes irrespective of the social consequences of those statements and of partnering in discussion with other people on the basis that you hold the discovery of truth to be a higher value than pushing your own agenda.[1]

The IDW champions free speech – discussion of this runs throughout this book. However, it is in Weinstein's remarks that we get the sense of what, for the IDW, is at the heart of the current free speech problem. There are two elements. Consistent with Andrew Doyle's remarks about the Salem witch trials that I mentioned in the Introduction, the first is that in 'IDW space', you are not afraid to speak your mind. Or, to put this in grander terms: you are not afraid to speak truth to corrupt power. The second is the other side of this: in IDW space, you do not turn your back on truth for the sake of 'pushing your own agenda' – for the sake of corrupt power.

It is no small thing that for Weinstein deception can be driven by both fear and opportunism. This leads us to consider that perhaps many of us start out small and say what we need to say to survive, but after being rewarded for our conformity, we ourselves become the zealots who enforce the orthodoxy. While reality is no doubt more complex than this, as we shall see, this form recurs again and again in IDW thinking. For example, Jordan Peterson often distinguishes between corrupt and healthy hierarchies. In corrupt hierarchies, power is got through conforming to specious dogmas; whereas in healthy hierarchies, it is based on competence, which is cognate with truth.

Michael Shermer, the founding publisher of *Skeptic* magazine, provides a similar although more superficial account than Weinstein of what characterises the IDW. Echoing John Stuart Mill, he writes, 'If by fiat I had to identify one central organizing principle [of the IDW] it would be a commitment to the search for truth and free speech as the royal road to it'.[2]

A third account that dovetails with these two is by IDW-sympathetic blogger Daniel Miessler. He writes, 'The unifying characteristic [of the IDW] was the willingness to … discuss controversial topics in Good Faith'.[3] I always nod whenever I hear 'in good faith'. Yet an instant later I recall, with dismay, that we are always accusing one another of being in bad faith. 'Good faith' is an invaluable concept, but like many invaluable concepts, it's easy to abuse. And it sure is hard to tell from one moment to the next whether we ourselves are in good faith.

## Loving Truth and All Knowledge

This leads us to a consideration of temperament and to the question of whether some people have a deeper regard for truth than others. Given the variability within most human traits, this is surely possible. Plato explored this long ago when, in *The Republic*, he discussed the philosophical character. He says things like '[true philosophers are] those who love to see the truth'.[4] Academic Kathleen Stock, who is in the Kuiper Belt of the IDW (a distant associate), was interviewed on the UK podcast Triggernometry in November 2021. Stock has become notorious in the UK for her involvement in the Transgender debate. One of the hosts, Francis Foster, asks her:

> Why didn't you give up? Why did you not think, you know what, life's too short, I've got this wonderful career at a great university, I could just shut my mouth, and I could just carry on with my work. Why didn't you do that?

After saying that issues such as children transitioning and maintaining women's spaces are important, Stock says: 'I just think partly it's my philosophical brain that will not accept inconsistency. Even to my own detriment, to some extent. I just can't have it'.[5] Do IDW figures have a greater regard for truth than most? I'm not certain. However, many certainly are willing to break taboos and talk about inconsistencies.

To linger with Plato, he also says, 'the man who is ready to taste every branch of learning, is glad to learn and never satisfied – he's the man who deserves to be called a philosopher, isn't he?'[6] The IDW is not merely concerned with trying to be faithful to truth in an abstract sense, it also has Plato's philosopher's characteristic of loving every branch of learning. While the IDW has spent many hours battling Identity Politics, Postmodernism, Political Correctness, and so on – perhaps to its detriment – a positive aspect of the IDW is that podcasts such as Rogan's, Peterson's, Harris's, and Fridman's feature conversations with experts from numerous fields, including the Sciences, Economics, History, and the private sector. This gives the impression that at the heart of the IDW is indeed the pursuit of truth. And if foes are battled along the way, this is not for the sake of the battle itself, but because the foes block the path to truth.

## Corruption

However, we do also need to consider the failures of the IDW in the realm of truth. Jordan Peterson is an excellent case study. Lex Fridman had Jordan Peterson on his podcast in August 2022. In it Fridman presents Peterson with one of Nietzsche's famous aphorisms: 'Battle not with monsters, lest ye become a monster, and if you gaze into the abyss, the abyss gazes also into you'.[7] The implication is that Peterson has spent too long battling monsters and gazing into the abyss and that this has corrupted him. Interestingly, in August 2022, Peterson himself released a podcast in which he invited two of his friends, Jonathan Pageau and Gregg Hurwitz, to criticise him. Hurwitz says:

So, you're one of the great minds of a generation. You have a transformative intellect. You have an ability to frame things in a way that makes people see things through epiphany that is altering – we've talked about the difference between the semantic and the procedural, and how you get things in a ritual: you know how to do that. If [he means 'But when'] you are on twitter you are insane. You are dealing with a monster that you don't know what it is ... Jonathan Haidt [a near-core IDW academic] manages to act like an adult ... He's got a more even temperament than you ... Jordan, you're in a video game that's designed by teams of addiction specialists to skew your opinions a bunch of ways and to make you angry and outraged and to make you represent views and say things in captured language that's offensive to the other side to drive polarization further. That's the medium.[8]

I struggle to adjudicate whether Peterson's often injudicious temperament is ultimately a bug or a feature – to borrow a phrase from Fridman. Hurwitz, giving some ground to Peterson, says, 'one of the things you said that I thought was valid is you said "look you have to work up a certain amount of vehemence to go up against the world"'.[9] But to what extent does this vehemence diminish Peterson's cause – to what extent does he continue to pursue truth and remain in good faith? And most significantly, what effect does he have on his immense audience? A major concern that Eric Weinstein raises is that IDW – 'heterodox' – figures become 'captured' by their audiences, who want their de facto leaders to support extreme positions rather than take a less exciting path that brings everyone closer to truth.[10]

Nietzsche, who, in his own writings, lacks an even temperament, says, 'Carefree, mocking, violent—thus wisdom wants us: she is a woman, she always loves only a warrior'. I love to see an intellectual warrior in flow state – being mocking and violent. Yet these characteristics must be tempered by being 'care-free'. Peterson does so well in the famous Cathy Newman interview which I will discuss in Chapter 6 because he remains open and light.

Once again, I don't have space in this book to closely analyse the various IDW figures and the controversies they have been embroiled in. However, as Eric Weinstein says about IDW types: 'Almost everyone loses his or her footing at some point'.[11] A key question is how much tolerance we have for this. We should have some, but not too much.

## Notes

1   Rebel Wisdom 2020 June 24: 0:09:02. We come across similar statements quite often. Lex Fridman on Joe Rogan speaks about Twitter's perceived left-wing bias. He says:

> It's not necessarily what they believe. What bothers me the most is the arrogance that they can know the truth or they can know what is and isn't misinformation. I think it's ok to be whatever, a capitalist or a communist, as long as you have a deep humility about your understanding of the world … You might bring them [ideals] up as part of a conversation. But like you know you have a sense that you might be very wrong. And that's the kind of humility that you have to bring to the table, and that's where you have to have actual diversity of ideas at the table. That's why I think Elon is a really good push back at Twitter against the sort of Woke culture, corporate culture, that nourishes Silicon Valley (The Joe Rogan Experience 2022 May 26: 1:26:25).

2   Shermer, Saide, & McCaffree 2019.
3   Miessler 2019.
4   Plato 2003 [380BC]: 475e.
5   Triggernometry 2021 November 22: 0:24:38.
6   Plato 2003 [380BC]: 475e.
7   Lex Fridman 2022 August 20: 0:00:00.
8   Jordan B Peterson 2022 August 26: 1:56:59.
9   Jordan B Peterson 2022 August 26: 2:01:26.
10   Rebel Wisdom 2021 June 30: 0:09:07.
11   Rebel Wisdom 2021 June 30: 0:06:22.

3

# What Was the IDW Defined Against?

Even though we find good and bad faith across the political spectrum, the IDW has mostly criticised what it sees as being a bad faith branch of the left side of politics. The problem has been referred to as 'Political Correctness' or 'Wokeness', but we have also heard the phrases 'the illiberal left' and 'the regressive left'. 'Wokeness' – or just 'Woke' – is the term du jure; however, people still say 'Political Correctness'. 'The regressive left' and 'the illiberal left' are heard less often.[1]

The term 'Political Correctness' originated in the Russian revolution of 1917. But it gained its current flavour amongst 1960s Leftists who were making fun of the dogmatism and humourlessness of the Leftists of the previous generation. They get points for this! For the last few decades, 'Political Correctness' has continued to be used to deride an excessively serious and censorious left.

'Woke', which is a slightly newer term, has a similar meaning as 'Political Correctness', but it also indicates something evangelical. Around the mid-2010s, 'staying Woke' was used in the context of Black Lives Matter to encourage people to stay awake to racial injustice. It then quickly came to be used in relation to other Social Justice movements such as #MeToo. But in this process, it became self-aware, and as with Skynet's own ascendence to self-awareness in the *Terminator* franchise, trouble followed. Consider this 2017 definition from The Evergreen State College in the United States (where Brett Weinstein had his incident). Being Woke is 'A state of enlightened understanding, particularly related to issues of race and Social Justice. Someone who is Woke is aware of issues of injustice and inequality.'[2] Right around the time people widely started using 'Woke' to describe their own enlightened state,[3] the term came to be used derisively by those who doubted the sincerity of those who applied the term to themselves.[4] That this was a rhetorical victory for the anti-Woke is demonstrated by the fact that people quickly stopped referring to themselves as Woke (in 2023 I attracted the ire of students for using the phrase 'the Woke Left' in a lecture). This shift in the meaning of 'Woke' can be seen in a December 2018 article by Andrew Sullivan in *Intelligencer*:

> And so the young adherents of the Great Awokening exhibit the zeal of the Great Awakening. Like early modern Christians, they punish heresy by banishing sinners from society or coercing them to public demonstrations of shame, and provide an avenue for redemption in the form of a thorough public confession of sin.[5, 6]

Returning to the IDW, in October 2021 on an IDW-related podcast, Decoding the Gurus, Sam Harris discussed the IDW. While objecting to the idea that the IDW was ever coherent, he concedes that all within it were allergic to 'Wokeness':

> [T]hose of us who are on the left or started out on the left, we've had a common experience which is [that] the most dishonest and the most vindictive assaults on our reputation that we've ever encountered have come from the left. The impossibility of conversation that has caused us to despair of even ever making an effort to communicate about anything that's substantial to anyone – that has been encountered when we're facing to the left, not to the right. As somebody who has spent a lot of time fighting with the far-right, at least on religious points ... [n]one of those encounters have ever been one-tenth as poisonous as what I've gotten from the left ... This is an experience people have had of socially being extruded from the body of the left by some kind of crazy rhetorical immune system that has gotten tuned up in response to very specific ideas.[7]

Similarly, Psychologist Jonathan Haidt says:

I do share something important with the loose web of people that you list [he is referring to the list of IDW candidates mentioned in the article in *Skeptic* about the IDW]. I think it is this: we are all fed up with a strain of illiberalism that is found on the left but that is nowhere near a majority of the left.[8]

The most articulate objection to Political Correctness and the illiberal left that I have encountered within the IDW was made by British public intellectual, Stephen Fry, within his opening statement as part of the Munk Debate on Political Correctness. When it occurred in mid-2018, it was surprising to see Fry on the same side as Jordan Peterson – Fry himself mentions this. But Fry's presence in the anti-Political Correctness camp reveals not only that it's possible to oppose Political Correctness and its close relative, Wokeness, without being on the right, but also that there is substantial common ground across the political spectrum (I suspect that many of our political values are not irreconcilably different, but rather, we give different weightings to values we all share). Fry says:

Naturally, I want racism, misogyny, homophobia, transphobia, xenophobia, bullying, bigotry, intolerance of all human kinds to end. That's surely a given amongst all of us. The question is, how is such a golden aim to be achieved? My ultimate objection to Political Correctness is not that it combines so much of what I have spent a lifetime loathing and opposing: preachiness …, piety, self-righteousness, heresy hunting, denunciation, shaming, assertion without evidence, accusation, inquisition, censoring. That's not why I'm incurring the wrath of my fellow Liberals by standing on this side of the house. My real objection is that I don't think Political Correctness works … I believe one of the greatest human failings is to prefer to be right than to be effective. And Political Correctness is always obsessed with how right it is without thinking of how effective it might be. I wouldn't class myself as a Classical Libertarian [I think he means 'Classical Liberal'], but I do relish transgression. And I deeply and instinctively distrust conformity and orthodoxy. Progress is not achieved by preachers and guardians of morality. But to paraphrase Yevgeny Zamyatin [author of *We*, which was one of the first dystopian political Science Fiction novels in the ilk of *Brave New World* and *Nineteen Eighty-Four*], by madmen, hermits, heretics, dreamers, rebels and sceptics.[9]

I sense the Platonic form in this. The fact that Fry mentions 'bulling' is telling. It reminds us that even if you are Woke, you can still be a bully. Thus, it's not enough to adhere to the dogmas of Identity Politics to be good.

## Notes

1   Joe Rogan and Peter Boghossian used 'regressive left' and differentiated it from older Liberalism in December 2015. Boghossian said it's going to get a lot worse before it gets better (The Joe Rogan Experience 2015 December 15: 1:32:53). He was right.

2   The Evergreen State College 2017.

3   Edinburgh Comedy Awards director, Nica Burns, provides a good example of 'Woke' being used unironically and non-derisively in the wild. She says she is 'looking forward to comedy's future in the Woke world' (Burns 2018). In 2016, Jack Dorsey, the then CEO of Twitter, appeared on an interview with a t-shirt with '#stayWoke' on it, along with the Twitter logo. Amusingly, in November 2022, Elon Musk found a closet full of old #stayWoke shirts at Twitter HQ. The t-shirt clearly didn't catch on (Musk 2022 November 23). Further, as we might expect, *South Park* recently depicted a future which is dominated by Woke comedy. One of the Woke Comedy jokes told by Jimmy, a stand-up comedian, is: 'What's the deal with these Mexicans? I mean, they have fabulous food, their country has amazing beaches, and they're really fantastic people' (Flard 2021 November 28).

4   Comedian Bill Burr, who is an IDW associate by virtue of his many appearances on Rogan and the subject matter he covers in his comedy, captures the corruption of the term 'Woke' in his Netflix comedy special 'Bill Burr Live at Red Rocks':

> What kind of a fuckin' idiot white person refers to themselves as 'Woke'? You know. If you actually were socially conscious, you'd realize that white people stole that word from black people … But you know what, I blame black people for that.
>
> One of them fucked up. They were at a party, there was white people there, and they let it slip out. 'Stay Woke' or however the fuck you say it. And some white person heard it, like, 'Ah, what was that? Oh, my God. "Stay Woke?" I wanna say that. I gotta say that around my white friends so they know that I'm down'. (Burr 2022: 0:08:06)

5   Sullivan 2018 December 7.

6   Michael Nayna made a documentary about Bret Weinstein's Evergreen

State College incident. In some of the footage, we see academics publicly performing their shame (Michael Nayna 2019 April 24: 0:05:00).
7    Decoding the Gurus 2021 October 30: 1:10:36.
8    Shermer, Saide, & McCaffree 2019.
9    TheMunkDebates 2018 June 2: 00:03:36.

4

# The Core Ideological Battle of the IDW

Elizabeth Nolan Brown, writing for the Libertarian publication, *Reason* ('free minds, free markets'), in yet another article that followed Weiss's 8 May 2018 article about the IDW, suggests that the IDW 'is just re-hashing old P.C. controversies in new media'.[1] This is true to a degree; although 'just' misses the mark. To properly understand the IDW, we need to recognise that beyond objecting to Political Correctness or being Woke, the IDW is fighting what it sees as being a civilisation-level battle over truth itself. This battle, which accounts to a considerable extent for the 'Intellectual' in 'Intellectual Dark Web', is fought between Enlightenment and Postmodern approaches to truth. While I will briefly outline the IDW's Enlightenment approach (I don't say much here because it comes up again and again throughout this book), the chapter will focus on the IDW's understanding and criticisms of the Postmodern approach.

As an aside, 'truth', and the closely related term 'knowledge', can be difficult to define. As I understand them, 'truth' refers to the things and events that constitute reality and the patterns of cause and effect that these things and events are a part of. Knowledge refers to grasping truth. In short, the truth is out there, and when we grasp it, we have knowledge. However, we can have declarative knowledge (knowing that water boils at 100 degrees Celsius), but we can also have procedural knowledge (knowing how to run down a hill after a wheel of cheese); the latter, precisely because it is not declarative, can be hard to pin down (like the cheese), as indeed is the knowledge found in art.

## The Enlightenment Approach to Truth

The basic IDW account of the Enlightenment approach to truth is that the aim of intellectual work is to get to the truth. Jonathan Haidt, in a 2016 speech in which he argues that universities suffer from a lack of viewpoint diversity, approvingly tells the story of when he arrived at Yale in 1981 and saw over the doorway the words 'Lux et Veritas' – light and truth.[2]

In a nutshell, for the IDW, we try to get to the truth by drawing on reasoning and evidence. As Helen Pluckrose from the Grievance Studies Affair (see Chapter 6) says, there is an 'expectation to give evidence for a claim – to make it reasoned'. Further, we negotiate our thoughts in the 'Liberal marketplace of ideas' – which ought to include universities and the media. By using this approach humanity progresses:[3] we cure diseases, create better political systems, travel into space, and so on.

## The Postmodern Approach to Truth

With the rise of Postmodernism, the veneration of truth, reasoning and evidence came to be seen as old-fashioned, or 'problematic', as they say today. There is an amusing 1990s Noam Chomsky video on YouTube about this. Chomsky is not in the IDW, yet he has appeared on Lex Fridman's podcast twice, and his attitude to Postmodernism puts him in the same epistemological ballpark as the IDW; in any case, he's close enough to earn an appearance in this book. Chomsky talks about two lectures he had recently given: the first at Birzeit University in Palestine, the second at an Israeli university:

> As we walked out he [a friend of Chomsky's] kind of laughed and he told me that most of the especially younger people liked it [the lecture] a lot, but he heard one critical – really critical comment – from a young woman faculty member who sort of liked the general political thrust of it, but told him it was very naïve. And I said, 'why was it naïve?' and he laughed and he said, well, it's because you said that people do things on moral grounds and you talked about truth. And that's old-fashioned nonsense. That's kind of this old Enlightenment stuff
>
> … Nobody does anything on moral grounds. It's all power plays. You know. Read Foucault. And so on and so forth, if you can understand it. And truth is kind of like an old-fashioned concept. You know,

> there's no truth … That stuff goes on all over. The next day I gave a talk at an Israeli university … One of the commentators was the dean. And he hated it of course. An historian. He also said it was naïve because I was talking as if there was an objectivity in history.[4]

The Israelis and Palestinians: politically divided, but united by Postmodernism. lol. Chomsky also says:

> there's a lot of material reward that comes from it [being a Postmodernist] – like if you are part of that system you can run around the conferences, get big professorships, and you know, all this kind of stuff – so there's a lot of conventional material reward, and it has this very radical look to it.[5]

So, for Chomsky, **Postmodernism = faux radical careerist relativism**. I tell ya, shit ain't changed. I show the Chomsky video to my students to make the point that you can be on the left and still believe in truth, reasoning, and evidence.[6]

The following is a summary of what, for the IDW, comes under the umbrella of 'Postmodernism' (these points arise repeatedly throughout this book):

- Epistemological (and moral) relativism. This refers to the belief that neither truth (nor morality) can be generalised. Related points include:
  - There is little or no human nature (this is known as the 'blank slate' view of the human brain).[7]

- Denying that we have access to reality. Related points include:
  - Truth claims, or even just language – or 'discourse' – do not represent reality, they construct reality to serve the interests of power.[8]
  - We cannot distinguish between facts and feelings.
  - Science (although not climate science) is just another discourse that serves the interests of power.

- Identity Politics. 'Identity Politics' involves believing that the key elements of a person's identity are determined by the groups to which he or she purportedly belongs rather than his or her individual characteristics and experiences. Amongst many other things, this can involve thinking that the less power a group has, the greater the group's access to truth.

- Being anti-West.

- Being reluctant to discuss ideas. According to the IDW, for Postmodernists, open discussion is not just unhelpful, it is dangerous because bad discourses perpetuate undesirable power.

Helen Pluckrose articulates many of these points in her appearance on Rebel Wisdom in October 2019:

> The main characteristics of it [Postmodernism] are a belief in the cultural constructedness of knowledge. So, knowledge isn't something that's out there to be found, it's something that humans make with their language. And this works in the service of power. So particularly the Postmodern ideas will go against Christianity, but also Marxism, and also Science. They will say these have undue power, they're accepted as truths, they're dangerous, and they want to pick them all apart. So, because of that we see understandings of categories that we've accepted as distinct, as actually blending into each other – the things like fact and fiction, reason and emotion. We're not separating these in Postmodernism. There's that really intense focus on language as dangerous – as a constructor of things. And we've got quite a loss of both humanism and individuality. We're not to see each other as fellow human beings with individual characteristics that we can like, dislike, agree with, disagree with. Now it's all about knowledge as attached to identity.[9]

Jordan Peterson, in his first appearance on Rogan in November 2016, identifies similar characteristics:

> The Postmodernists – that's a philosophical community, let's say – believe that the entire point of human categorisation is power. And that dialogue between people is only a power dialogue. And that there's no real reality outside of interpretation. And that basically what we do is exchange interpretive viewpoints to ratchet up our dominance and status, and that's that. Biology is an ideology and the idea of the objective world is an ideology, and science is an ideology.[10]

There is a much longer story to tell here about how Postmodern ideas and Identity Politics evolved, at least in part, out of Marxist ideas that were articulated over a century ago. The short of it is that Marxism held that how societies produce things – the 'economic base' – affects everything from politics to culture – the 'superstructure' – and that once the workers gained control of the means of production a better world would be created. Notably, Marxism emphasised collective identity – in its case: class – and was often revolutionary in spirit. Newer Marxist ideas associated with Gramsci and the Frankfurt School increasingly stressed that ideology and culture played a role in maintaining unequal class relations; that is, workers were not just materially oppressed, they were brainwashed. Then, with the rise of Poststructuralism in the 1960s, the Marxist focus on class was replaced by the vaguer concept of 'power' (today 'privilege' has replaced 'power'), and 'ideology' became 'discourse'. With Poststructuralism, the materialism of Marxism (worrying about the means of production) was swept away, and even to speak about reality or truth became odious. Yet the Marxist attraction to collectivism and revolutionary, utopian thinking remained. And this is largely where we are now. Where once a better world was to be brought about by the workers seizing the means of production, now a better world will be brought about by those groups who have less privilege transforming discourse.

To give an example of the Postmodern approach to knowledge – just to show that the IDW isn't making it all up – many points mentioned in this section can be seen in the following run-of-the-mill 2012 Postmodern academic paragraph from International Relations (Postmodernism has colonised every academic field):

> The main targets of the 'reflexive critique' are positivism's adherence to 'truth as correspondence', its understanding of knowledge as 'representation' and its separation of subject and object, and of facts and values. Against these core positivist epistemic stances, the 'reflexive turn' was meant to signify IR's awareness of the historicity of knowledge, and of the inherently normative or ideological nature of IR's underlying theoretical premises, modes of theorizing and scholarly ethos.[11]

Here, Postmodernism appears as the 'reflexive critique', and 'positivism' is the representative of the Enlightenment.

The point of appending 'reflexive' to 'critique' (beyond the simple pleasure of writing with redundancies and signalling group membership) is to imply that Enlightenment types – 'positivists' – are operating at a lower level: they may critique things, but their critiques are not 'reflexive' or properly self-aware. For the naïve positivists, then, which includes Marxists, truth claims correspond with things and events in reality; whereas for the superior reflexives, this is not so. The same point is being made by the objection to 'knowledge as representation'. In both cases, the Postmodern denial that we have access to reality is implied; that is, truth claims do not correspond with something in reality and knowledge does not represent reality. Here also we see grounds for epistemological and moral relativism: if truth and knowledge are not grounded in reality, then we have no basis for elevating one claim above another.

The objection to the positivist separation of subject and object is more of the same. However, it is here that the anti-science flavour becomes stronger. The scientist – the subject – in trying to get to the truth takes care to remove his or her bias to better grasp whatever object he or she is studying. This is the point of science (#theoriginalreflexivecritique). As the oft-quoted Richard Feynman remarks: 'The first principle is that you must not fool yourself – and you are the easiest person to fool'.[12] But in the Postmodern world, subjectivity cannot be removed (you'd think that at this point the Postmodernists would resign their academic positions and retire to the commune because they cannot justify their salaries). The same claim is being made in the objection that 'facts' cannot be separated from 'values'. It is this point that Ben Shapiro is attacking with his tag line: 'facts don't care about your feelings'. The suggestion that knowledge has historicity (quite the word) is yet more of the same, but here we get the sense that knowledge flows from culture or language – from 'discourse' – rather than from reality (but if this was true, we ought to call this so-called knowledge 'opinion' – but down this path also lies unemployment). A significant implication is that older works do not contain knowledge; rather, they merely reproduce the bigoted ideas of the past. Which is why we don't need them. Amongst all this, there is also the implication that there is not much point in studying history itself because history has historicity – I encounter very few history buffs amongst the ranks of Postmodern academics.

We can rehash all this, and continue working through the paragraph, using two useful words: *is* and *ought*. For Enlightenment types, much of life involves trying to understand what *is* so that we can better decide how we *ought* to act.[13] For example, we need to know the road rules so that we can figure out how we ought to drive, or a doctor needs to know how the body works so that he or she can operate successfully. In the Postmodern universe, claims about how the world *is* merely reflect people's interests about how they wish the world *ought to be*. This is what is meant by 'normative'. So, claims about the nature of reality are really just about people trying to get what they want – they are about power. Whence 'ideological'.

As mentioned by Chomsky, Foucault, one of the major figures in Postmodernism, popularised these ideas – at least in the academic realm – in the 1960s and 1970s. The following remarks from his book *Discipline and Punish* provide a good sense of Postmodern thinking:

> We must cease once and for all to describe the effects of power in negative terms: it 'excludes', it 'represses', it 'censors', it 'abstracts', it 'masks', it 'conceals'. In fact power produces; it produces reality; it produces domains of objects and rituals of truth.[14]

The crux of all this is that from the Postmodern perspective, the point is *not* to try to understand the nature of reality – what *is* – and then determine *what we ought to do* based at least in part on what *is*. Instead, because there is no *is*, the point is to begin by assuming that you are right and put your energies into changing how people talk and think because whatever passes for reality is constituted in culture, in language, in discourse. Peter Boghossian addresses this problem when speaking at Portland State University on a panel with Heather Heying, Helen Pluckrose, and James Damore. Objecting to 'activist academics', he says 'They think they've found the truth, there's no need to seek it, they are activists. But your epistemology has to come before your activism. Why you are doing activism matters'.[15]

This brings us to the final point about Postmodernists' aversion to debate. Back in 2005, International Relations academic John Mearsheimer made the following observation about 'Post-Cold War idealists' (his name for 'Postmodernists'):

> Post-Cold War idealists have a different strategy for changing the world [than their Cold War counterparts]. They believe that the master causal variable is discourse, not reason itself. It is not enough to have the better argument [the approach of earlier idealists]; rather, one wins the day by having the only argument. Specifically, they maintain that how we talk and think about the world largely shapes practice.[16]

These remarks provide a clear sense of what many – not just those in the IDW – are concerned about. In a world without truth or knowledge, in a world where we do not have access to reality, in a world where language conjures reality into existence, there is no place for arguing, just as there is no need to study history or the classics or science. There is only the totalitarian mission of transforming discourse because it is from discourse alone that the ills of the world are derived.

But how does all this actually work? I mean, Postmodernism really doesn't make sense. For instance, if reality is so hard to discern, then why is it so easy to work out who has power or privilege? And isn't the whole point to end oppression as it exists in reality? The following is my distillation of what is going on.

As discussed, in Postmodern epistemology, there is no distinction between subject and object, between facts and values. To steel-man Postmodernism, collapsing these distinctions helps to make the entirely reasonable point that sometimes powerful people lie to serve their interests. However, you don't defeat a liar by saying there is no truth. And this brings us to the real goal of Postmodernism: by collapsing these distinctions, a sinister yet elegant reversal becomes possible. If subject cannot be separated from object, if facts cannot be separated from values, then the Postmodernist himself or herself is justified in treating his or her own feelings, intuitions, hypotheses, and so on, as if they were facts – as if they were knowledge. **Thus, the tool that was putatively developed to undermine the powerful is now used to protect the power of Postmodernists.** This is the Postmodern sleight of hand. But what kind of a world is it if we cannot speak truth to power – if we can only speak power to power? It is a world of chaos.

Jordan Peterson makes similar points in his appearance with Bret Weinstein on Rogan in September 2017, when talking about the student mob at Evergreen State College (see Chapter 6):

> Part of the reason that the only thing that the Postmodernists believe in is power is because that helps them justify their arbitrary use of it under any circumstances whatsoever … So it's not surprising that you see this manifested in that mob-like behaviour of the students. It's right in accordance with everything they're being taught.[17]

So much more could be said about the battle between Enlightenment and Postmodern approaches to truth.[18] But I will limit myself to a couple more remarks. While Postmodernism has its uses – culture can be propaganda – it is, ultimately, just another form of corrupt power. Corrupt power always works the same way: once it has been attained it wants to be unaccountable. Consider that one of the (now) amusing things the Bolsheviks did when they gained power following the 1917 Russian revolution was to ban unions. Why would workers need a mechanism to fight for their interests when the Bolsheviks were the party of the workers?

I've been quite black and white in this section. There are a range of intensities with which Postmodernism is practiced. For example, more moderate Postmodernists can be upbeat about our ability to discern reality; however, their Postmodern inclinations are revealed in, say, an aversion to weighing positives and negatives about a phenomenon. I regularly encounter this with colleagues' and students' deep contempt for the West (except Postmodernism). They will provide evidence to demonstrate that the West is bad – and sometimes it is good evidence – but they will bristle if asked to weigh pros and cons. I also regularly encounter the 'blank slate' view of the human mind in everything from Constructivism in International Relations (for Constructivists, the international realm will be transformed by changing norms) to the idea that never dies: gender is a social construction (though this construction rarely seems to be so odious that the person asserting it has abandoned trying to look attractive in conventional ways). I'll return to the problem of pinning down the excesses of Postmodernism in my discussion of the 'Motte and Bailey Doctrine' in Chapter 7.

## Further IDW Objections to Postmodernism and Its Heirs

On Sam Harris's podcast in January 2018 (titled 'The Intellectual Dark Web' – it is on this episode that Eric Weinstein coined the name 'Intellectual Dark Web'), in talking about what bothers him most about the times, Ben Shapiro makes a clear critique of the relativism that lies at the heart of Postmodernism. He laments the loss of 'human reason' and 'objective truths', both of which he claims have been replaced by 'radical subjectivism'. He says:

> [People will] toss reason out altogether. They'll say your specific bias as a person prevents you from even having a reasonable conversation. Your white privilege or your background or your ethnicity – all of this prevents us from even discussing on a one-on-one level. I can recognise my background having an impact on how I think. But if that is supposed to be a conversation stopper, then how exactly are we supposed to have a conversation?[19]

Here, Shapiro finds a useful middle ground. He concedes that background affects what we think but indicates that this does not prevent us from working together to get to the truth. Harris provides a pithy paraphrase of Shapiro's remarks, saying, 'That's why Identity Politics is so toxic, in my view. Because if identity is paramount, communication is impossible'.[20]

Jonathan Haidt makes a point that is similar to Boghossian's previously mentioned remarks about 'activist academics'. Haidt objects to 'motivated scholarship' and states that if a scholar wants to undertake research to support his or her political agenda, then he or she will almost always succeed.[21] He argues that 'motivated scholars' succeed because the mechanisms of 'institutionalised disconfirmation' – typically peer review – aren't working. This is because parts of academia are now dominated by scholars who share the same political views and who uncritically support one another's work (seems we need to be more critical of the reflexive critique). In making these arguments, he presents data that demonstrate American universities are increasingly dominated by left-wing scholars. Haidt says all of this not because he is on the right – he votes Democrat – but because, once again, he thinks that truth should be the goal or telos of universities. Haidt, invoking standard Enlightenment ideas, says that humans are 'biased and flawed and often shallow and silly [...] but when we push against each other we challenge each other and we get better – we get smarter – together'. He then makes his key argument: 'On this view of human nature, on this view of intellectual life, a university must have viewpoint diversity and it dies – it dies – if it has political orthodoxy and a monoculture'.[22] The point is that the Postmodern sleight-of-hand helps to support the political monoculture by generally weakening standards.

Steven Pinker made a compatible critique of the left 20 years ago (Pinker himself could be IDW 'patient zero' rather than Douglas Murray – but where do we stop with such things: Richard Dawkins? Christopher Hitchens?). Early in *The Blank Slate*, Pinker presents a range of 'blank-slate' claims that he deems 'preposterous'. He then writes:

> This is the mentality of a cult, in which fantastical beliefs are flaunted as proof of one's piety. That mentality cannot coexist with an esteem for the truth, and I believe it is responsible for some of the unfortunate trends in recent intellectual life.[23]

The only significant shift between then and now, and arguably one of the reasons why the IDW became prominent, is that the 'unfortunate trends in recent intellectual life' Pinker speaks about are no longer limited to esoteric academia. They now underpin the excesses of the left in the Culture Wars and can be found throughout the organs of Western society, including governments, schools, and corporations.

Bret Weinstein makes this point at the end of Michael Nayna's documentary about the Evergreen State College incident. In Weinstein's remarks, we also see the concern that the Postmodern turn is a civilisation-level threat:

> I keep being invited to talk about free speech on college campuses and every time I'm invited I make the same point, which is this isn't about free speech and this is only tangentially about college campuses. This is about a breakdown in the basic logic of civilisation and it's spreading, and college campuses may be the first dramatic battle but of course this is going to find its way into the courts. It's already found its way into the tech sector. It's going to find its way to the highest levels of governance if we are not careful. And it actually does jeopardise the ability of civilisation to continue to function…. These ideas [which are all related to Postmodernism] were wrong when they first took hold in the academy. And instead of shutting them down, we created phony fields that act as a kind of analytical affirmative action where ideas that

do not deserve to survive are given sustenance. These ideas are so toxic and so ill-conceived that to the extent they are allowed to hold sway **as if one truth is equal to every other truth, right, my truth is as good as your truth,** to the extent that that idea is allowed to pervade other institutions on which civilisation depends, civilisation will come apart, so we have to fight this, and don't get the sense that it is just about college campuses or kids overacting because, um, that ain't what this is. This is far more important.[24]

## Notes

1   Brown 2018 May 14.

2   Gravitahn 2016 December 6: 0:01:36.

3   Rebel Wisdom 2019 October 7: 0:02:08.

4   Chomsky's Philosophy 2015 September 13: 0:02:06.

5   Chomsky's Philosophy 2015 September 13: 0:00:55.

6   Postmodernism today isn't quite the same as what it was in the 1990s. While its relativism and focus on language and power has been retained, in its newer Social Justice incarnation, there is a little less obscurantist language. Helen Pluckrose discusses this on the Rebel Wisdom (Rebel Wisdom 2019 October 7: 0:03:00) and in greater depth in her and James Lindsay's book, *Cynical Theories* (2021).

7   Several IDW figures come from fields that are founded in the belief that human nature exists. Core figures Bret Weinstein and Heather Heying, and associate Richard Dawkins are Evolutionary Biologists. Gad Saad is an Evolutionary Psychologist. A foundational IDW discussion about human nature occurs between Bret Weinstein and Jordan Peterson on The Joe Rogan Experience 2017 September 1.

8   Helen Joyce, author of the book, *Trans: When Ideology Meets Reality*, says the following about Postmodernism's emphasis on language on Jordan Peterson's podcast: '[In the Postmodern turn], the language takes precedence over the bedrock material itness of things' (Jordan B Peterson 2022 September 13: 0:04:48). Andrew Doyle, speaking on the Triggernometry podcast, says the following about the link between the various strands of Identity Politics and Postmodernism:

> I see it as a kind of hydra – with many heads – because you've got a strand about race, gender – and all these things are different. Critical Race Theory is very different from Queer theory, say, but they all come from the same well-spring. They all come from the same fundamental Postmodern

assumptions that, for instance, our understanding of reality is constructed through the language that we use. That's why they are all obsessed with language and the manipulation of language (Triggernometry 2022 September 8: 0:40:08).

9   Rebel Wisdom 2019 October 7: 0:00:31.

10  The Joe Rogan Experience 2016 November 28: 0:04:01.

11  Hamati-Ataya 2012: 671.

12  Feynman 1974.

13  We should keep in mind that some *oughts* cannot be derived from what *is*. But this is a deeper philosophical discussion.

14  Foucault 1991 [1975]: 194.

15  Freethinkers of PSU 2018 February 26: 0:39:18. IDW associate Matt Taibbi also speaks about this phenomenon. Impersonating the orthodox-left position he says, 'We've decided something, right? We're not going to discuss it anymore.' Then critiquing this he says: 'So if you discuss it, you're in the bad zone … There are just so many of these places in the cultural landscape that are no fly zones.' Taibbi mentions this in relation to discussing Transgender issues and also the 'Lab Leak Hypothesis'; the latter refers to the possibility that the COVID-19 virus escaped from a lab – for a period in 2020 and 2021 it was taboo to mention this. 2021 December 7: 1:17:45.

16  Mearsheimer 2005: 145.

17  The Joe Rogan Experience 2017 September 1: 0:04:32.

18  Helen Pluckrose and James Lindsay's book *Cynical Theories* provides an extensive treatment of the battle, as do many parts of Pinker's *The Blank Slate, The Better Angels of our Nature* and *Enlightenment Now*.

19  Sam Harris 2018 January 6: 0:16:10.

20  Harris 2018 January 6: 0:18:15.

21  Gravitahn 2016 December 6: 0:04:12.

22  Gravitahn 2016 December 6: 0:00:34. More recently, Steven Pinker made the same points:

> Academia in particular has become notorious for having a political monoculture increasingly, especially in Humanities faculties and Science faculties and Public Health faculties. There are fewer and fewer people who would call themselves a Conservative or even Centrists. It's moving inexorably leftward. Unless you believe that the left has the truth about everything. In which case we don't need science. Just ask a left-wing pundit. And we have the answer. If you don't believe that, you are committed to the idea that we need diversity of ideas, of viewpoints. Not just diversity of gonads and skin colour. But diversity of beliefs. The most important kind of diversity there is (Big Think 2023 March 23: 0:27:27).

23  Pinker 2019 [2002]: x.
24  Michael Nayna 2019 April 24: 0:22:11.

5

# The Politics of the IDW

## The Media's Mislabelling of the IDW

It is easy to think that the IDW is just another right-wing player in the Culture Wars. Certainly, articles from the left-wing media have made the case that the IDW is associated with the right, even the far-right. In response to Bari Weiss's 8 May 2018 article, *The Guardian*, on 10 May 2018, published a piece for their 'Pass Notes' section (Pass Notes is 'A quick chat designed to tell you everything you need to know about a story you don't need to know about'). The headline referred to the IDW as 'The supposed thinking wing of the Alt-Right'[1] and suggested that all within it shared the value of 'hardcore Libertarianism', and that the IDW included demagogic right-wing figures such as Milo Yiannopoulos and Alex Jones (these figures have appeared on Rogan, but it is a long bow to draw to say they are in the IDW). And while the piece did moderate its position by stating that those in the IDW 'come from both the right and sometimes left extremes [I'm not sure who they think is from the left extreme – maybe Bret Weinstein and Heather Heying] of the political spectrum' and mentioning that 'mainstream intellectuals' such as Steven Pinker are often included, the sentiment in the headline carries the day.

Vox[2] also published an anti-IDW article on 10 May 2018 by Professor Henry Farrell. The headline was, 'The "Intellectual Dark Web", explained: what Jordan Peterson has in common with the Alt-Right'. The subheading was, 'A controversial *New York Times* article describes several popular white intellectuals as marginalized "renegades"'. 'White intellectuals' is telling. The author is lamentably playing Identity Politics: judging people by characteristics such as the colour of their skin and their biological sex rather than the arguments they make – the content of their character. As the article goes on to state, what really drives the IDW is resentment about the loss of status that their identity group has experienced in recent years. On this point, Farrell writes, 'It's hard for erstwhile hegemons to feel happy about their fall'. And a section in bold in the article describes the IDW as 'A group united mainly by its disdain for "multiculturalism"'.[3] Finally, Michael Brooks, who was a co-host of the podcast *The Majority Report* published a book in 2020 titled, *Against the Web: A Cosmopolitan Answer to the New Right*.[4]

In relation to all of this, Steven Pinker's term 'The Left Pole' is useful. He mentions it while lamenting that free speech has become associated with the right wing. He says:

> Just as when you are at the North Pole, all directions are South, the Left Pole is a mythical spot, from which all directions are right. So any opinion that does not conform to the orthodoxy of the Left Pole is branded right wing.[5]

Because those in the IDW challenge left orthodoxics, especially in relation to Identity Politics and Postmodernism, it appears to some on the left as if they are a part of the right. (While I'm mentioning Pinker, in *The Better Angels of Our Nature*, Pinker jokes about left-leaning Social Scientists 'studying Conservatism as if it were a mental defect'.[6])

There is no doubt that the IDW has spent more time criticising the left than the right. But the complexity lies in the fact that many associated with the IDW have repeatedly said they are on the left, and voiced support for left-wing policies such as public education and health care, social safety nets, and universal basic income. Perhaps there is nothing more dangerous for the Woke left than the criticisms made by other Progressives – rather than taking these criticisms seriously, these other Progressives must be nullified by being branded 'Alt-Right' or 'Conservative'. Eric Weinstein and Joe Rogan talked about this in November 2018. Weinstein had just said that he was worried he would get shut off Twitter. The conversation unfolds thusly:

*Rogan:* Are you worried about getting shut off?

*Weinstein:* I'm always worried.

*Rogan:* But you don't say anything inflammatory. You're a very logical and reasonable guy. So, you think it's really gotten to that point?

*Weinstein:* Well yeah, I'm actually worried that by being logical and reasonable I have more of a risk because the things I am saying –

*Rogan:* You're also a recognized intellectual and very left-wing. You're Progressive.

*Weinstein:* Yeah.

*Rogan:* So why would they shut you off?

*Weinstein:* Oh, I think because they're much more worried about a Progressive who says the current Progressiveness is absolute stupidity. That's much more dangerous than some right-winger who's always against anything that's Progressive.[7]

While in the remainder of this section I will detail the political groupings within the IDW, in large part those within the IDW can be classed as Liberals. However, the term 'Liberal' is confusing. In the United States, people who are seen as Woke are often derogatorily referred to as 'Liberals' by the right. And then there is the term 'Classical Liberal' which encompasses a range of traditional Liberal values, such as free expression, but which slides in the Libertarian direction insofar as Classical Liberals are wary of government regulation of markets. As I use the term, Liberals value individual freedom but also believe there is a role for government in ensuring all people in a society have a reasonable opportunity to flourish – to be free. Thus, Liberals occupy a broad chunk of the middle of the political spectrum. Those on the left, such as Sam Harris, value government more than those on the right, such as Ben Shapiro.

## The Centre-Left within the IDW

The modal political position in the IDW is somewhere around the centre-left; although there is another bump around the centre-right where Jordan Peterson and Ben Shapiro reside. Those in the IDW who occupy this centre-left position include Joe Rogan, Eric and Bret Weinstein,

Sam Harris, Heather Heying, Jonathan Haidt, Helen Pluckrose, Peter Boghossian, and associates such as Matt Taibbi, Bill Burr, and Dave Chappelle. My general sense is that these people do not move further left because even though they support various left-wing causes, they will not subsume individual identity into collective identity, which occurs as you slide further left; whence the disdain for Identity Politics and an older foe: Communism. But also, they despise Wokeness.

If these people within the IDW are critical of parts of the left, then this is a case of the left getting its own house in order. We see this in remarks from Helen Pluckrose and James Lindsay in *Cynical Theories*:

> Though the problem to the right is severe and deserves much careful analysis in its own right, we have become experts in the nature of the problem on the left. This is partly because we believe that, while the two sides are driving one another to madness and further radicalisation, the problem coming from the left represents a departure from its historical point of reason and strength, which is liberalism. It is that liberalism that is essential to the maintenance of our secular, liberal democracies.[8]

In a similar vein, when Helen Pluckrose and Peter Boghsossian appeared on the Rebel Wisdom podcast in October 2019 titled 'Fighting Postmodernism from the Left', Pluckrose says, 'I think there's going to be a big pushback against Social Justice and I want it to come from the Liberal left, rather than the populist right'.[9] Steven Pinker also makes a similar point. Having indicated that he was horrified by the election of Trump, he says:

> Even if, like myself, you were appalled, horrified, by the results of the election last November, that's all the more reason to make sure that we don't set up academia and information technology as an institution that is perceived as so oppressive that people will react to it. We can't be less intelligent, less open to argument, less reasonable, less rational, than Donald Trump.[10]

A point that arises sometimes within the IDW is that the far-right is more dangerous than the left, and there is a danger that if the left – which really ought to know better – goes too far, then the far-right will be antogonised. About this, in September 2017, Peterson says, 'The continual clawing of new ground underneath the radical Leftist rubric, especially in universities, is starting to produce an extraordinarily dangerous counter position'.[11]

Rogan, whose politics are indicative of the centre-left within the IDW, has made many statements about his politics. In October 2018, when talking with James Lindsay and Peter Boghossian about the Grievance Studies Affair, he says:

> I get accused of being Alt-Right all the time. I lean so far-left: universal healthcare, universal basic income, free schooling … I believe in a lot of socialist ideas. But I'm right wing because I make fun of people that want to study problemisation of dogs fucking [he is referring to one of the hoax articles from the Grievance Studies Affair] … If you look at whether I support gay rights, women's rights, I'm on board, all of them … Take more of my taxes. I can afford to pay more if I really believe that people are going to get real health care and real education … I would be very happy.

Lindsay and Boghossian say: 'We're the same'.[12]

Rogan also had Bernie Sanders on his podcast in August 2019 and endorsed him to be the candidate for the Democratic Party for the 2020 US election.[13] Also appearing on his show were Democratic candidates Andrew Yang and Tulsi Gabbard – Gabbard has been on Rogan six times; she is, as I have suggested, the central IDW political figure.[14] In relation to Trump, on Lex Fridman's podcast in July 2022, Rogan said:

> And by the way, I am not a Trump supporter in any way shape or form. I've had the opportunity to have him on my show more than once. I've said no. Every time. I don't want to help him. I'm not interested in helping him.[15]

We can gain a further insight into the left wing of the IDW by considering some remarks by Philosopher Slavoj Žižek. Žižek is not really IDW, but I would locate him closer to the core than Chomsky, in that in April 2019 Žižek debated Jordan Peterson (4,249,872 views on YouTube as of 12 October 2022),[16] and there are several videos on YouTube of Žižek talking about figures in the IDW, such as Sam Harris. But most significantly, he does not like Political Correctness and Identity Politics. Speaking at Seton Hall University, the inimitable Žižek says:

> Political Correctness is, for me, a typical petit-bourgeois excess, which really tries to continue to obfuscate economic issues ... I think that Cultural Marxism, if by this we mean the culturalization of the left from late 80s onwards, this is what enabled Trump. We all know. And in Europe, because the left, this Postmodern left, which is terribly afraid to be connected with real working class – they like minorities, they like whatever – third world nations, and so on, they of course, as we all know, they neglected your own working class, that's why today, and it's a tragedy, in Europe, for example, which European party did most for actual working class in Europe now – it's horror – Law and Justice, the Polish arch Conservative – Kaczyński, the brothers, one died – party where precisely on behalf of right wing Populism, they did things that no moderate Leftist today dare to do: they lowered retirement age, they expanded healthcare, they made better credits for students, and so on and so on. So in this sense for me, I support them totally. It was an obscenity. Do you remember, two three months before Trump was elected, the big topic in left Liberal media was how to solve the problem of toilets with Transgender people ... I think that this total neglect of concerns of ordinary working people was a catastrophe. And that's why I like Bernie Sanders.[17]

For Žižek, as for quite a few in the IDW, the left has abandoned class concerns for bourgeois Identity Politics.

(Those who support Identity Politics are aware of the argument that Identity Politics led to the election of Trump – the argument is common enough. Suzanna Walters, in her article 'In Defense of Identity Politics' says that Identity Politics wasn't to blame for the election of Trump; rather, Trump's success was about 'male and white supremacists endlessly reasserting both their interests and their universality'.[18] Sigh. The Culture Wars.)

Andrew Doyle makes a similar point to Žižek's:

> For me, unless you are concerned about class issues – pushing working class people up, social mobility, economic inequality and trying to redress that – if you're not interested in those things, I don't think you're left wing. In any meaningful sense. So the whole Identitarian move-

ment – the whole LGBTQIA nonsense – the Critical Race Theory nonsense – all of this stuff, is essentially an upper middle class pursuit. It has got nothing to do with being left wing at all. I would argue it's more right wing, because it's concerned with posh people and their interests.[19]

He also points out that Labour in the UK used to be anti-EU; thus leaving the EU was a natural policy for it:

Jeremy Corbyn [the leader of the Labour Party from 2015-2020] was campaigning for 40 years to get out of the EU. And all of a sudden all my left-wing friends were saying, we're really pro-EU. They were really pro this trading block, this undemocratic, bureaucratic, trading block, that has Capitalism at the heart of its constitution. This isn't a left-wing stance.[20]

Reinforcing the idea that the establishment left has been losing its focus on class, Bernie Sanders in March 2023 on Bill Maher's show, says:

When FDR was president, when Truman was president, even when JFK was president, you go out on the street and you say to people, 'which party represents the working class of America'. Most people I think – agree? [he's seeking Maher's agreement] – would have said the Democratic Party. Today you go out on the street and that is not the sentiment. In fact, the Republican Party probably has more adherents than the Democrats.

Maher asks: 'How did that happen?' Sanders replies:

I'll tell you how it happened. Because thirty years ago the Democrats said, 'Hey, the Republicans are getting all this corporate money, we want it too! Let's go out and get it. And let's forget about the people working 50 or 60 hours'.

Earlier Maher had referred to Sanders' book in which Sanders says that the Democratic Party 'abandoned their cause to the beautiful people'.[21]

In relation to all of this, the term 'Woke Capitalism' is significant. Ross Douthat coined the term in an article in the *New York Times* on

28 February 2018.[22] It refers to the corporate embrace of left-wing issues that relate to race and gender. Implied in the term is the idea that corporations are very happy to make 'costless gestures' – to use the term that Matt Taibbi used when critiquing the US Democratic Party[23] – that pander to the politics of their market. Ours is a difficult time to make sense of. It's strange that the corporate world is so strongly aligned with the so-called radicals of the university. But then with Chomsky's remarks about Postmodernism in mind, it's not strange at all: The so-called radicals from the university aren't radical. On this point, academic Camille Paglia, who is an IDW distant associate, is ruthless. She derides the 'pseudo-Leftists' and 'frauds' of academia and says:

> These people who manage to rise to the top at Berkely, at Harvard, at Princeton – the idea that these people are radical. They are career people. They are corporate types who love the institutional context. They know how to manipulate the bureaucracy which has totally invaded and usurped academia everywhere. These people are company players. They could have done well in any field. They love to sit in endless committees. They love bureaucratic regulations.[24]

I know that the *ad hominem* argument is frowned upon. However, I think it has its uses. For years, as I was trying to make sense of all this (before I relised there were others who thought the way I thought), I kept encountering Postmodern academics who styled themselves as radicals, but who seemed banal and middle of the road. Corporate types. The thing is, my philosophical values are present in how I live my life. Thus, for better or worse, my life is an advertisement of my philosophy. I believe this is the case for most people. Whence the value of the *ad hominem*.

## The Centre within the IDW

The second political position within the IDW sits around the centre, but it approaches the centre from four or five related angles. I'm not certain who to put in this 'position'; I suspect the 'angles' resonate with many in the IDW. The first angle is described by the term 'Radical Centre'. Steven Pinker was talking about this in late 2018.[25] The word 'centre', much like 'centre-left', combines broadly Progressive values with a liking for being enterprising. And 'radical' indicates that rather than being at the centre because of political apathy, the person is there because he or she has thought hard about politics and decided there are pros and cons on both sides; or indeed, he or she deals with problems on their own merits rather than buying into a political package. Joe Rogan echoed this in March 2023 when talking with Michael Malice:

> I think we just need to figure out why we are in these ideological rifts that are so fucking polarising and rabid. I think we need to figure that out. I think that's possible. Just like I think the hippie movement came out of nowhere in the 50s, I think there's like a radical, rational Centrist movement that could come about today. I really do. I think there's enough people like you and I that just think this is bananas. This subscribing to one predetermined pattern of behaviour and fucking rules of thought. And the other one is like polar opposite of it.[26]

The second angle, which could just about be merged with the first, is old-fashioned open-mindedness. Dr Robert Malone, who was a dissenting voice during the COVID pandemic, appeared on Rogan in December 2021. Whether or not one believes his concerns about COVID vaccines, his remarks towards the end of his appearance on Rogan about Rogan's politics help to consolidate our understanding of IDW politics:

> So Joe … you're one of the few voices that has an audience that is not Democrat or Republican or black or white or vaccinated or unvaccinated – or all these dipoles that we create artificially. And you are trying to speak to that persuadable middle and do so with an open heart and an open mind and in a world in which all of the information is being so carefully manipulated and so pervasively distorted.[27]

Lex Fridman delivered an inspiring endorsement of open-mindedness in December 2021 at the beginning of the podcast in which he interviews the CEO of Pfizer, Albert Bourla:

> Please allow me to say a few words about truth and human nature. Specifically, about two groups of people throughout history that seek to lay claim to the truth. The first group will tell you that they possess the truth. That the government will save you, the company will save you, the science, the authorities, the experts, the institutions will save

you. The second group too will tell you that only they possess the truth. That the government will hurt you, the company will hurt you, the science, the authorities, the experts, the institutions will hurt you. Both groups have the benevolent and the malevolent, their heroes and their charlatans, and I think the hard truth is that no one in this world can tell you with absolute certainty which is which. You have to use your mind. This is the burden of being human. Of being free. Don't blindly follow any leader. Neither the emperor, nor the martyr who points out that the emperor has no clothes.[28]

A third angle is being willing to criticise your own side. This doesn't exactly put someone at the political centre, but it shows a willingness to step outside tribal dogma in the direction of the centre. Making this point, Weiss, in her 2018 article, says, 'There is no direct route into the Intellectual Dark Web. But the quickest path is to demonstrate that you aren't afraid to confront your own tribe'. In January 2023, we heard this point again on Lex Fridman's podcast. Fridman says, 'What's hard to do is to speak up when everybody else is silent'. Jeremi Suri, with whom Lex is in conversation, adds, 'And to speak up against those who you thought were on your side'. Lex says, 'It's a lonely place. It's a painful place. That's why walking in the centre is tough: you get attacked from both sides. It's a wonderful wonderful journey'.[29] Ben Shapiro, the most Conservative figure in the IDW, is in the IDW in part because he was willing to criticise the right.[30] And on Rogan in October 2022, Tulsi Gabbard describes how she increasingly fell out of favour with the Democratic Party as it became clear she would not toe the party line, but wanted to think for herself.[31]

A fourth angle follows from the third: being politically homeless. Quite a few within the IDW started on the left but have become estranged from it. Christina Hoff Sommers describes this on Rogan in November 2015:

> Not only was I once a radical, but I'm sympathetic to Leftists because – some of the people closest to my heart are very left wing, but they're not haters, they're not – they don't take whole groups of people and impugn them as evil.

Rogan says, 'I'm very sympathetic to a lot of the ideas that left-wing people have – I don't know if I consider myself left wing or Libertarian or what – I'm kind of in the middle –' Sommers says, 'You're probably like me: I'm homeless, politically homeless'.[32] Returning to Gabbard on Rogan in October 2022, Gabbard announced that she was leaving the Democratic Party and becoming an Independent.[33] She states that within the party there is a 'cult-like atmosphere'[34] and that people are too afraid to stand up for what they believe in because of the ramifications. She also says that the Democratic Party that once 'welcomed and encouraged this marketplace of ideas' does not exist anymore. Rogan asks Gabbard, 'Is there any courting of you by the Republican party?' She replies, 'Not that I know of'. Rogan asks, 'You have no interest'. Gabbard replies, 'No no'.[35] She goes on to say that the Republican Party is itself divided. But she does identify what she sees as being some good aspects of the Republican Party. She says that the party has 'turned more towards Populism [in a positive sense] and fighting for working people,' and she also speaks positively about 50 Republicans in Congress who opposed the US waging a proxy war against Russia and notes that no Democrats opposed the spending bill that was under consideration. Both of these points are interesting: supporting workers and opposing war were once strong Democratic policies. In May 2022, Conservative YouTube personality, Brett Cooper – who is a young, female version of Ben Shapiro – gleefully mentions several disgruntled Liberals who 'feel like they are without a party': Elon Musk, Joe Rogan, Russell Brand, Tulsi Gabbard, and Bill Maher.[36]

The fifth angle, which perhaps more than any other, may well contribute to the political novelty of the IDW is Joe Rogan's statement (I can't find on which episode he says it!) that he thinks like a Democrat but lives like a Republican.

## The Right within the IDW

I have much less to say here about the politics of the right within the IDW than I do about the IDW's left and centre politics. This is because what is most politically interesting about the IDW is that while the IDW is ostensibly anti-left, many associated with it are on the left, or at least they resist joining the right. Exploring this gives us insights into our political moment. The political right within the IDW is more familiar, even if the right itself is undergoing something of a change by championing free speech and being increasingly connected with the working class. The figures on the right in the IDW include Ben Shapiro, Jordan Peterson, Douglas Murray, Dave Rubin, and Gad Saad.

A notable aspect of the right within the IDW is religiosity. The obviously religious figures are Shapiro and Peterson. The religiosity of both seems to drive, or at least go hand-in-hand with, their Conservatism and more traditional values, such as Shapiro's strong anti-abortion stance.[37] I will say more about the relationship between the IDW and religion in Chapter 16.

The dominant right-wing aspect of the IDW is its championing of individual responsibility. While I will discuss this in more detail in Chapter 14, the broad sense, even amongst those on the left of the IDW, is that even though the world is unfair and ought to be improved, focusing on one's grievances with the world – 'activism' – rather than trying to make something of one's self, can be damaging. For some, such as Rogan, this championing of individual responsibility is flavoured by a Libertarian-style rugged individualism.

Beyond religion and individual responsibility, some of the other IDW positions that I will explore in Part 2 can be construed as right wing, but this is sometimes only because they stand in opposition to Woke positions that have come to be indicative of the left. Included in this is the IDW belief that there are biological differences between men and women beyond obvious physical differences. Then there is the Transgender issue (see Chapter 16); being concerned about children transitioning or Transgender women competing in women's sports are not necessarily right-wing positions, but such causes have come to be championed by the right.

## Populism within the IDW

A final political dimension of the IDW to consider is Populism. Populism is often a pejorative term. We have seen this in the context of the Trump phenomenon and also Brexit. Often when people say 'Populism' they mean that stupid racist people have been beguiled by an ogrish demagogue. And yet there is more to Populism than we might first think. As we have just seen, Tulsi Gabbard used 'Populism' in a positive sense to indicate a regard for the people. While the meaning of the term is contested, Populism can be understood, at least from the point of view of populists themselves, as the virtuous people standing against the corrupt elites. Interestingly, we can have both right- and left-wing Populism. For the right, the corrupt elites are found in government and the intellectual and cultural classes – from academia to Hollywood. For the left, they are found in the corporate world. As should already be clear, the IDW believes that many of our elites are corrupt, whether they are within academia, the media, the corporate world, or government. Thus, we could think of the IDW as a broad-based populist movement.

Those more inclined towards Populism are Joe Rogan, Jordan Peterson, Ben Shapiro, Dave Rubin, Bret Weinstein, Heather Heying, and, perhaps most of all, Russell Brand – if we include him in the IDW. We might even include Bernie Sanders if he were IDW – recall his objection to 'the beautiful people?' Others in the IDW are wary of elites; however, they are more circumspect in their criticisms. We have already seen in this chapter that Lex Fridman has said that there is no easy choice to be made between the establishment and the antiestablishment. And as we will see later, Eric Weinstein makes a similar argument. The point for Lex Fridman, Eric Weinstein, and also Sam Harris, is that while some of the elites who run our institutions are corrupt, many aren't, and ultimately, we need our institutions. The slide towards Populism can be both necessary and perilous. Elites everywhere ought to be scrutinised, but it's important to put the brakes on before we start indulging in unfounded conspiracy theories.

## The Left and Right of Politics Ain't What They Used to Be

To finish, as I have already touched on, the IDW also sometimes mentions that there has been something of a reversal in the left and the right wing. There are two parts to this reversal. First is the left's reduced interest in class. In many respects, we do now have a 'Woke Capitalism' that is characterised by radical ideas about gender and race that were developed in the academy being enthusiastically endorsed by the corporate world. It's odd. Recall that Žižek says: 'Political Correctness is, for me, a typical petit-bourgeois excess, which really tries to continue to obfuscate economic issues'. Second is the left's now censorious nature. About this, Rogan says:

But that's what the left used to be about. The left used to be about, like, freedom. It was more like freedom of speech. Freedom of expression. Think about the comic books that came from the left … Bizarre wild shit the right would never create. But then somewhere along the line the roles reversed. And I don't even know if people realised it … Today if you are going to be a person who had a controversial comic book, you would most likely be on the right.[38]

We see this shift within the long-running show *South Park*. *South Park* started out more on the left – it had a New Atheist feel to it – but is now increasingly praised by the right; recently in Australia the right-wing Sky News was energetically discussing the episode that made fun of the royals, Harry and Meghan, who are widely considered to be Woke.

The broad point is that perhaps the distinction between left and right as we once knew it: workers versus capital, wild freedom versus stuffy Conservatism, no longer exists. Given this, perhaps we really ought to treat individual issues on their own merits, rather than pick a side. Rogan, speaking with Francis Foster and Konstantin Kisin in July 2022, says 'Nuance is difficult. Looking at things for what they really are is complicated. It's complex'. Kisin replies, 'It's much easier to pick a team, man'.[39]

## Notes

1   The 'Intellectual Dark Web' – the supposed thinking wing of the Alt-Right 2018.

2   While I am telling myself to keep my powder dry, the drums of the Culture Wars beat loudly in my head. As I was drafting this paragraph on 7 July 2022, at the top of the page, in a pane where *Vox* was soliciting donations, were the words, 'Explaining the best ways to do good has never been more important.' The hubris. Once again, it is easy to understand why 'Woke' ('A state of enlightened understanding') rapidly became a pejorative term. Compare this with the following description of the mission of the Australia paper, *The Sydney Morning Herald:* 'The Herald is proudly committed to fearless, independent and accurate journalism as Australia's number one news brand, whilst generating high-quality and informed opinions and debates to help readers make up their own minds.' Vox will explain to its readers how to do good. The Herald, in contrast, aims to present opinions and debates that help readers themselves determine what they think.

3    Farrell 2018.

4    Brooks 2020.

5    Only Love 2017 August 24.

6    Pinker 2011: 800.

7    The Joe Rogan Experience 2018 November 16: 3:49:35.

8    Pluckrose and Lindsay 2021: 12.

9    Rebel Wisdom 2019 October 7: 0:03:39.

10   Enlightainment 2018 August 1: 0:04:08.

11   The Joe Rogan Experience 2017 September 1: 0:13:29.

12   The Joe Rogan Experience 2018 October 31: 0:32:52.

13   The Joe Rogan Experience 2019 August 6.

14   Yang: JRE #1245 (2019 February 12). Gabbard: JRE #1170 (2018 September 11), #1295 (2019 May 14), #1391 (2019 November 26), #1599 (2021 January 21), #1880 (2022 October 11).

15   Led Fridman 2022 July 4: 0:19:18.

16   Manufacturing Intellect 2019 April 27.

17   Seton Hall University 2018 November 2: 1:27:44.

18   Walters 2018: 483.

19   Triggernometry 2022 December 26: 0:25:04.

20   Triggernometry 2022 September 8: 0:29:32.

21   Real Time with Bill Maher 2023 March 4: 0:03:01.

22   Douthat 2018 February 28.

23   Taibbi 2020 June 29.

24   Jordan B Peterson 2017 October 3: 0:11:17.

25   Pinker 2018 December 18. Daniel Miessler (2019) also thinks of IDW politics as being of the 'Radical Centre'.

26   The Joe Rogan Experience 2023 March 8: 1:08:25.

27   The Joe Rogan Experience 2021 December 31: 2:45:00.

28   Lex Fridman 2021 December 19: 0:00:00.

29   Lex Fridman 2023 January 26: 1:48:16.

30   This is discussed in Sam Harris 2018 January 6.

31   The Joe Rogan Experience 2022 October 11: 1:06:30.

32   The Joe Rogan Experience 2015 November 179: 2:16:39.

33   The Joe Rogan Experience 2022 October 11: 1:00:55.

34   The Joe Rogan Experience 2022 October 11: 0:58:00.

35   The Joe Rogan Experience 2022 October 11: 1:11:08.

36   The Comments Section with Brett Cooper 2022 May 24: 0:00:00.

37   The Free Speech Club 2018 November 16.

38   The Joe Rogan Experience 2023 March 8: 0:14:30.

39   The Joe Rogan Experience 2022 July 27: 0:17:07.

6

# The Beginnings (and Possible Ending) of the IDW

### The Multiple Origins of the IDW

What were the origins of the IDW? There is no single right answer to this question. A confluence of factors and circumstances contributed to its identification and rise.

### *The IDW has always been around.*

The first answer is that the IDW has always been around in some form. As I have mentioned, in some of the backlash articles responding to Weiss's May 2018 article, the authors suggest that there is nothing new about the IDW. Elizabeth Nolan Brown claims that the '"Intellectual Dark Web" Is Just Rehashing Old P.C. Controversies in New Media',[1] and Jonah Goldberg sees the IDW as being just another instance of Liberals becoming disillusioned by the Liberal orthodoxy.[2] Such points are reasonable; though I don't think they detract from the IDW: similar problems continue to arise (humans don't seem to change all that much); thus we would expect similar responses.

Going back a few decades, Steven Pinker, in his 2002 book *The Blank Slate*, challenged the Postmodern assumption that the human mind is a blank slate. In 1996, Physicist Alan Sokal's hoax article, 'Transgressing the Boundaries: Towards a Transformative Hermeneutics of Quantum

Gravity' was published in the Postmodern journal *Social Text*. In the article Sokal satirised Postmodern jargon and the familiar Postmodern claim that science is a social construction (I still come across this claim today). And for several years in the 1990s, the journal *Philosophy and Literature* awarded prizes for the worst sentences produced by Postmodern academics. A notable winner was Postmodern gender scholar, Judith Butler (I'm ashamed to say that I understand the sentence).

Looking further back, Monty Python's *Life of Brian* and *Holy Grail* have a strong IDW flavour. The movies satirise the self-importance and ineptness of far-left groups but also the excessive violence of unaccountable power – it is not easy to pigeon-hole Monty Python as left or right. The 'What have the Romans ever given us?' scene from *Life of Brian* is as relevant as ever. In it, John Cleese's character, Reg, who is the leader of the revolutionary group, The People's Front of Judea, asks what the Romans have ever given the people of Judea. As he pauses for effect, his followers begin to make suggestions: the aqueduct, the sanitation, the roads (to which Reg says, 'well yeah, obviously the roads, I mean, the roads go without saying, don't they'), irrigation, medicine, and so on.[3] Reg's one-sided contempt for the Romans is similar to the current antipathy for the West in the Woke world.

There are many historical figures with whom the IDW shares something. Orwell is admired by several within the IDW. Like the IDW, he was a Leftist who was critical of the excesses of the left. *Animal Farm's* 'Four legs good, two legs bad' is an earlier incarnation of our own Identity Politics, in which good and evil are determined by identity markers, such as skin colour, biological sex and whether or not one has a disability. And the immortal 2 + 2 = 5 from *Nineteen Eighty-Four* reminds us of the mad statements that we now must endorse, such as the paradox 'Transwomen are women'.

Then there is Nietzsche, who, like the IDW, was wary of running with the herd, and knew that people grasp at power by claiming to be victims. But Nietzsche also had the meta-awareness that when we fight monsters, we ourselves can become monsters.

Even Shakespeare has something of the IDW about him – or the IDW has something of Shakespeare about it. Shakespeare's works pursue the truth of the human condition; they do not seek to condemn the heretic. Sonnet 66 (see the epigraphs to this book), despite being written over 400 years ago, perfectly describes our current cultural moment.

And beyond all of these is Plato, whose philosopher seeks to know the patterns that describe reality, and who knows how easy it is for the philosopher to be corrupted by the chattering and temptations of the crowd.

But all this can be abstracted. For humanity, there is an eternal interplay between truth and power. When power is founded on truth, it is good. But whenever power becomes corrupt, truth objects. A sympathetic reading of the IDW is that it is just another manifestation of truth objecting to corrupt power. The unsympathetic reading is that Political Correctness and Identity Politics are just fine – they are on the side of truth – and the IDW is merely a manifestation of corrupt power attempting to retain power. Again, as Henry Farrell writes, 'It's hard for erstwhile hegemons to feel happy about their fall'.

### The IDW is a continuation of the New Atheist movement.

The second answer is that the IDW was a continuation of the 'New Atheist' movement that was prominent in the 2000s. The New Atheist movement included proto-IDW figure Christopher Hitchens (Hitchens died before the IDW matured) and IDW figures Sam Harris, Ayaan Hirsi Ali, and Richard Dawkins. We also saw the involvement of IDW associate Stephen Fry. Further, near-core IDW figures James Lindsay and Peter Boghossian both promoted atheism in the early 2010s and wrote books and articles on the subject. And as we have seen, the earlier days of the IDW (the mid-2010s) was partly characterised by figures such as Douglas Murray, Sam Harris, and Ayaan Hirsi Ali objecting to aspects of Islam at a time when such objections were taboo. However, the central distinction between the New Atheists and the IDW is that where the New Atheists used reason to attack religion, the IDW has used reason to attack Wokeness – which, for the IDW, is a new religion. I shall return to all this in Chapter 16.

### Campus politics reached critical mass.

The third answer is that in the early 2010s campus politics reached a critical mass and began to spill over into broader society and this precipitated a push-back. Hypotheses abound about what caused the explosion of Woke politics on campus and in the wider world.

Jonathan Haidt and Greg Lukianoff, in their book *The Coddling of the American Mind*,[4] see the change in campus politics as being driven by students who grew up online, and who were, because of this, more fragile than previous generations and more inclined to draw strength from a mob-based victimhood. This inclination dovetailed perfectly with the Identity Politics and Postmodern ideology that had been simmering in academia for decades.[5]

In October 2022, Lex Fridman and Balaji Srinivasan (in a very long podcast [7:47:51!])[6] discussed Paul Graham's thoughts about the transformation in the media landscape in the early 2010s and how this led to the eruption of Wokeness in the wider world. In a Tweet on 7 June 2019, Graham wrote: 'Hypothesis: Although some newspapers can survive the switch to online subscriptions, none can do it and remain a politically neutral "newspaper of record." You have to pick a side to get people to subscribe'.[7] Graham is referring to the *New York Times*, which, rather than being a 'newspaper of record', has, according to IDW figures and others, become a driver of Woke politics. The point is that as social media undermined traditional news media, traditional news media had to exploit polarisation to continue to make money; once again, we see the belief that capitalism lies behind Wokeness. Graham reproduces a 'New York Times Word Usage Frequency (1970–2018)' set of graphs originally produced by David Rozado. These graphs show the prevalence of various words in the *New York Times*. Whereas words such as 'education', 'universities', and 'schools' jump around throughout the period, words such as 'sexism', 'racism', 'kkk', and 'inequality' shoot upwards from a low base around 2013. Srinivasan states that traditional media such as the *New York Times*, 'took all these weapons that had been developed in academia to win status competitions in Humanities departments and they just deployed them'. Echoing my earlier analysis, Srinivasan says that 'Wokeness is the combination of Foucauldian deconstruction and civil rights'.[8]

2024 Republican Presidential Candidate Vivek Ramaswamy has a similar hypothesis. Speaking on Jordan Peterson's podcast in March 2023, Ramaswamy suggests that the explosion of Woke politics beyond the university was driven by corporations after the 2008 Global Financial Crisis. Ramaswamy argues that post GFC, corporations integrated

Identity Politics, with a focus on race and gender, to appease the left and thus divert attention from their own ongoing exploitation of the poor.[9]

It was in the early 2010s that Joe Rogan began to have academics such as Gad Saad on his podcast to discuss the minutiae of campus politics (Saad's first appearance was 8 July 2014). In July 2022, Rogan, when discussing IDW subject matter with Francis Foster and Konstantin Kisin, said that he had been talking about Woke culture on his podcast since 2012 and made the point that many of the things the IDW has been concerned about were, at that time, largely isolated to universities.[10] On several occasions, Rogan has said that people would say to him: Why are you worrying about campus politics? Rogan's reply was: Campus politics won't necessary stay on campus. Rogan was the canary in the coalmine.

### Trump was elected president.

The fourth answer is that the IDW gained further momentum when Donald Trump was elected president of the United States. We can think of the IDW as a response to the excesses of the left that were themselves a response to the excesses of Trump. But then, as Žižek argues, Trump himself was a response to the excesses of the left. Rogan, in November 2016, when talking with Peterson, says: 'Ironically, I really truly believe that one of the big factors in Trump's rise to power is that people are sick of this oversimplification, this ridiculous ideology, coming from the left … So they've chosen an Identity Politics that opposes the Identity Politics that they think is disgusting'.[11]

## IDW Origin Events

While we can, as I have just been doing, explore the rise of the IDW in sociological terms – that is, see it as a part of broader social forces – we can also identify several IDW origin events that brought various IDW figures to public awareness and helped to cement the conviction amongst many people that there was a serious problem with parts of the left.

### Sam Harris argues with Ben Affleck about Islam.

Date: 2014 October 7

For many years following the US invasions of Afghanistan and Iraq, there was a taboo on the left about criticising Islam. This was understandable because racism directed at Muslims was widespread and helped to support the wars. I recall saying things like, 'yes, the 9/11 terrorists were Muslims, but this does not mean that all Muslims are terrorists'. However, the taboo made it difficult to distinguish between unreasonable and reasonable criticisms of Islam. In October 2014, Sam Harris, continuing his New Atheist work, appeared on Real Time with Bill Maher and criticised Western Liberals for themselves failing to criticise the illiberal aspects of the Muslim world.[12]

The following is indicative of Harris's position:

> Liberals have really failed on the topic of theocracy. They'll criticise white theocracy; they'll criticise Christians … But when you want to talk about the treatment of women, homosexuals, free thinkers, and public intellectuals in the Muslim world, I would argue that Liberals have failed us. The crucial point of confusion is that we've been sold this meme of Islamophobia, where every criticism of the doctrine of Islam gets conflated with bigotry towards Muslims as people. It's intellectually ridiculous.

Such remarks were not unusual for Harris. However, what made this a foundational IDW event was the response of actor Ben Affleck, who was also a guest on the show. Affleck was clearly agitated by Harris and lashed out at him. For many, this encounter provided an illustration of the dogmatic nature of left-wing politics. This episode was all the more popular because Affleck was seen as being a member of the Woke Hollywood elite that smugly considers itself to be a guardian of Progressive morality. Recall again Bernie Sanders' objection to the Democratic Party becoming the party of 'the beautiful people' at the expense of workers.

### Bret Weinstein is mobbed by students at Evergreen State College.

Date: 2017 May

Bret Weinstein, along with his wife Heather Heying, was a professor at Evergreen State College. The college had traditionally held a 'Day of Absence' in which Black students stayed away from campus. However, in

2017, there was a push to change this. Rather than black students staying away in protest, the idea was that white students would be asked to stay away. Weinstein opposed this.[13] In his own protest letter he wrote:

> There is a huge difference between a group or coalition deciding to voluntarily absent themselves from a shared space in order to highlight their vital and under-appreciated roles (the theme of the Douglas Turner Ward play *Day of Absence*, as well as the recent Women's Day walkout), and a group or coalition encouraging another group to go away. The first is a forceful call to consciousness which is, of course, crippling to the logic of oppression. The second is a show of force, and an act of oppression in and of itself.... On a college campus, one's right to speak — or to be — must never be based on skin color.[14]

In response to this, on Tuesday 23 May, hundreds (I'm not certain of the numbers) of students protested against Weinstein, and effectively took over the college.[15] The story of this spread, with even left-leaning news outlets such as *Vice* covering it in a way that presented Weinstein in a positive light.[16] The story is compelling because Weinstein is clearly not a right-wing racist (he has a history of fighting racism that involved personal cost), and we get the sense that both students and staff are using Identity Politics and Postmodern rhetoric to pursue corrupt power. Mike Nayna's documentary about the event is available on YouTube.[17] There is also footage on YouTube of the students arguing with Weinstein.[18] What stands out most for me is that none argue about what Weinstein said in his email, even though it was this email that precipitated the events. The corruption of the students is evident in one of the better-known scenes. In it, the president of the college, George Bridges, is told by students to stop gesturing when he is addressing them – the ridiculous implication is that his gestures are intimidating. When he puts his hands down, the students laugh derisively, giving the strong impression that the whole episode is a cynical power game.[19] The episode became a foundational IDW event when Weinstein appeared on Rogan in June 2017, two weeks after the incident. Bret Weinstein's early appearances on Rogan are, like Peterson's and Eric Weinstein's appearances, canonical: they established so much that we now consider to be the way of the IDW.

***James Damore is fired by Google.***

Date: 2017 August

In July 2017, James Damore, then an employee at Google, circulated a memo[20] in response to Google's diversity policies – Google had solicited feedback. The memo, which discusses why there were fewer women than men in tech and what can be done about this, came to be widely shared within the company. On 7 August 2017, two days after *Gizmodo* published a story on the memo,[21] Damore was fired. In the memo Damore argues that Google is an 'ideological echo chamber' in which all inequalities in outcome ('disparities in representation') are attributed to oppression, such that other factors, which could include population-level differences that are a result of biology, are ignored. In the memo, Damore makes several suggestions about how Google can take these population-level differences into account to improve 'representation' in the company.

The episode is foundational for the IDW for several reasons. Most significantly, Damore, like Steven Pinker and many others associated with the IDW, does not hold to the 'blank slate' view of the human mind with respect to biological sex. And like other IDW figures, he broke the taboo in polite society against speaking about such things. Related to this, Damore clearly endorses the Enlightenment tradition, which holds that to solve problems, the nature of reality – the nature of the problems – needs to be determined (recall that in the Postmodern tradition, problems come from discourse and are thus solved by changing discourse). Damore also speaks about the importance of 'viewpoint diversity', saying that it is arguably the most important type of diversity. Finally, Damore comes across as a political Centrist – he says that he is not interested in day-to-day politics and is more interested in ideas and how to bridge the divide between the two sides.[22]

About the episode *The Guardian* wrote, 'Google's sexist memo has provided the Alt-Right with a new martyr'. While it is debatable that the memo is sexist, it is likely true that the episode provided the Alt-Right with a new martyr. Though, it also provided the IDW with further evidence that its concerns were well-founded. Many of us have spent decades arguing against the Postmodern assertion that there are no biological differences between men and women beyond physical appearance, and episodes such as the Damore firing reveal the bad faith that we believe we've been struggling against.

Damore appeared on Rogan shortly after he was fired (2017 September 6). Notably, Bret Weinstein and Jordan Peterson had appeared together on Rogan just five days earlier, and Eric Weinstein would appear on Rogan for the first time a month later.[23] Damore also joined with Heather Heying, Helen Pluckrose, Peter Boghossian, and Bret Weinstein on 17 February 2018 in a talk at Portland State University[24] (this was some months before the 'Grievance Studies' affair, involving Pluckrose and Boghossian, became public).

### Jordan Peterson is interviewed by Cathy Newman.

Date: 2018 January 19

The most significant IDW origin event, besides Weiss's article, was Jordan Peterson's interview by Cathy Newman on Britain's *Channel 4 News*.[25] Peterson had already gained fame through his opposition in 2016 to Bill C-16 that was passed by the Parliament of Canada. Peterson was concerned that the Bill would make the use of gender pronouns 'compelled speech', which would undermine free speech. Peterson then appeared on Rogan for the first time in November 2016. Both Peterson's opposition to the Bill and his Rogan appearance are themselves IDW origin events (so much of this book can be found in Peterson's first Rogan appearance), but the Newman interview stands out because of how Newman herself responded to Peterson.

Early in the interview, Newman questions Peterson about the pay gap between the sexes at the population level. Peterson provides nuanced responses to her questions, stressing that there is no simple explanation for the pay gap. Newman repeatedly mischaracterises what Peterson is saying, prefacing her comments with 'You're saying …' This became a meme.

Peterson becomes more relaxed as the interview progresses. At one point Newman, attacking Peterson's position about men and women and employment, says, 'Because a lot of people listening to you will just say, are we going back to the dark ages?' Peterson laughs lightly – there is little malice – and replies, 'That's because they're actually not listening, they're just projecting what they think'.[26] He says 'they're', but it's clear he also means 'you are'. While Peterson's remarks are a blow, the laughter is a bigger blow. How does one respond when the person one is arguing with has been taken by a demon, or, as Peterson puts it in a later interview, is 'animus possessed'?[27] In this later interview, Peterson says, 'If you engage in the argument on the terms they've defined, you lose. It doesn't matter whether you win or lose. You lose as soon as you engage in the argument'. His gentle laughter was the best way to respond to the demon. Shortly after, as Newman continues to mischaracterise what he is saying, Peterson calls her remarks 'silly'. He doesn't say she is being ridiculous or preposterous or insane. Just silly. This works because it is clear to many who watch that her arguments are silly. Thus, Peterson defeats Newman not only on the level of argument – propositionally – but on the level of performance.

The most watched part of the interview (YouTube has a feature where you can see which parts of the video have been most replayed) relates to free speech. Newman famously asks, 'Why should your right to freedom of speech trump a Trans person's right not to be offended?'

Peterson pauses, then replies, 'Because in order to be able to think you have to risk being offensive'.[28] It's a strong response to give under pressure, and this is one of the main reasons Peterson has become such an icon: very few of us hold up in the heat of intellectual battle, especially when faced with a disingenuous interlocutor. Peterson is right. If we only say what others want to hear, then our words will not be committed to getting to the truth and solving problems; they will only be committed to corrupt power.

Directly after this, Peterson says, 'I mean, look at the conversation we are having right now. You're certainly willing to risk offending me in the pursuit of truth. Why should you have the right to do that? It's been rather uncomfortable'. He is then gracious: 'You're doing what you should do, which is digging a bit, to see what the hell is going on. And that is what you should do. But you are exercising your freedom of speech to certainly risk offending me. And that's fine. More power to you, as far as I'm concerned'.

Newman begins to respond: 'But you haven't sat there …' She pauses, struggling to find a way to continue the interview. **In what is the supreme moment for the IDW, Peterson says, 'Ha, gotcha'.** We then see a glimmer of Newman's humanity. She gives a genuine smile and says, 'you have got me, you have got me …' But alas, she resets herself and the humanity vanishes. But this too is telling. In a different branch of the multiverse, at this point Peterson and Newman become friends and Newman says what she really thinks, rather than continuing to be the mouthpiece for the orthodox-left.

But there is more. Later Newman talks about Peterson comparing Transgender activists with Mao. She says, 'This is grossly insensitive'. Peterson sticks to his guns, calling both 'left-wing totalitarians'. Newman says, 'There's no comparison between Mao and a Trans activist'. Peterson says, 'Why not?' Newman says, 'Because Trans activists aren't killing millions of people'. It really does seem that Newman has this point won. But Peterson goes on to say, 'The philosophy that drives their [Trans activists'] utterances is the same philosophy that already has driven us to the deaths of millions of people'. Newman says, 'Ok, tell us how that philosophy is in any way comparable'. It's almost like we are watching a movie – Newman thinks she is on such firm ground that there is no way Peterson can prevail. Peterson says:

> Sure, that's no problem. The first thing is, is that the philosophy presumes that group identity is paramount. That's the fundamental philosophy that drove the Soviet Union and Maoist China and is the fundamental philosophy of the leftwing activists. It's Identity Politics. It doesn't matter who you are as an individual. What matters is who you are in terms of your group identity.

Once again, we sense that we are getting to the heart of the matter. But Newman replies, 'You're just saying things to provoke, aren't you?'[29] It's tough. Peterson is right about Identity Politics being a common philosophy. But then he is also being provocative. Identity Politics has caused, or at least been used to justify, the greatest horrors of last century. But it is arguably scaremongering to link the relatively mild contemporary incarnations of Identity Politics with the atrocities committed by Stalin, Mao and Hitler. Addressing this point, Steven Pinker in *Enlightenment Now* says, 'The totalitarian governments of the 20th century did not emerge from democratic welfare states sliding down a slippery slope, but were imposed by fanatical ideologues and gangs of thugs'.[30] Thus, while we should certainly challenge Identity Politics' and Postmodernism's degradation of Liberal values, we also ought to avoid unnecessarily exacerbating the Culture Wars. But I don't know. How dangerous is the Woke mind virus? Perhaps the threat is not Identity Politics itself, but what happens once Identity Politics has degraded our Liberal democracies.

To conclude, Peterson's performance is exemplary of the way of the Intellectual Dark Web – mostly for the better but also, to a degree, for the worse. Peterson is presented with numerous talking points, each of which has an orthodox-left position that is protected by a taboo against considering other perspectives. For each talking point, he presents a thoughtful dissenting perspective. His arguments are not flawless, yet Newman almost entirely fails to engage with anything Peterson says, which generates the unfortunate impression that she is speaking corrupt power to truth. This is the supreme origin event for the IDW because Newman is not a flaky Hollywood actor, nor is she a green student, nor a spineless executive who is worried about how his or her corporation appears to a blood-thirsty activist class. She is an intelligent and respected journalist working for a reputable British – not American – news outlet. When the IDW argues that substantial parts of the mainstream media have been captured by the Woke or illiberal left, Newman's interview is, for them, emblematic of the problem.

***Bari Weiss's article, 'Meet the Renegades of the Intellectual Dark Web' is published in the New York Times***

Date 2018 May 8

I won't say much more about Weiss's article – it is easy to read online. The point is that Weiss popularised the name 'Intellectual Dark Web', and introduced many IDW figures, such as Joe Rogan, Jordan Peterson, Eric and Brett Weinstein and Heather Heying to a wider audience, and clarified several IDW talking points. The first paragraph of the article states:

> Here are some things that you will hear when you sit down to dinner with the vanguard of the Intellectual Dark Web: There are fundamental biological differences between men and women. Free speech is under siege. Identity politics is a toxic ideology that is tearing American society apart. And we're in a dangerous place if these ideas are considered 'dark'.[31]

One point to note is that Weiss writes 'vanguard'. This reminds us that there is a core to the IDW, and that spreading out from this are innumerable associates, such as Weiss herself, and legions of acolytes who share the IDW's concerns.

### The Grievance Studies Affair becomes public.

Date: Mid 2017 – 2018 October 2

By the time the 'Grievance Studies Affair' became public, Bari Weiss's article had been published, the name 'Intellectual Dark Web' had been established, and many IDW figures had become well known. Thus, the Grievance Studies Affair isn't exactly an IDW origin event. However, it is one of the most significant events for the IDW, and it established Helen Pluckrose, James Lindsay, and Peter Boghossian as major IDW figures. But above all else, it must be mentioned because of what it targeted.

Consider the four events I have just mentioned (Weiss's article aside). The Harris event struck at Hollywood – insofar as Affleck is metonymic of Hollywood. The Bret Weinstein event struck at students – or student-activists. The Damore event struck at the corporate world. The Peterson event struck at the media. But the Grievance Studies Affair struck at the heart of the beast: academic publishing. All the other areas could almost be forgiven for being partisan – Hollywood, students, the corporate world, maybe even the media. But academics, more than all the rest, ought to be committed to truth.

In the Grievance Studies Affair, Helen Pluckrose, James Lindsay, and Peter Boghossian wrote and attempted to publish numerous bogus academic articles to draw attention to what they saw as being poor scholarship in areas of academia contaminated by Postmodernism,[32] such as Sociology and Cultural Studies as well as disciplines concerned with gender, race, sexuality, being fat, and so on. Boghossian, Pluckrose, and Lindsay say the following about the hoax:

> To be clear up front, we think studying topics like gender, race and sexuality is worthwhile. And getting it right is extremely important. The problem is how these topics are being studied right now. A culture has developed in which only certain conclusions are allowed. Like those that make whiteness and masculinity problematic. The fields we're

concerned about put social grievances ahead of objective truth. So as a simple summary, we call the problem 'grievance studies'.[33]

Beyond drawing attention to poor scholarship, the concern was to highlight that people are gaining employment and being promoted because of this poor scholarship. There was also the broader concern that people who gain degrees in 'grievance studies' fields go on to get jobs beyond universities and the ideas spread.

Out of 21 hoax articles, four were published, three more were accepted but not yet published, and another four had the status of 'revise and resubmit' – which means they would likely have been published. One other was under review and nine had been rejected. The titles of some of the published, accepted or 'revise and resubmit' articles include: 'Human Reactions to Rape Culture and Queer Performativity at Urban Dog Parks in Portland, Oregon' (this article received an award), published in *Gender, Place & Culture*; 'Who Are They to Judge? Overcoming Anthropometry and a Framework for Fat Bodybuilding' in *Fat Studies*; and 'When the Joke Is on You: A Feminist Perspective on How Positionality Influences Satire' in *Hypatia*.

I won't say more about the episode here as I have already covered some of the core issues in Chapter 4, and I will continue to return to them throughout the book. But the episode is significant not only because of the enormous coverage it received but because it highlights the IDW's concern with upholding Enlightenment values; in particular, the belief that we ought to determine the nature of reality before we decide how to act, rather than beginning by assuming that we understand reality and that our course of action is righteous.

## The End of the IDW?

If we were to identify an end of the IDW, it would be in the weeks and months after Trump was defeated in November 2020. The drama surrounding Trump's defeat played a part in the IDW fracturing; though at the same time, I suspect the idea of the IDW just got old for the people involved and everyone else.

On 18 November 2020, Sam Harris turned in his 'imaginary membership card' to the IDW. In his podcast titled 'Republic of Lies', he says:

> [T]here are many people in my circle – friends and colleagues and podcast guests … many of them are almost exclusively focused on the problem of the far-left. And this is causing them to significantly discount the harm that Trump has caused … Some of these people are Trump supporters, but many aren't. And they have been taking the Trump team's allegations that the election was stolen through massive voter fraud way too seriously. And they are extending a principle of charity to Trump and to the rest of his team that is frankly delusional. Again, there is a needle to thread here, and many people do not appear to even see it, insofar as I've noticed what others in the so-called Intellectual Dark Web have been saying. It's generally not something I want to be associated with. I don't want to single anyone out in particular. But allow me to turn in my imaginary membership card to this imaginary organisation. The IDW was always tongue in cheek, from my point of view. It was a funny name for a group of people who were willing to discuss difficult topics in public, mostly on podcasts, but it never made sense for us to be grouped together as though we shared a common worldview. I never saw much downside to it, and I didn't much think about it. But in the aftermath of this election, with some members of this fictional group sounding fairly bonkers, I just want to make it clear that I'm not part of any group.[34]

Harris's remarks were part of a growing quarrel between him and certain IDW figures, including Gad Saad and Dave Rubin, who were relatively upbeat about Trump. Gad Saad, 11 days earlier, on 7 November, as part of the quarrel, had made a satirical video in which he mentions the IDW and ironically repudiates any connections he may have had with Trump. In heavy-handed fashion, he states that Trump is worse than Hitler, ISIS, the Khmer Rouge, and so on.[35] The quarrel was petty and unpleasant.

On 2 October 2021, on The Rubin Report episode titled, 'Why Did the IDW Fall Apart? Gad Saad, Peter Boghossian, Michael Shermer', Saad says the following:

> But the members of the IDW, without mentioning any, that you would think are all committed to truth, to intellectual diversity, to the scientific method, they too can be parasitised by various idea pathogens. And that's been my biggest disappointment, and that's why I frankly wanted to disassociate from some of the folks because if you are a

true intellectual, there has to be a bent towards deontological ethics – there are certain things that are absolutely incontestable, that you are never going to yield on. For example, if you truly believe in freedom of speech, you can't be a consequentialist and say, 'well, of course I'm a strong believer in freedom of speech, but not when it comes from the ogre Trump' [Saad is almost certainly talking about Sam Harris here].[36]

Saad's sentiments sound impressively lofty, but as they are caught up with petty IDW in-fighting, it is hard to give them weight.

Eric Weinstein was also involved in this IDW endpoint. While continuing to be active on Twitter, and continuing to appear on various podcasts, Weinstein's own podcast, The Portal, released its last episode on 2 December 2020, titled: 'Cashing Out My Trump and IDW Positions'. There is a poetic rightness to this, seeing as Weinstein himself coined the term 'Intellectual Dark Web' (and it is episode 42 and featured Douglas Murray!). Let us consider Weinstein's remarks about Sam Harris leaving the IDW:

My friend Sam Harris attempted to very publicly exit the so called IDW. That's a bit tricky since it doesn't fully exist, and almost no one in it talks about it all that much in 2020 … Before this I heard public remarks about Sam's inability to understand reality from more than a few people that dismayed me. But in true IDW fashion, I'm not going to talk directly about who made those remarks because the ideas were the problem, and the idea that Sam was not capable of seeing reality is frankly silly … Sam did not name or shame anyone who named and shamed him … He stuck to the ideas in true IDW fashion. And as Sam's friend, Christopher Hitchens once said … 'A gentleman is defined to be a man who is never rude by accident'. And Sam is very much a gentleman. Which brings me to what Sam is doing wrong. You don't leave the IDW by being civil, focusing on ideas, foregoing the ability to stick it to others, holding to your true convictions, or getting things right. I'm sorry, but that's just not how this works at all. I shouldn't have to explain this, but you do it instead by being publicly dismissive of members of your group, rather than their ideas. Trolling. Not paying attention to shifting situations like the election [i.e. Trump's loss and his claims that the election was stolen], getting captured by your audience, or getting it wrong and not noticing. If the

> IDW is a protocol [a way!] as much as it is a group of humans, Sam continued to behave as a gentleman, while others were far closer to trying to leave the group by at least testing the above boundaries … The IDW … doesn't really exist. Maybe it never did. And it was all just a dream and a tongue in cheek bad joke of mine that took on a life of its own for a while. But it's possible that there's still some reason we go back to the IDW every now and then'.[37]

Here at the end, we see that as much as the IDW was a thing that people belonged to and talked about, it was also a protocol – a way. Thus, while we can argue that the IDW ended in late 2020 or early 2021, the way endures.

Another 'end of the IDW' event – or in this case, anti-event – was the disappearance of Jordan Peterson. In early-mid 2019 Peterson vanished from public life because of family and health problems. Writing for *The Weekend Australian* on 30 August 2020, Caroline Overington, at the conclusion of her article 'What the hell happened to Jordan Peterson?', captures the come-down felt by at least some Peterson fans: 'Some have suggested he [Peterson] was never more than a charlatan but, for others, the feeling is one of understandable disappointment, like he somehow talked the big talk and turned out not to have the answers. Like anyone does'.[38] While Peterson is an ambivalent figure, no one attacked Identity Politics and Postmodernism the way he did. And insofar as the IDW is above all else about championing Enlightenment values in the face of Leftist dogmas, the loss of Peterson took the wind out of the IDW's sails.

Of course, we now know that Peterson returned – a little more religious and Conservative, but as strong as ever. Upon his return he joined Ben Shapiro's Daily Wire. Peterson appeared on Rogan in January 2023 and performed confidently. But here's the really interesting point: at the start of the podcast, Peterson and Rogan are talking about Peterson's suits – Rogan had once gently mocked Peterson for his formal dressing.[39] Peterson said that one of his suits had several heads embroidered within it: Rogan's, Bret Weinstein's, Ben Shapiro's, Russell Brand's (interesting that Brand is there), and Sam Harris's. With an upbeat tone, Rogan says: 'That whole Intellectual Dark Web thing'.[40]

But I say once again that even if no one uses the name 'Intellectual Dark Web' anymore, writing in 2023, I do not get a strong sense that it has come to an end. Most of the figures who were associated with it remain immensely popular and controversial, and the same issues continue to be discussed; albeit with the addition of COVID and climate change material. Further, many of the IDW figures are still talking with or at least about one another. For example, in March 2023, Sam Harris appeared on Lex Fridman's podcast, and the two spoke at length about Bret Weinstein and Joe Rogan, and Eric Weinstein was also mentioned.[41] And early 2023 also saw Eric Weinstein appearing on Rogan. From the point of view of the acolytes, very little has changed.

## Notes

1   Brown 2018 May 14.
2   Goldberg 2018 May 8.
3   Monty Python 2009.
4   2018.
5   Haidt spoke about this on Real Time with Bill Maher (2018 October 27).
6   Lex Fridman 2022 October 21.
7   Graham 2019 June 7.
8   Lex Fridman 2022 October 21: 6:34:09.
9   Jordan B Peterson 2023 March 21: 012:55.
10  The Joe Rogan Experience 2022 July 27: 1:44:45.
11  The Joe Rogan Experience 2016 Nov 28: 0:58:13.
12  Real Time with Bill Maher 2014 October 7.
13  There are other events like this; however, the Evergreen incident stuck a little more in the IDW imagination than others. Probably because Joe Rogan quickly got behind Weinstein. Another notable incident was the Erika and Nicholas Christakis Halloween email at Yale. Erika, in an email, questioned an email from college administrators that told students to be careful about what they wore on Halloween. Amongst other things, Erika asked students to consider whether they really wanted to be told what to do by the university bureaucracy. However, her email, which clearly falls into the Liberal realm of supporting freedom of expression, caused an enormous backlash by Yale students. The link to her email and two news articles that discuss events are in the reference list: Christakis 2015; Christakis 2016; Friedersdorf 2016. Nicholas Christakis appeared twice on Rogan; although this was some years after the event (episodes #1274 [2019 March 18] and #1566 [2020 November 18]).

14  Volokh 2017 May 26.

15  Weinstein explains what occurred in his first appearance on Rogan (The Joe Rogan Experience 2017 June 3).

16  In the Reference List I include a link to Fox's and Vice's coverage of the event. VICE News 2017 June 17; Fox News 2017 May 27.

17  Michael Nayna made a film about the Evergreen episode. Michael Nayna 2019 January 18.

18  Benjamin A Boyce 2018 July 17.

19  Michael Nayna 2019 March 7 0:24:24.

20  Damore 2017.

21  Conger 2017.

22  CNBC 2017 August 16: 0:10:33.

23  The Joe Rogan Experience 2017 September 6.

24  Freethinkers of PSU 2018 February 26.

25  Channel 4 News 2018 January 17.

26  Channel 4 News 2018 January 17: 0:15:07.

27  Channel 4 News 2018 January 17: 0:09:12.

28  Channel 4 News 2018 January 17: 0:22:12.

29  Channel 4 News 2018 January 17: 0:24:24.

30  1Pinker 2019: xvi.

31  Weiss 2018 May 8.

32  James Lindsay and Peter Boghossian explained what they did on The Joe Rogan Experience 2018 October 30.

33  Michael Nayna 2018 October 3.

34  Sam Harris 2020 November 19: 0:03:02.

35  Gad Saad 2020 November 7: 0:00:00.

36  The Rubin Report 2021 October 2: 0:14:53.

37  The Portal 2020 December 2: 0:47:25.

38  Overington 2020.

39  The Joe Rogan Experience 2017 September 1: 0:00:00.

40  The Joe Rogan Experience 2023 January 28: 0:01:11.

41  Lex Fridman 2023 March 15.

7

# Interlude: Challenges in Evaluating Others and Ourselves

Before I move to the second part of the book, I want to step back and consider some of the challenges involved in evaluating the claims made by the IDW and the IDW's opponents – and also the challenges involved in making sense of our own politics. These meta-discussions, which draw on the IDW's own meta-discussions, mostly involve the relationship between truth and power.

## The Slip from Truth to Corrupt Power

A phenomenon that has interested me for decades – I wrote my PhD dissertation about it – is when a truthful statement, or better still, an endeavour that has its roots in truth, is bleached of its truth content and comes to serve corrupt power. I say 'corrupt power' because often truth and power work together, such as when a competent person, like a doctor or an engineer, makes decisions, or when people protest against genuine injustice.

Ibsen explores this phenomenon in his play *An Enemy of the People*. Doctor Stockman – the one who stands alone against the mob – at one point says:

The life of a normally constituted truth is generally, say, about seventeen or eighteen years, at most twenty; rarely longer. But truths as elderly as that have always worn terribly thin. But it's only then that the majority will have anything to do with them; then it will recommend them as wholesome food for thought … All these majority truths are just like salt meat that's been kept too long and gone bad and mouldy. That's at the root of all this moral scurvy that's going about.[1]

A familiar chilling historical example of the phenomenon is Robespierre, one of the characters thrown up by the French Revolution. I am confident there was truth in the French Revolution; which is to say, even though I struggle to make sense of what exactly caused it, I do think it was motivated to a considerable extent by the worthy desire for power to be more widely shared amongst the French population. Yet despite the virtuous impulse of the revolution, in the midst of it came 'The Terror', in which over 10,000 people were executed or died in prison without trial – without due process.[2] Robespierre supported many values that we today uphold, such as the abolition of slavery and universal (albeit male) suffrage. Yet as a member of The Committee of Public Safety (what a name!), he said the following in favour of the violent tactics of the revolution:

> If the spring [basis] of popular government in times of peace is virtue, the springs [bases] of popular government in revolution are at once *virtue and terror*: virtue, without which terror is fatal [baneful]; terror, without which virtue is powerless. Terror is nothing other than justice, prompt, severe, inflexible; it is therefore an emanation of virtue; it is not so much a special principle as it is a consequence of the general principle of democracy applied to our country's most urgent needs.[3]

So, when things get heavy, it's ok to kill lots of people without asking too many questions, because it's for a good cause. The ends justify the means.

At the other end of the spectrum of horror are bureaucracies. Even though I know that humans are often craven sheep, I still struggle to fathom what goes on in the HR department within my university. There are whole teams of people driving initiatives to systematise tasks that have been easily managed for centuries by one competent admin person. There is something true in the bureaucratic impulse: it is generally good to systematise tasks and ensure that processes are fair. But somewhere along the line the impulse is corrupted, and the aim of the bureaucracy becomes to grow itself.

It's all versions of the same phenomenon: truth slips into corrupt power. Funnily enough, this is also what interests Postmodernists. When they claim, following Foucault, that power produces truth, they are identifying that when some people make claims about how the world is – what is true – they are merely pursuing power and are not saying anything about how the world is. However, what makes all the difference for Enlightenment types is that they think that truth exists and we can approach it, even if we can never grasp it in its entirety. The Postmodernists throw the baby of truth out with the bathwater of corrupt power, and having done this, they then protect their own corrupt power by saying there is no truth.

Returning to the IDW, the IDW has pushed back against truth slipping into corrupt power primarily in academia and the media. But at the same time, some in the IDW, and many of the IDW's acolytes, have arguably themselves been corrupted.

IDW associate David Fuller and Eric Weinstein discussed the danger of IDW-type figures losing their grip on truth on Fuller's Rebel Wisdom in July 2021. Fuller asks: 'Do you think that … you might have had too much of a focus only on the faults of the mainstream and not enough on the faults of the alternative?' Weinstein testily replies, 'Appreciate that. Just as I have sung your praises about being early, give me at least that I may have introduced the concept of "audience capture" because I've been worrying about the same thing from the beginning'. He goes on to say that 'It's important to have a certain amount of antagonism … with one's own audience', and 'I've taken my own podcast off the air at times because … I don't want to be enmeshed in certain battles'.[4]

It is difficult to say with confidence who in the IDW has been captured by his or her audience. Sam Harris spoke about audience capture with Lex Fridman in March 2023. He says that he was concerned that Bret Weinstein had succumbed to audience capture in relation to the COVID pandemic. Harris points out that Weinstein produced around 100 podcasts about COVID despite there being numerous other things he could talk about.[5] Were Bret Weinstein's podcasts indicative of audience capture? – Was he pandering to populists who were overly sceptical about both governments and the pharmaceutical companies that produced the vaccines, or was he onto something?

So how do we spot corruption in others and ourselves? This is one of the great questions. One way is to try to grasp the 'form' of corrupt power. But what is a 'form'? As we read in *The Republic*, for Plato, there is the realm of opinion and the realm of knowledge. While Plato believes that opinions are better than ignorance, there is still something insubstantial about them: they belong to the world of 'multiplicity and change'. In contrast, knowledge relates to 'eternal, unchanging things' – these eternal, unchanging things are the forms.[6] So, the point is to recognise that many problems are problems not because of their *sui generis* characteristics, but because they are yet another instance of corrupt power, where corrupt power is power that is not founded on some incarnation of truth, such as expertise. Once we grasp the form of corrupt power, it becomes easier to recognise that corruption can happen to anyone, and that saying good words is not only no protection against corruption but it can be indicative of it. The point is not to follow the dogma, but to be more supple. The Tao that can be told is not the eternal Tao.

A second way is to think about our own emotional states. In *The Empire Strikes Back*, Luke Skywalker and Yoda have a conversation about the challenge of perceiving corruption within ourselves:

*Luke Skywalker:* Is the dark side stronger?

*Master Yoda:* No, no. Quicker, easier, more seductive.

*Luke Skywalker:* How am I to know the good side from the bad?

*Master Yoda:* You will know … when you are calm, at peace … passive. A Jedi uses the Force for knowledge and defence … never for attack.[7]

Returning to *The Republic*, Plato presents similar ideas when discussing how to identify the 'philosophic character' (for Plato, a philosopher is the one who is able to grasp the form of things): 'You must see it [the philosophic character] has no touch of meanness; pettiness of mind is quite incompatible with the constant attempt to grasp things divine or human as a whole and in their entirety'.[8] I've certainly been at my worst when I've been agitated, and I've noticed that when teaching, students very quickly sense this and do not respond positively – when I am agitated they are much more inclined to attack me. And I find that when I am calm and magnanimous the students allow me to explore controversial topics; I even win one or two over to my cause.

A third solution comes from the IDW itself. It involves neither philosophical abstractions nor emotions, but instead exploits our relationship with the physical world: 'having a relationship with the unforgiving'. Bret Weinstein speaking with Joe Rogan explains what is meant by this:

> There's a tremendous danger in a socially mediated world in which those who are successful are successful because some social thing has told them that they are correct. Because you can be dead wrong, seem correct, and move ahead in a social world. Whereas if you're doing carpentry – if you're in some sort of competition – the nature of the beast is one that will tell you when you've got it wrong, and therefore it will allow you to actually improve your insight in whatever form you have it. So I'm a tremendous fan of the idea that even if your world is largely socially mediated you have to make sure that some part of it isn't. And you are confronting something real enough to tell you when you're confused so that you can learn how not to be confused.[9]

There are many examples of the unforgiving. Quite a few IDW figures do Jiu Jitsu: Joe Rogan, Sam Harris, Lex Fridman, Russell Brand, and Peter Boghossian. There is no equivocating in Jiu Jitsu. Whether you win or lose is revealed by the activity itself; it is, as Boghossian says on Rogan in December 2015, 'a truth-seeking community'.[10] Eric Weinstein, on Rogan in November 2018, mentions hiking in the wilderness and having no easy way to get out.[11] Peterson, in his book *12 Rules for Life*, mentions skateboarding. And interestingly, Diogenes Laërtius' *Lives and Opinions of Eminent Philosophers* mentions that Plato may have wrestled in his youth;[12] thus, the lover of knowledge himself was also a lover of the unforgiving – though this is speculative!

I am strongly attracted to the idea that subjecting oneself to the unforgiving has salubrious effects in the realm of truth. I imagine that immense good would come from people regularly spending a few nights in the wilderness, or even just running regularly and competitively or something similar. Though maybe it's the other way around: those who love truth are attracted to unforgiving activities – so perhaps subjecting people to wilderness ordeals won't improve their epistemology. Regardless, it would be illuminating to examine the correlation between people's epistemologies and their recreational activities – if such a study were possible to design.

A fourth solution also comes from the IDW: 'first-principles reasoning'. First-principles reasoning involves reducing a problem to its fundamental elements and building a solution from these elements. The most notable proponent of first principles reasoning within the IDW is Elon Musk. He says:

> The normal way we conduct our lives is we reason by analogy [Musk doesn't mean 'reasoning using analogies']. We are doing this [whatever we are doing] because it is like something else that was done. Or it's like what other people are doing … Slight iterations on a theme … It's mentally easier to reason by analogy rather than from first principles. First principles is a kind of a Physics way of looking at the world. You boil things down to the most fundamental truths and say, 'what are we sure is true?' – or as sure as is possible is true, and then reason up from there. That takes a lot more mental energy than [reasoning by analogy].[13]

In the realm of ideas, if we keep questioning whatever we believe, perhaps we can make our way, if not to fundamental truths, then at least to fundamental assumptions.

Yet reasoning is a funny old thing. Often, we think we are reasoning – even from first principles – and we are doing nothing of the sort – we are pursuing corrupt power. Cathy Newman's interview with Jordan Peterson had a veneer of reasoning, but much of the time Newman makes a straw man of Peterson's arguments. A very different example of the failure of reasoning is the glorious 'She's a witch' scene from Monty Python's *Holy Grail*. In this scene, a medieval knight leads a peasant mob through a nonsensical chain of reasoning to determine whether a woman is a witch. Later, the knight is conversing with King Arthur who had become involved and who had given the unforgettable answer, 'a duck', to one of the knight's questions. The knight asks Arthur: 'Who are you who are so wise in the ways of science?'[14] Alas, it is because reasoning and science do go awry that some Postmodernists suggest that science is a social construction. Yet as always, we ought not to throw the baby out with the bathwater. The antidote to bad reasoning is not to abandon reasoning, but to reason better.

All of this returns us to a fifth and familiar solution: the foundational IDW way of discussing our ideas with others – especially those with whom we disagree. We might not be able to recognise when we ourselves have been corrupted, but if we open ourselves to criticism, we might have a better shot.

### Problems with Proportion

Problems with proportion arise regularly when considering the IDW. An often-encountered question is: how many people really are Woke? For opponents of Wokeness, it's easy, or even attractive, to imagine the Woke are everywhere – to imagine that the body snatchers have got to everyone. Jonathan Haidt was implicitly commenting on this problem of thinking the Woke are everywhere when he said 'we [the IDW] are all fed up with a strain of illiberalism that is found on the left but that is nowhere near a majority of the left'.[15]

But we can take this point further. Granted, events such as those at Evergreen State College were ridiculous. But most other universities have not experienced such events. And even if many other universities do have problems with freedom of speech, perhaps these problems are overblown. As mentioned, I learned fear and silence following my early encounters with Identity Politics at university. But I now think that I was at fault for letting myself be cowed. If, when I was a student, I had always calmly spoken my mind whenever I encountered what I thought to be corruption in academics and not indulged my fears about what might happen to me if I spoke up, I may well have been fine. And even if I wasn't, I'm certain there would have been unexpected dividends for speaking up, the most important being a stronger sense of self: when we do not act when we ought to, we are diminished (this was Hamlet's problem[16]).

However, the question of proportion can tilt another way. Joe Rogan, in conversation with Konstantin Kisin and Francis Foster in July 2022 asks, 'But how many people are accepting this [Woke ideology]?' Kisin says, 'It depends what you mean by "accepting", Joe. In the Soviet Union, most people knew that the system was bullshit, right? But they went along with it anyway'. Kisin goes on to say that many of us have dual identities. We have our public views and our private views. Kisin also says, 'Do you know how many comedians who used to hate us on the comedy circuit for starting Triggernometry now contact us and say, "actually, you guys were right" … They won't say anything in public'.[17] Here, the issue is that while not many people are true believers, many more go along with Wokeness to avoid rocking the boat. About this, ex-British academic Kathleen Stock says, 'A small number of people can have a very loud and powerful chilling effect. And you do become frightened. Social ostracism is a very powerful weapon. I think it's probably hard-wired into us to fear it'.[18] A similar point is made by Edward Gibbon in *The Decline and Fall of the Roman Empire:*

> [T]he tyrant of a single town, or a small district, would soon discover that an hundred armed followers were a weak defence against ten thousand peasants or citizens; but an hundred thousand well disciplined soldiers will command, with despotic sway, ten millions of subjects; and a body of ten or fifteen thousand guards will strike terror into the most numerous populace that ever crowded the streets of an immense capital.[19]

Arguably, across the world, a relatively small number of zealots have an immense effect on the political landscape.

### The Motte-and-Bailey Fallacy

Now I return to the challenge of battling Postmodernism. Many are familiar with the concept of straw man arguments: mischaracterising someone's argument or position to knock them down more easily. But a lesser known yet important companion of the straw man argument is the 'Motte-and-Bailey Fallacy'. This concept occasionally appears in IDW circles – Eric Weinstein mentioned it when talking with Joe Rogan in February 2023.[20] The term 'Motte-and-Bailey Fallacy' was coined by Nicholas Shackel in his 2005 proto-IDW article, 'The Vacuity of Postmodernist Methodology'.[21] For those who remember their Year 8 history, 'mote and bailey' refers to a motte-and-baily castle. In such a castle, the motte is a hill within the castle with a tower upon it – the keep. The bailey is the rest of the land within the castle wall. The bailey is the preferred place to be because it's spacious, sunny, and there are things to do, like practice sword-play or groom horses (I'm just thinking of *Game of Thrones*). The motte is cramped and gloomy. But when the castle is attacked, one must retreat to the motte which is easier to defend. In the realm of ideas, when we are with our comrades, we are inclined to make extreme and difficult to defend claims – as mentioned, Pinker suggests that 'fantastical beliefs are flaunted as proof of one's piety'. We all do it. And naturally, our comrades don't mind because they do the same. This is life in the bailey. But when pressed by non-comrades, we moderate our extreme claims and make them defensible, even banal. This is life in the motte. When we moderate our claims, our non-comrades call off the attack. But once they are gone, we head back to the bailey and start running our tongues again.

An example is when people say things like, 'Language does not refer to reality' – a colleague of mine recently said, with a flourish, 'There is nothing behind representation'. An obvious response to a person severing the link between language and reality is to point out that the person themselves often presents evidence to support what he or she is saying, and that this indicates a belief that reality exists and that it can be got at using language. He or she might then say, 'I didn't mean that language does not refer to reality, but just that sometimes people misrepresent reality to suit their interests'. This is entirely defensible to the point of utter banality.

Straw man arguments are easy to deal with: you clarify your position. But it's much harder to deal with motte-and-bailey scenarios because there is nothing firm to attack: your opponent's position is always shifting. This is why Postmodernism has had such a long life.

### Dunbar's Number

Now for a very different approach to the problem of truth and corrupt power: Dunbar's number. 'Dunbar's number' refers to the number of people that a tribe in human prehistory could sustain before it cleaved.[22] The central conjecture is that beyond a certain number, individuals in the tribe could not know all the other individuals in the tribe, and this would lead to instability. People typically cite the number as being 150; however, this has become something of meme – there is a range. But for this discussion, the number doesn't matter.

Bret Weinstein, in his conversation with Rogan in December 2017, suggests that Dunbar's number is a foundational concept.[23] Daniel

Schmachtenberger, who is another IDW Kuiper Belt figure – a distant associate – provides an account of Dunbar's number on Lex Fridman's podcast:

> Up to a certain number of people, everybody can know everybody else pretty intimately … Everybody can know everyone intimately enough that if your actions made anyone else do poorly, it's your extended family. And you're stuck living with them. And you know who they are. And there's no anonymous people. There's no 'just them' and 'over there'. And that's one part of what leads to a kind of tribal process where what's good for the individual and good for the whole has a coupling. Also, below that scale, everyone is somewhat aware of what everyone else is doing. There's no groups that are very siloed. And as a result, it's very hard to get away with bad behaviour. There's a forced kind of transparency. And so you don't need the state in that way. But lying to people doesn't actually get you ahead. Sociopathic behaviour does not get you ahead. Cause it gets seen.[24]

We ought to be wary of being armchair anthropologists – it's important to be sceptical of neat-sounding theories. Nonetheless, Dunbar's Number has immense appeal for helping us think about problems of accountability in large populations. In the distant past, our immediate environment was close to being a closed system. But now we can draw our livelihood from a corporation that has a negative impact on some other part of the world, or we can gain status by presenting a false view of our life on social media. Or similarly, we can be a serial exploiter of people – for money, sex, whatever. And if or when we are found out, we just move on. In a world with billions of people, relationships are, alas, an inexhaustible resource. We just need to be sufficiently psychopathic so that we don't have to answer to our consciences.

Arguably the various institutions and checks and balances in the democratic system, such as the rule of law and the free press, help to ensure accountability, and thus they allow larger societies to exist without cleaving. Religion likely also plays a role here.

But Dunbar's number is also relevant to the question of whether the IDW and the broader Culture Wars are guilty of generating unnecessary controversy and making matters worse by encouraging us to focus on problems over which we have little control. Speaking with Jordan Peterson in May 2021, Stephen Fry discusses the problem of being aware of the diverse problems of the world:

> [I]f you take a load of mice and put them on a Perspex tray and float them on the water, because they are unaware of the risk they're in they move around randomly and their random movement makes the tray even – they [are] just randomly moving around. If you scale it up and put humans on it, they sink within seconds because they think 'oh we're tipping, we must run to this end'. And of course they all run to that end. And so it tips over. In other words, consciousness of the problem, attempting to deal with it, being aware of it, is the biggest problem of all, and that's something new to us because in the old days we lived in small groups who just didn't know how awful humanity was, what sins we were committing, how dreadful we were making the world. It was only through the telecommunication and through the, you know, the recent development of the global village or whatever you want to call it … that we have actually become aware and are now likely to be running around in that tank and causing it to fall over.[25]

However, all this is yet another grey area. While worrying about problems far from us over which we have little control can lead to futile and even damaging Culture Wars, having a global awareness arguably also moderates our feelings towards distant others – this is foundational to the Liberal world.

To finish, the concept of Dunbar's number alerts us to the possibility that in any larger society, there is a serious problem of truth and power becoming untethered from each other because there is a lower cost for people lying or even just being incompetent. From an optimistic perspective, many of the institutions we have developed function to keep truth and power tethered to some degree. But as the IDW often argues, these institutions can themselves become corrupt.

## Notes

1   Ibsen 1999: 77.

2   As Chaliand and Blin (2016: 5) write, 'the Law of 22 Prairial prohibit[ed] witnesses and legal representation for the defense and authoriz[ed] the Revolutionary Tribunal to pass death sentences on the basis of conviction alone'.

3    Modern History Sourcebook 1997 [1794].

4    Rebel Wisdom 2021 June 30: 0:10:02.

5    Lex Fridman 2023 March 15: 2:58:13.

6    Plato 2003 [380BC]: 484b.

7    John Mercano 2017 December 17.

8    Plato 2003 [380BC]: 486a.

9    The Joe Rogan Experience 2017 December 20: 0:20:32.

10   The Joe Rogan Experience 2015 December 15: 0:40:03.

11   The Joe Rogan Experience 2018 November 16: 0:09:47.

12   Diogenes Laërtius 2018 (3rd century CE): 114.

13   Innomind 2013 December 4.

14   NM05 2006 March 14.

15   Shermer, Saide, & McCaffree 2019.

16   Roberts 2022 April 20.

17   The Joe Rogan Experience 2022 July 27: 1:41:57.

18   Triggernometry 2021 November 22: 0:41:56.

19   Gibbon 2008 (1782 Written, 1845 Revised): Chapter 5, Part I.

20   The Joe Rogan Experience 2023 February 22: 3:56:32.

21   Shackel 2005. The term 'motte-and-bailey fallacy' gained popularity in the greater IDW sphere when Scott Alexander wrote about it on his 'Slate Star Codex' blog (2014 November 3).

22   Dunbar 1992.

23   The Joe Rogan Experience 2017 December 20: 1:44:25.

24   Lex Fridman 2021 June 14: 3:04:46.

25   Jordan B Peterson 2021 May 18: 1:09:36.

# Part Two: The IDW in More Detail

8

# IDW Criticisms of Universities and Media and Battles for Free Speech

There is a magnificent document to which I return from time to time: 'A declaration of the independence of cyberspace', produced in 1996 by John Perry Barlow.[1] It is magnificently bad, being guilty of the worst crime, aesthetically speaking, that writing can commit: earnestness. And yet its utopian vision of Cyberspace gives us something to measure our moment against. It begins by saying, 'Governments of the Industrial World [I do like the excessive capitalization], you weary giants of flesh and steel, I come from Cyberspace, the new home of Mind'. This is most of it, really. In classic Cyber-Libertarian style, it bangs on about how Cyberspace is – or will be, or ought to be – free from government interference, and it talks about forging a new Social Contract. However, it is the following that interests me most: 'We are creating a world where anyone, anywhere may express his or her beliefs, no matter how singular, without fear of being coerced into silence or conformity'. And: 'We are creating a world that all may enter without privilege or prejudice accorded by race, economic power, military force, or station of birth'.

It is interesting how things have gone. We certainly see people expressing their singular beliefs on the internet. But at the same time, when people's Cyberselves are linked with their real-life selves, which they often are, people do not express their beliefs without fear. And yet, for the millions who have been attracted to IDW-type figures, Cyberspace has lived up to its promise. Against the other weary giants: the traditional media and universities, the internet has provided a space for much that cannot be said to be said.

Barlow's declaration is echoed on the 'About' page of the British IDW-associate YouTube show Rebel Wisdom:

> In these times of change, we can no longer trust the traditional media to make sense of the world. The old gatekeepers are losing their power. A new counter culture is filling the void, driven by a great intellectual awakening. Facilitated by new technology, it's made a new kind of conversation possible; more in-depth, more open and more democratic.

We also find the familiar opposition to Postmodern relativism: 'In a time where truth has become whatever you want it to be, we believe in the rebellious, Transformative power of genuine truth'.[2]

Making a similar point, but objecting to universities rather than the media, Peter Boghossian speaking on Rogan in October 2018 says:

> If you want to get back to constructive politics – to get back to people having conversations – and that's the thing: I think one of the reasons that your show's been so successful, is it's a combination of authenticity with – you're totally willing to have conversations with no holds barred – you can't have that in the academy. So people need to go to you to hear these thoughts. And to wrestle with ideas and to engage.[3]

However, some in the IDW indicate that they are wary of the Libertarian romance of thinking of the system as bad. In Chapter 5, I included some remarks by Lex Fridman to this effect. Speaking on Rebel Wisdom in July 2021, Eric Weinstein makes the same point:

> [I am] very worried about protecting the credibility of the heterodoxy [free thinkers]. And we're going to have to confront the fact that our audiences want us to do things that are not safe, not good, because of the fact that they want a Schelling point [a clear point around which people can coalesce] which either says 'the man is right', or 'the man is trying to stick it to us', and neither of these Schelling points is viable. Congratulations, you've entered the wilderness of Modernity.[4]

At its best, the IDW threads the needle. At its worst, it slides into a dubious Cyber-Libertarian-Populism.

## Criticisms of Traditional Institutions

But let's be clear. While Eric Weinstein is not some gung-ho Libertarian, he has serious concerns about our institutions. On the same Rebel Wisdom interview, he says, 'I believe our institutions are degrading – they are greatly degraded. I cannot stand the leadership class'.[5] Similarly, on Rogan in November 2018 he says:

> What I think is we have a crisis in expertise. Institutional expertise is at an all-time low. Nobody really trusts any of our institutions to be an authoritative source of ground truth. That's not to say that everything the institutions say is wrong or everything the experts say is wrong – far from it – it's just that there are almost no experts or institutions that aren't willing to distort facts in order to pursue institutional goals.[6]

The sense we get from this is that experts, who almost always reside within institutions, often go about their business as they ought to; however, once the political wind is blowing in a certain direction, they will compromise their regard for truth for the sake of political expediency, i.e., their careers.

Weinstein clarified his thoughts about our institutions with venture capitalist Peter Thiel on the first episode of his podcast The Portal in July 2019.[7] (In some ways, this was the high point of the IDW. We had encountered Weinstein on Rogan, and here he was, the renegade mathematician who had introduced the name 'Intellectual Dark Web', starting his own podcast.) Both Weinstein and Thiel share the belief that meaningful growth stopped in the late 60s or early 70s. They grant that computing and communication – 'the bit' – has advanced, but argue that much else has not. In Physics, for instance, Weinstein contends that our knowledge of the atom has barely increased in 50 years, and elsewhere, Weinstein has been critical of String Theory (there is an ongoing discussion within the IDW about whether String Theory has merit). Further, Weinstein argues that since the 1970s there has been no real wage growth for the lower classes. It's a plausible hypothesis.

But the major point for this chapter is that for Weinstein, this lack of growth has affected institutions, in particular universities. Weinstein says that institutions have an 'embedded growth obligation'.[8] For universities, this means that it has been assumed that universities will continue to produce knowledge, as they did through the early and middle parts of the 20th century. But the problem is that there is not nearly enough new knowledge to go around:

> We structured almost everything on an expectation of growth and then this growth that was expected ran out, or wasn't as high or as stable or as technologically led as before, [and this] has a pretty surprising implication. Which is – let's not dance around it – it feels like, almost universally, all of our institutions are now pathological.

To this, Thiel adds 'and the incentives have been for the institutions to derange and to lie'. Thiel also says:

> There's probably a way the universities could function if they did not grow. You'd be honest. Most people in PhD programs don't become professors. Maybe you'd make the PhD programs much shorter. Maybe you'd be much more selective. You'd let fewer people in. There would be some way you could adjust it and the institutions could still be much healthier than they are today.[9]

A little earlier Thiel talks about specialisation:

> The political cut I have on … specialization is always that if you analyse the politics of science, the specialization should make you suspicious. If it's got harder to evaluate what's going on, then it's presumably gotten easier for people to lie and to exaggerate.[10]

Thiel mentions String Theorists and quantum computer researchers, and says he is sceptical about how highly such people speak of their own specialisations.

### Criticisms of the University

**Political Homogeneity.** Here, Weinstein and Thiel are focusing on the Sciences. But from where I stand in the Arts and Social Sciences it is, I fear, far worse. As the Grievance Studies Affair went some way to revealing, there are numerous sub-disciplines within the Arts and Social Sciences that are politically homogenous echo chambers. From the perspective of IDW figures such as Helen Pluckrose, James Lindsay, and Peter Boghossian, the purpose of these sub-disciplines is not to create knowledge, but for the participants in the sub-discipline to huddle together and advance their careers. These sub-disciplines are almost necessarily underpinned by Postmodern ideology and its offshoots because the best way to support weak claims is to deny there is truth and to push the point that knowledge is attached to identity; thus, so long as the group agrees, a dubious claim can count as knowledge. Rogan, in October 2018, in conversation with Lindsay and Boghossian about the Grievance Studies Affair, does not hold back:

> What we're talking about – what was ridiculous is – there's many fields of studies that you can get legitimate degrees in that are absolutely preposterous. Literally filled with nonsense, taught by nonsense people, who live in these nonsense bubbles, and then they give these degrees, and these people go out in the real world and they infect things.[11]

Elsewhere Weinstein and Thiel use the term 'Ponzi Scheme' to describe what happens in institutions. In a managed fund Ponzi Scheme such as Bernie Madoff's, older investors are paid out with the money invested in the fund by newer investors rather than from the fund's own successful investments. In the university, established academics train their students to cite the articles and books they and their colleagues write, and also to learn the jargon, and the students are rewarded with good marks and a pathway into the institution. While academia isn't exactly a traditional Ponzi Scheme, the common point is that in both, there is no real value: citations and money, respectively, fly around, creating the impression that something valuable is happening, but it is an illusion. Weinstein uses the term 'Kayfabe'[12] to describe this illusion. The term was originally used to describe how in professional wrestling staged performances are presented as authentic. And it all works, even though the audience knows that the performances are staged. Though perhaps it works precisely because everyone knows that the performances are staged.

I don't think that the Arts and Social Sciences are lost. People continue to do good research in which claims about the world are substantiated using reasoning and evidence. But activist academia is prominent, and in my experience, few will stand against it. And the Postmodern corrosion of what we once valued very much continues. Steven Pinker, who also thinks that universities are not lost (he says, 'I don't think that universities or media outlets or the deep state is rotten to the core'), nonetheless expresses similar concerns about their declining credibility:

> As universities have driven out the various dissidents and heretics and heterodox thinkers, often in comically outrageous episodes that get replayed endlessly in popular right-wing outlets, the credibility of the university gets corroded, and by extension, public health agencies, media outlets ... If universities don't establish their credibility – if they develop a well-earned reputation for drumming out anyone who disagrees – they'll be blown off by leaders – they'll be blown off by the majority of the population. And I think that our institutions have done a poor job of safeguarding their credibility. And instead by following the natural tendency to form their own tribe – [a] tribe of right thinking people – they have blown off people in power and huge portions of the population.[13]

For Pinker, a major concern with all this is that when the universities are correct, such as about anthropogenic climate change, they aren't believed. It is a 'boy who cried wolf' thing. And while it is possible for intellectuals such as Steven Pinker, Eric Weinstein, or Jonathan Haidt to recognise the strengths and weaknesses of our institutions, as I have mentioned, many everyday people get a sense of some of the crazy things coming out of universities and they flee to the populist right.

Returning to the phenomenon of Cyberspace, Weinstein suggests that we now have two systems running: the institutions, and whatever is occurring in Cyberspace:

> We have two separate parallel systems. Now this podcasting experiment that you and I are now part of provides for a very unscripted, out of control, narrative, and there's this parallel institutional narrative, that seems to exist in a gated form [Weinstein also uses the terms 'Gated Institutional Narrative' and the 'Distributed Idea Suppression Complex' or DISC] where the institutions keep talking to each other

and ignore this thing that's happening that has reached more and more people. So you effectively have multiple narratives, one of which almost no one needs to believe, it's just that the institutions need to trade kind of lies, deceptions, back and forth amongst themselves. How is it that these two things can be kept separate? It's like a real wrestling league and a professional wrestling league, side by side.

Thiel replies: 'If they came into contact, then they wouldn't both be able to exist'.[14] Apart from one or two colleagues with whom I discuss such matters in whispers, the contempt amongst my fellow academics for IDW figures is immense – they ensure that there is no meaningful discussion of IDW ideas. (I also always think of Thiel's remarks in relation to what happened to this book with its first publisher. Of course it could not be permitted to exist in the academic realm.)

**Tenure.** Tenure refers to having a job for life in academia. As with so much that I discuss in this book, tenure is arguably a case of truth slipping into corrupt power; that is, tenure was once a good idea, but now it's far from clear that it serves a good function. We see some of the IDW's concerns about tenure in the October 2018 discussion between Joe Rogan, James Lindsay and Peter Boghossian about the Grievance Studies Affair:

*Rogan:* How are your peers treating this [the Grievance Studies Affair]?

*Lindsay:* From academic people I've had two kinds of responses. Some of those are like 'oh you guys'. The overwhelming of them are the same thing over and over again. I mean a lot of people. '[whispering] Thank you so much for doing this, but I can't. Don't tell anybody. I'm trying to get a job. I'm up for tenure. I can't talk. Thank you'. And that's everywhere. It's everywhere. You can't proceed through academia now unless you bow to this stuff.[15]

With Lindsay's remarks in mind, the first point about tenure is that it is a tragedy that many don't gain tenure because they are bold, but because they either exploit the orthodoxy, or don't rock the boat (we are back with Bret Weinstein's original point about what constitutes 'IDW space' – see Chapter 2). A colleague of mine suggested that academics are, perhaps by disposition, craven. I think this is largely true. Yet these are the people supposedly driving the creation of knowledge and educating our youth.

A second point about tenure is revealed in the following:

*Rogan:* The whole thing [tenure] sounds preposterous. That you could keep a job for life.

*Lindsay:* The idea was supposed to be that you work your ass off for a few years – it was supposed to be to defend academic freedoms. You get tenure, then you can go forth and put out some crazy ideas – really dig into some stuff – and they can't fire you for maybe coming up with weird stuff. And then people would argue about it. But now it's kind of become the situation where people get in their job and you can't get rid of them.[16]

The purpose of tenure was to protect academic freedom, with the idea that academics with tenure would be able to boldly pursue truth. Now tenure protects academics who boldly pursue tenure, or worse, the kind of vengeful power that is indicative of slave morality – see Chapter 11. The pursuit of truth has slipped into corrupt power.

People might argue that tenure is working exactly as it should. After all, academics are putting out crazy ideas. But the concern is that the crazy ideas are not being discussed – at least not within the university. Boghossian, talking about his own teaching experiences, says, 'There's no questioning. And it's something for me that makes me deeply uncomfortable when my students can't ask questions. They're just uncomfortable to voice their opinion about things'.[17]

**Theory, Hypothesis, and Idea Laundering.** The IDW sometimes talks about the abuse of the word 'theory' within academia. In the technical sense, a 'theory' is an account of the way the world works that is well supported by evidence. An example is Einstein's General Theory of Relativity, which continues to be upheld by observation after observation, from the orbit of Mercury to gravitational waves. In contrast, an idea about how the world *might* work is an 'hypothesis'. One issue is that in everyday language we say 'theory' when we mean 'hypothesis'. This vagueness has been capitalised upon in the Arts and Social Sciences. Joe Rogan and James Lindsay discuss this. Rogan says, 'Theory ... I love that word ... What are you saying? ... Once you say that [i.e. call something theory] you're good. You can say something ridiculous, and then say "feminist theory", and they're like, oh it's in feminist theory'.[18]

A particularly dodgy practice that is strongly encouraged at university is employing 'theoretical frameworks'. Common sense tells us that theorising (hypothesising) involves trying to describe, and sometimes explain the causes of, events and patterns in reality. Further, having developed a theory (an hypothesis), we expect to continually test it against reality to determine whether it is accurate. It's a back-and-forth process. However, when a theoretical framework is employed, we use our favourite theory (hypothesis) to entirely explain some aspect of reality. For example, I might choose to analyse how the world responded to COVID using a feminist theoretical framework. I would unfailingly find sexism everywhere. But note that this is not the same as exploring how women fared during COVID. The latter is a reasonable open-ended question (and perhaps we would find sexism everywhere). The former involves beginning by assuming your conclusion – there's no genuine analysis of data. When supervising and marking students' dissertations I often have to explain such things. However, no one wants to hear about it because fifty years of Postmodernism within the academy has institutionalized confirmation bias, and the students know which way the political wind is blowing, and what they need to do and say to succeed.

Returning to the IDW, Lindsay makes similar points:

> Let me throw them [Postmodern academics] an olive branch. So much of the stuff they come up with is a creative idea. Maybe there's something to some of this stuff, right? But what they're putting forward is hypotheses. And then they're treating them as conclusions ... But they're not testing it [the claims they make]. Instead of testing it, they're concluding it and using theory to do so.[19]

Lindsay gives the example of the TV show *South Park*:

> *South Park* presents these ideas ... These ideas are [for the Woke left]

'problematic' – that's the big word. Theoretically that's a problem. Why? Because … they literally believe that use of language creates the power dynamics that define society. So *South Park* is using language and imagery that creates a power dynamic that makes people more comfortable being racist. Boom. Theory. Done. No test needed. No even attempt to test.[20]

Lindsay mentions a term coined by Bret Weinstein: 'Idea Laundering'. This is used to describe how the corruption in academia functions:

They [academics] come up with these ideas. They start with their conclusion. And they push it through. It gets published. It's like the academic equivalent of money laundering. So how does money laundering work? You take some money you got – ill gotten money. You put it through this shell company or this thing or the other thing, and it comes back to you and now it's had a legal trail that makes it legit, right? Well here [in academia] you take some prejudice, you write it down as an academic paper, you publish the thing, it gets the academic stamp on it – it's the gold standard of knowledge now – and now this prejudice you started with now looks like legitimate knowledge. It can go straight in the classroom, it can go straight to activists or policy makers. It's a real problem …[21]

Lindsay goes on to say that in response to one of their spoof papers from the Grievance Studies Affair, the reviewer had said, 'This paper is an important contribution to knowledge'. This is amusing on several levels. As I touched on before, while Postmodernism has undermined the idea that truth exists (again, truth is produced by power), it has, bizarrely, retained the concept of 'knowledge'. It's quite the paradox. Traditionally, knowledge has been understood as 'justified true belief'. This is a decent enough definition. And regardless of what we think about the terms 'justified' and 'belief', the key point is that when we have knowledge, it is about something that is true. But then this paradox is exactly what is required for all those in the Postmodern tradition to maintain their careers: they need to publish, and what is published must be something rather than nothing, whence the need for it to contribute to knowledge. Yet the only way to get poorly-supported claims over the line is to degrade truth (and reasoning and evidence). What a time to be alive!

## Criticisms of the Media

The IDW arose partly in opposition to problems in academia. But it was also a response to a partisan mainstream media, whether this be *CNN*, *BBC*, *Fox*, or the *New York Times*. As mentioned, of all media sources, it is the *New York Times* that is most attacked by the IDW. As Russell Brand says, when in conversation with journalist Seymour Hersh in February 2023, 'A short time ago you could rely on an organization like the *New York Times* for anti-establishment, radical reporting – now they are a mouthpiece of the establishment'.[22]

Two stand-out IDW figures in the world of reporting are Bari Weiss (2 Rogan appearances) who brought the IDW to a broader audience with her 8 2018 May article, and Matt Taibbi (4 Rogan appearances). Weiss used to work for the *New York Times* (resigned July 2020) and Taibbi for *Rolling Stone* (resigned April 2020). Both now publish through the independent online publishing platform, Substack, which uses a subscription model.

Recently, both, along with some other journalists, were asked by Elon Musk to review and report on a collection of internal Twitter documents. Interestingly, as Taibbi says on Rogan in February 2023, mainstream media has stayed away from the so-called 'Twitter Files'.

*Rogan:* Has no mainstream media source covered the Twitter files?

*Taibbi:* Not really. No. They've done hit pieces on me and on Elon and on Bari, but they haven't covered the stuff in the stories … No matter what you think about me or Elon Musk or whatever, the stuff in the files is clearly newsworthy. If you didn't know, the idea that the FBI and Homeland Security having a system of sending moderation requests to every internet platform in the country – the idea that that's not a news story is insane to me … You have to make a conscious decision not to do that story. Which they've done.[23]

Taibbi then says that in one hit piece, the *Washington Post* described him as a 'Conservative journalist', but quickly changed this following a Twitter backlash. Taibbi is far from Conservative. Taibbi also says that he was accused of doing PR for the world's richest man (Musk). One of several similar tweets was by Mehdi Hasan from US news company

MSNBC. Hasan said, 'Imagine volunteering to do online PR work for the world's richest man on a Friday night, in service of nakedly and cynically right-wing narratives, and then pretending you're speaking truth to power'.[24]

In this section, I will provide a sense of the IDW's objections to the mainstream media by discussing Bari Weiss's *New York Times* resignation letter, and some remarks made by Taibbi during his most recent appearance on Rogan in February 2023.

**Bari Weiss's NYT Resignation Letter.** In her resignation letter,[25] Weiss says she was hired by the *New York Times* to bring in voices that would not otherwise appear, including Centrists and Conservatives – Weiss says she is a Centrist. She mentions a number of people, including IDW figures Ayaan Hirsi Ali, Heather Heying, and Glenn Loury, that she brought to the *New York Times*. She then makes the following typical IDW statement:

> Lessons that ought to have followed the election [of Trump] —lessons about the importance of understanding other Americans, the necessity of resisting tribalism, and the centrality of the free exchange of ideas to a democratic society—have not been learned. Instead, a new consensus has emerged in the press, but perhaps especially at this paper: that truth isn't a process of collective discovery, but an orthodoxy already known to an enlightened few whose job is to inform everyone else.

Weiss then talks about the bullying she allegedly experienced, mentioning, amongst other things, coworkers who insisted that she be rooted out if the company is to be inclusive (as is often the case, inclusivity and diversity are upheld by ensuring a political monoculture). She writes: 'I do not understand how you [the *NYT*] have allowed this kind of behaviour to go on inside your company in full view of the paper's entire staff and the public'. It is experiences such as these that remind me, once again, that what we ought to care about is the *form of corrupt power* (see Chapter 7): whether we are talking about racism or Wokeness, the process is the same: once someone is deemed to be in the wrong tribe, he or she can be treated badly without the perpetrators suffering any repercussions. It is licensed cruelty.

Mirroring the point that Pluckrose, Lindsay, and Boghossian were making in the Grievance Studies Affair, Weiss writes: 'If a person's ideology is in keeping with the new orthodoxy, they and their work remain unscrutinized. Everyone else lives in fear of the digital thunderdome'.

Weis asserts that the problems at The Times are not indicative of the majority, but that this majority is 'cowed'. She says, 'standing up for principle at the paper does not win plaudits. It puts a target on your back. Too wise to post on Slack, they [her cowed coworkers] write to me privately about the "new McCarthyism" that has taken root at the paper of record'.

Towards the end, she quotes Adolph Ochs. Ochs said that he bought the *New York Times* in 1896 'to make of the columns of the New York Times a forum for the consideration of all questions of public importance, and to that end to invite intelligent discussion from all shades of opinion'.

**Matt Taibbi on the Corruption of Journalism.** Matt Taibbi worked for *Rolling Stone* until April 2020. As he says in his conversation with Rogan in February 2023, he knew he didn't have a future at the magazine anymore when he was told not to touch the story about Trump's potential collusion with Russia. As Taibbi tells it, he had written some articles in which he voiced his doubts about whether the collusion had occurred. In a strongly anti-Trump environment, this was perceived as helping Trump.[26] In June 2020, Taibbi published an excoriating critique of Robyn DiAngelo's *White Fragility*.[27] Interestingly, at the time of writing this (February 2023), Taibbi's review is hardish to find on Google (search terms: 'Matt Taibbi White Fragility'): it is buried some way down the second page. However, on Duck Duck Go, which seems less corrupt for the moment, the article is the top result. As it should be.

Taibbi, in his conversation with Rogan in 2023, revisits many points made by Weiss. But he has several additional insights that add depth to our understanding of how, according to the IDW, things have gone wrong in journalism.

He talks about how several decades ago journalists had an adversarial relationship with the politicians they reported on: '[They would say] "Our job is to ask difficult questions and if we have difficult truths, we've got to report those things." The press has to have its own mission or else it's not legitimate'. Now, according to Taibbi, this is not the case:

> The new generation of journalists who have come in, they imagine themselves, because they're socially the same people they're reporting on – they hang out in the same circles, they go to the same parties – the idea of not being let behind the rope line is an atrocity to them … They see their role as helping to explain the point of view of power.[28]

Taibbi describes how, for him, journalism ensures that non-conforming individuals are managed:

> You see coming up in the business that when somebody tries to buck the system and tries to force through an unpopular story or refuses to write a story that's not true, or does anything that the others don't like, they see that those people are moved out of the business sooner rather than later. They just sort of end up being washed out with reputations for being difficult people … They kind of just squeeze you out. There's no particular thing that happens. And that sends signals down the ranks of people in journalism that if you want to get ahead, just keep doing the shit that we want you to do. You don't have to be a genius to figure out what that is. Just keep doing it and, you know, you'll eventually rise up through the ranks and before you know it you'll have your own show, you'll be running a desk, but you won't have anything to say. Because early on you'll have made the decision to abandon your individuality. That's the key to the whole thing. It's not people who are making these big decisions to sell out when they're 50. They make the decision to sell out when they're 22 or 23. At the very start. When they first see it. And they understand how the business works. And they start climbing. That's when they sell out. So by the time they get to be older, it's who they are.[29]

Here, we see the point that returns again and again within the IDW: if you think for yourself, and follow your curiosity and ask questions, you get in trouble. But what really catches my attention in Taibbi's remarks is that people sell out when they are in their early 20s, and that having sold out, when they finally get into a position of power, they don't have anything to say.

Taibbi hits some more deep points:

I think younger people have less tolerance for phoniness – or at least, historically they did; it's been a little weird lately … People who are going to go into journalism when they are 18 or 19 – once upon a time they all wanted to be Woodward and Bernstein or Sy Hersh, or Hunter Thompson. They just wanted to be a rule breaker. Someone who told the truth. And consequences be damned. Because that's what it's about. It's about being free and speaking your mind. What is it William Blake said? Always be ready to speak your mind and a base man will avoid you. That's what journalism is. You derive power from your willingness to say the unpopular true thing. And that's an attractive idealistic thing for a young person. But if they see that path closed, they're not going to go into – why would you go into journalism, and try to work at *The New Yorker* or *MSNBC*, if you know that you are never going to get to do that. But [on the internet] you can create your own show with almost no overhead and do the same thing and have a much bigger impact and you'll have a bigger audience even.[30]

And so here we are, back at the Declaration of the Independence of Cyberspace. However, Taibbi does also say that he thinks those in power will do much more in the future 'to try to prevent things like your [Joe Rogan's] show from breaking out'.[31]

## IDW Battles for Free Speech

Much of this book is about free speech. But here is a good place to say a few more words about it. Specifically, every IDW figure I mention has his or her own story about free speech. Here are some examples.

Joe Rogan's podcast is immensely popular because Rogan discusses topics that are often avoided in the media, academia, and polite society.

Jordan Peterson's battles have often been about free speech. Once again, in his interview with Cathy Newman, Newman asks Peterson: 'Why should your right to freedom of speech trump a Trans person's right not to be offended?' Peterson's now iconic reply is: 'Because in order to be able to think you have to risk being offensive'.[32]

Jonathan Haidt founded the Heterodox Academy, which is concerned with upholding 'diversity of viewpoint' (its tag is 'great minds don't always think alike'). The point is that the diversity that so many currently advocate involves supporting a diversity of identities so long as there is a homogeneity of viewpoints amongst these identities. Or as

Peter Boghossian puts it:

> They [the academy] have redefined the word 'diversity'; they've rede-
> fined the word 'inclusion'. But to people outside the academy, they
> think 'oh, diversity, it's a great thing'. But that's not what it means. It
> means when everybody has the same ideas about something.[33]

Ayaan Hirsi Ali, as she explains on Rogan, received strong support
from the media for her 2015 book, *Heretic*. But she struggled to gain
any support for her 2021 book, *Prey: Immigration, Islam, and the Erosion
of Women's Rights*. She mentions that one of the causes for her reduced
support was her own support of author JK Rowling – see Chapter 15.
Her publisher said that Hirsi Ali would have to generate publicity via
podcasts (funny how podcasts are legitimately illegitimate – or something like that).[34]

Richard Dawkins had his own deplatforming experience at Berkeley,
when radio station KPFA cancelled a book event with Dawkins in July
2017. About this, on The Rubin Report, Dawkins says:

> I lived in Berkeley – I lived there for two years – this was a Liberal
> beacon at a time in the late 60s when Berkeley was the home of free
> speech – the Free Speech Movement was 1963 [it was 1964]. How
> have the mighty fallen. Berkeley the home of free speech now the
> home of suppression of free speech.[35]

Steven Pinker, in support of Dawkins, says the move 'handed a precious
gift to the political right, who can say that left-leaning media outlets enforce mindless conformity to narrow dogma, and are no longer capable
of thinking through basic intellectual distinctions'.[36]

Bret Weinstein was driven out of Evergreen College for himself attempting to make such a distinction: it is one thing for Black people to
stay away as a protest. It is another thing for White people to be asked
to stay away.

The difficulty with the free speech issue at the moment is that there
is no clear proscription against certain speech. Rather, there's a continuum. Towards one extreme people sometimes lose their jobs for speaking
their mind, as happened to James Damore, or they are in some other
way 'cancelled', or perhaps they receive death threats or occasionally ex-

perience violence. Further along are the experiences of Bari Weiss at the *New York Times*, or those that Matt Taibbi describes. Here you don't immediately lose your job, but the institution makes it difficult for you and you are eventually extruded (this has been my experience over the last two decades as I've moved in and out of academia). Then, there is the vast middle ground of self-censorship, which ranges from people who hold their tongues with great reluctance because of fear or because it is not the right time to fight, to those who hold their tongues because they know it will benefit them. Consistent with Taibbi's remarks, my impression is that we humans have a remarkably acute sense of taboos: we don't need to hear much before we know which way the political wind is blowing.

We can also put the silencers of speech on a continuum. First, we encounter the people we just passed: those who hold their tongues when injustices are occurring around them. Then, we come to those who police the taboos because it is better to attack than be attacked. And at the extreme are the zealots who take pleasure in twisting the knife. The lovers of cruelty.

## Mill's *On Liberty* (and a Defence of Writing Essays)

I completed my PhD in 2009. I couldn't see how I could obtain an academic position while writing about what mattered to me (truth slipping into corrupt power), so I got a job teaching academic writing. This led me to think a lot about how to write a good essay. Sometimes students would ask: 'Why do I need to write essays? They don't prove anything. I want to study science'. At first, I didn't have a good answer. But then I realised that an essay is like much of life. In life we are constantly required to provide solutions to problems even though our understanding of the problems is incomplete. This is the case with everything from deciding who to vote for to trying to be a good parent. How do we come up with a solution to a problem about which we inevitably have an incomplete understanding? To the best of our ability, we explore the complexities of the problem and the range of possible solutions. We then select, or devise, the best solution. And if we are producing an essay about the problem, we lay out this process in writing.

As I became familiar with the IDW, I came across Jonathan Haidt speaking highly of John Stuart Mill. I'd read Mill, but never really studied him. The following are two oft-cited remarks:

> He who knows only his own side of the case knows little of that. His reasons may be good, and no one may have been able to refute them. But if he is equally unable to refute the reasons on the opposite side, if he does not so much as know what they are, he has no ground for preferring either opinion.[37]

And:

> The peculiar evil of silencing the expression of an opinion is, that it is robbing the human race; posterity as well as the existing generation; those who dissent from the opinion, still more than those who hold it. If the opinion is right, they are deprived of the opportunity of exchanging error for truth: if wrong, they lose, what is almost as great a benefit, the clearer perception and livelier impression of truth, produced by its collision with error.[38]

However, what pleased me the most was:

> [T]he only way in which a human being can make some approach to knowing the whole of a subject, is by hearing what can be said about it by persons of every variety of opinion, and studying all modes in which it can be looked at by every character of mind. No wise man ever acquired his wisdom in any mode but this; nor is it in the nature of human intellect to become wise in any other manner.[39]

Upon reading this I laughed to myself and thought: this is the same as essay writing! But then of course it is because we write essays to help us think through problems and, with any luck, acquire wisdom. I like that Mill says, 'No wise man ever acquired his wisdom in any mode but this'. Is it not obvious, then, that we need free speech to solve our problems and become wise, because it is only through free speech that we can explore all the potential dimensions of a problem?

Alas no, it is not obvious. Mill is operating within an Enlightenment paradigm, which assumes that we have access, albeit imperfect, to reality, and that by weighing perspectives, we can get a better sense of reality, and then from this, better decide how to act.

In the Postmodern paradigm, as we saw in the quotation in Chapter 4, it is wrong to think that truth claims correspond with reality, or –

which amounts to the same thing – knowledge is representation. Rather, knowledge has *historicity*, which is a coy way of saying that truth claims are really just about power. So, the upshot? In the Postmodern paradigm, there is no reason to consider reasons. Again, there is only powerful people using their putative reasons to shape reality in the way that suits them. Their speech – their discourse – thus does violence because it shapes the world. It is not to be weighed. It is to be silenced. Perhaps not many would openly endorse such sentiments. And yet our institutions are hobbled by taboos that seem founded on the assumption that to speak anything other than the orthodoxy is to bring evil into the world.

## Notes

1   Barlow 1996.
2   Rebel Wisdom n.d.
3   The Joe Rogan Experience 2018 October 31: 0:40:16.
4   Rebel Wisdom 2021 July 30: 0:02:50.
5   Rebel Wisdom 2021 July 30: 0:01:50.
6   The Joe Rogan Experience 2018 November 16: 3:00:30.
7   Eric Weinstein 2019 July 20.
8   Eric Weinstein 2019 July 20: 19:12.
9   Eric Weinstein 2019 July 20: 19:31.
10   Eric Weinstein 2019 July 20: 18:28.
11   The Joe Rogan Experience 2018 October 31: 0:01:52.
12   Weinstein 2011.
13   Big Think 2023 March 23: 28:18.
14   Eric Weinstein 2019 July 20: 0:26:09.
15   The Joe Rogan Experience 2018 October 31: 0:28:35.
16   The Joe Rogan Experience 2018 October 31: 0:29:12.
17   The Joe Rogan Experience 2018 October 31: 0:30:23.
18   The Joe Rogan Experience 2018 October 31: 18:11.
19   The Joe Rogan Experience 2018 October 31: 0:18:32.
20   The Joe Rogan Experience 2018 October 31: 0:20:05.
21   The Joe Rogan Experience 2018 October 31: 0:49:13.
22   Russell Brand 2023 February 19: 0:21:21.
23   The Joe Rogan Experience 2023 February 13: 1:44:54.
24   Hasan 2022 December 3.
25   Weiss 2020 July 14.

26   The Joe Rogan Experience 2023 February 13: 1:08:06.
27   Taibbi 2020 June 29.
28   The Joe Rogan Experience 2023 February 13: 0:33:54.
29   The Joe Rogan Experience 2023 February 13: 0:41:44.
30   The Joe Rogan Experience 2023 February 13: 0:49:03.
31   The Joe Rogan Experience 2023 February 13: 1:17:54.
32   Channel 4 News 2018 January 17: 0:22:12.
33   The Joe Rogan Experience 2018 October 31: 45:08.
34   The Joe Rogan Experience 2021 March 2: 0:00:00.
35   The Rubin Report 2017 August 9: 0:01:53.
36   Flood 2017 July 24.
37   Mill 2011 [1859]: 53.
38   Mill 2011 [1859]: 33.
39   Mill 2011 [1859]: 36.

# 9

# Individuals and Populations
## An Introduction

The following chapters will explore three frequently encountered IDW talking points: biological sex and employment, racism and police violence, and Intersectionality. However, each chapter will sit within a broader discussion of statistics. This is because, for the IDW, in relation to these topics, many people make questionable inferences about the relationship between (i) individuals and populations or (ii) one population and another or (iii) the nature of the distribution within a population. Examples of each are (i) when an individual is judged not on his or her character, but on some characteristic such as skin colour or sex; (ii) when an average difference between populations is construed to mean that all individuals in one population are different from all individuals in another population; (iii) when we think that because some people with a certain characteristic excel, all people with that characteristic excel. But before I get to the issues, I will introduce a few basic concepts in statistics that the IDW draws upon.

When we are talking about populations, we are referring to a group of people who share one or more characteristics. So, we could be interested in 'females' or 'Australians' or 'people aged between 20 and 30' or 'female Australians aged between 20 and 30'. Often, we want to know how individuals in a population vary according to some other characteristic. For example, for any of the just mentioned characteristics we could measure income. Having done this, we can begin to speak meaningfully about the relationship between the populations and the variable.

First, we can describe the general nature of the distribution. See Figure 1. If the distribution is 'normal', then the mode, median, and mean will be the same. The mode is the most common score, the median is the middle score, and the mean is the average score. These three measures of central tendency will shift around depending on whether the distribution is left- or right-skewed. When a distribution is skewed, sometimes 'median' is a more meaningful measure of central tendency. This is the case when we talk about house prices. We could focus on 'mean' house prices, but the issue is that a small amount of very expensive houses, which hardly anyone can afford, push the mean up (house prices are right-skewed), when really, it makes more sense to know what the median or middle house price is, seeing as most house prices fall closer to this than the mean. An obvious but essential point about distributions is that for most characteristics, there is, as the word 'distribution' suggests, variability. A case where there is no meaningful variability would be something like 'number of heads per New Zealander'.

Second, we can observe whether a population distribution is more bunched or spread out (see Figure 2). An important aspect of this is what occurs at the tails – the extremes. When scores are more bunched, there are fewer individuals at the tails than when scores are less bunched.

Third, we can observe how different populations compare with one another. For many characteristics we are interested in, populations overlap. When populations heavily overlap, we can say that the populations

## Figure 1. Different Distribution Shapes

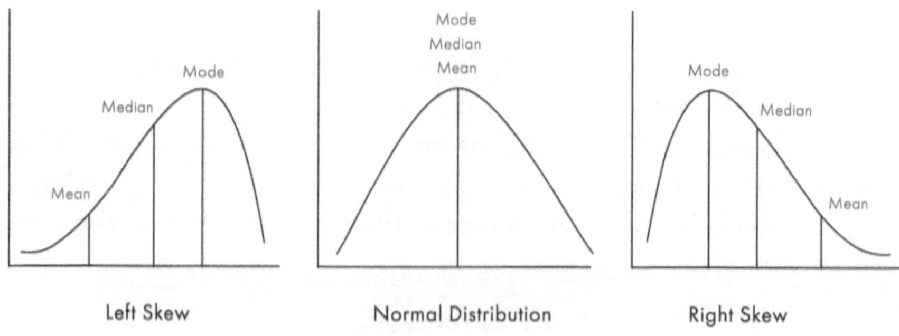

## Figure 2. Variability within Populations

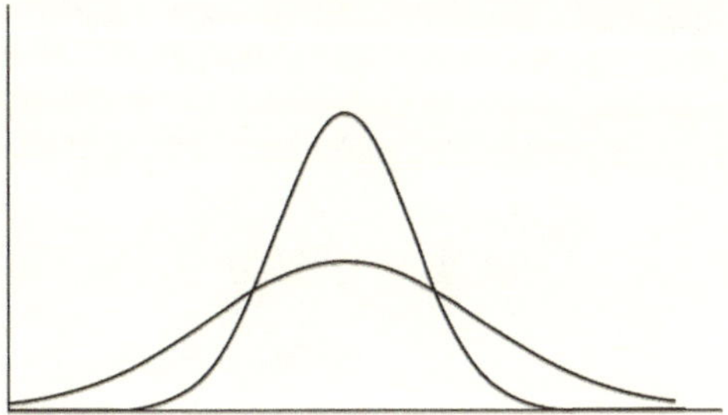

## Figure 3.  Overlapping Populations

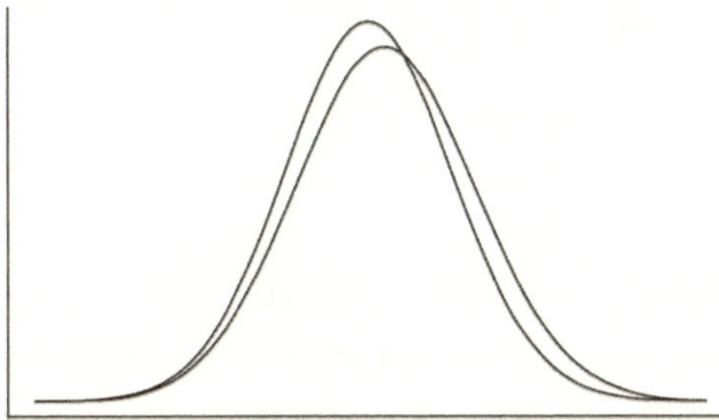

are similar. But even when populations heavily overlap, such as in Figure 3, there are meaningful differences.

In Figure 3, even though the populations are very similar, there is a difference between the means, medians, and modes. Further, the higher curve is a little more bunched, and the tails of the two curves are different: the tails of the lower curve contain more individuals – this is more noticeable on the positive side. This point is worth pausing on because of its substantial implications. Del Giudice, speaking about gender differences, says, 'Even when male and female distributions are largely overlapping in the region surrounding the mean of a trait, individuals with extreme values of the same trait may still be predominantly male or female'.[1]

## Note

1    Del Giudice 2015

10

# Individuals and Populations 1
## Biological Sex and Employment

This chapter will focus on two already mentioned IDW episodes: the James Damore memo and Peterson's conversation with Cathy Newman. Both were concerned with inequalities of outcome between the sexes in employment.

### Equality of Opportunity versus Equality of Outcome

When we see differences between populations in relation to some variable, such as the incomes of men and women, we naturally want to understand why such differences exist. Often, in relation to such matters, we talk about equality of opportunity and equality of outcome. When equality of opportunity exists, all people have the same opportunity to pursue a certain path. Much can be said about what constitutes the 'same opportunity'. When equality of outcome exists, people end up with the same outcome. Two questions can be asked: (i) When outcomes are unequal is this because there was a failure to ensure equality of opportunity? (ii) For whatever interests us, should we attempt to ensure there is equality of opportunity, equality of outcome, or possibly neither. In relation to the first question, a frequently encountered IDW position, as articulated by Steven Pinker while defending James Damore's memo, is '… we can't use differences in representation – that is, something short of exact fifty fifty – as proof of discrimination'.[1] In other words, we need to be cautious in how we make sense of inequalities in outcome; such inequalities are not necessarily due to obvious failures to ensure equality of opportunity. In relation to the second question, the IDW strongly supports equality of opportunity, but is wary of pushing for equality of outcome.

## The James Damore Memo and the Sex Ratio among Google Software Engineers

Once again, Damore's memo discusses how to interpret the fact that the ratio of male to female software engineers at Google was four to one. Talking on a panel at Portland State University in February 2018 with IDW figures Heather Heying, Helen Pluckrose, and Peter Boghossian, Damore expresses the mainstream view at Google as follows: 'The population has 50% women. Google has 20% women. Therefore sexism'.[2] In other words, Google attributed inequality in outcome to equality of opportunity failing because of sexism. This sexism could be in the hiring process and/or the environment within Google.

The first lines in the memo are:

> I value diversity and inclusion, am not denying that sexism exists, and don't endorse stereotypes. When addressing the gap in representation in the population, we need to look at population level differences in distributions. If we can't have an honest discussion about this, then we can never truly solve the problem.[3]

The obvious point is that if we assume that inequality in outcome is a result of sexism in the hiring process and a company's culture and it isn't, then we will struggle to change the inequality if that is what we want to do. As Damore, Pluckrose, and Heying argue, two other causes of inequality of outcome ought to be considered which lead to population-level differences: biological differences and broader cultural differences.

### Biological Differences

The IDW often argues that there are biological differences between women and men that extend beyond physical characteristics. Once again, in saying this, the IDW is repudiating the 'blank slate' position that is indicative of Postmodernism or, to use the term introduced by the panel, 'Social Constructivism'.[4] Here, understanding the statistics of populations is vital. Heying says, 'across cultures, men tend to be more interested in things, and women tend to be more interested in people'.[5] Heying is not suggesting that all men are one way and all women are another.[6] Rather, two overlapping distributions are being described. We could imagine that Figure 10.3 in the previous chapter is measuring interest in 'things' for women (higher curve) and men (lower curve). The point that is often made within the IDW is that when considering employment, we need to focus on the tails. If each of us gravitates towards activities that interest us and, along with this, that allow us to exploit our strengths, then small biological differences at the population level will lead to noticeable inequalities in participation in certain areas of expertise. As Heying says, 'So what you find is that women are actually increasingly overrepresented among the Life Sciences, and underrepresented in the Sciences that deal with non-organic things like Chemistry, like Physics, like Maths, like Engineering'.[7]

(As Pluckrose and Heying were speaking, several people walked out in protest, sabotaging the audio system on their way out. Outside, one of the protesters says, 'even the women in there have been brainwashed', and another says, 'we should not listen to fascism, it should not be tolerated in civil society, Nazis are not welcome in civil society'. Peter Boghossian, objecting to the sabotage and addressing the protests says, 'This is a university. If we cannot have this conversation here, we can't have it anywhere'. Amusingly, Boghossian also says, 'That sort of behaviour is unacceptable in civilised society'.[8])

### Broader Cultural Differences

Heying says that to try to understand the causes of unequal representation of software engineers in Google, we should also consider what occurs in broader society:

> The comparison population [for employment patterns at Google] – in statistics what we would call the 'expected value' – is not the sex-ratio of people in the population, because your average person isn't qualified to be a software engineer, so what should we look at for your expected

value? We've got the observed value of four to one sex ratio of software engineers in Google and across the tech sector, and it doesn't sound great – it sounds way off the one to one we know the human population to be at. But maybe we should look at the number of people – the ratio of people who are actually prepared for the job, the ratio of people who are likely to be applying for the job in the first place. And for me, the best proxy is, people earning degrees in computer science. So if you look at the educational data for higher ed, from the early 70s through last year, people earning bachelors degrees, masters degrees and PhDs in Computer Sciences, you have it climbing – the sex ratio – women start at around 11% or so, climbing up to around 35% in the mid 80s, and then slowly declining to their current level of female degrees in computer sciences, at about 20%. Which means that at the very least, Google is hiring software engineers at exactly the same ratio that universities are producing software engineers. Which tells you that there is no discrimination at Google with regard to the sex ratio of software engineers that are being hired.[9]

The point is that even if there are no biological differences between men and women at the population level, we must look beyond organisations themselves if we want to identify the causes of inequality of outcome. Perhaps, there are cultural factors that cause men and women to gravitate towards different degrees and professions, but such culture-wide influences are different to hiring policies and organisational environment. And how, or even whether, we should try to change them is a different discussion. Consider the questions of how or whether we should ensure that more men become nurses or more women become truck drivers.

With all of this, we can end up in a strange place. Peter Boghossian says, 'Why would we want to force someone to do something they don't want to do anyway?'[10] Pluckrose adds:

It maintains sexism. If we are assuming that the choices that men make are the ultimate absolute best choices, we are making men the default humans. The only reason women aren't doing exactly what men are doing, in exactly the same way, is because they are doing something wrong, or they are being conditioned into not thinking the right way. Because really, they should be just like men. But in fact, the areas that women dominate: healthcare, education, Psychology, publishing, these are all hugely influential areas on society. They are important.[11]

Heying makes a related point that is often made by Jordan Peterson: 'In those countries where equality of opportunity has been most democratised, roughly speaking, Scandinavia, you have people choosing more and more traditional gender roles for their careers'.[12] We also see the IDW reacting to the questionable deployment of Postmodern thinking in episodes such as the Damore memo. Recall the Postmodern belief that claims about how the world *is* do not – and maybe even cannot – describe how the world is, but rather, shape the world to serve interests. This is reflected in a headline of an article in *Cosmopolitan* in August 2017: 'The Viral Google Memo Is About the Stereotypes That Hold Women Back. James Damore put into writing the type of thinking that has kept women out of the workforce throughout history'.[13] Heying implicitly attacks this angle while discussing the claim that there is variability within populations by saying, 'It's not normative, it's just a truth'.[14] Later, Peter Boghossian says, 'The main confusion I see is the inability to understand the difference between stereotyping and talking about population distributions'.[15] This continues to be challenging territory. Certainly, stereotypes have been used to discriminate against women. But it does not follow from this that there are no differences at the population level between what interests men and women. And if such differences in interests exist, it is not certain what causes them.

Speaking explicitly in terms of equality of opportunity and outcome, Boghossian says: 'All of us are advocating for equality of opportunity. As John Rawls says, public education of the first rate … My own belief is that healthcare falls under that umbrella'. He and others on the panel then go on to object to pushing for equality of outcome. Boghossian says this would involve 'sending the worst singers to the best singing schools',[16] and Damore objects to having quotas based on characteristics such as sex. I largely share these views; however, I'm not certain that quotas are always unhelpful. But this is a long discussion.

### Jordan Peterson and Cathy Newman: The Gender Pay Gap

Jordan Peterson's discussion with Cathy Newman is also concerned with inequalities in outcome.[17]

Newman raises the issue of the gender pay gap. She says, 'The gender pay gap stands at just over 9%'.

Peterson replies, 'Multivariate analysis of the pay gap indicates that it doesn't exist'. These are not well-chosen words. Peterson here is guilty of exploiting the Motte-and-Bailey fallacy.

Newman replies – and this could be her high point of the interview – 'But that's just not true, is it. I mean, that 9% pay gap, that's the gap between median hourly earnings between men and women. That exists'.

Peterson replies: 'But there's multiple reasons for that [this is much more accurate than stating that the gap doesn't exist]. One of them is gender, but it's not the only reason. If you're a social scientist worth your salt you never do a univariate analysis. If you say women in aggregate are paid less than men, ok, then we break it down by age, we break it down by occupation, we break it down by interest, we break it down by personality.'

It is notable that Peterson mentions 'interest' and 'personality' – this is consistent with what was discussed by the IDW figures in relation to the Damore memo.

There is a bit more back and forth, then Newman says, 'You keep on talking about multivariate analysis. I'm saying that 9% pay gap exists. That's a gap between men and women. I'm not saying why it exists. But it exists. If you're a woman, that seems pretty unfair'.

Peterson replies, 'You have to say why it exists'. Here again we see the battle between the position that inequality of outcome is proof of discrimination – unfairness – and the position that inequality of outcome might have causes other than discrimination. Peterson claims there are about 18 factors that predict differences in income and says, 'There is prejudice – there's no doubt about that – but it accounts for a much smaller proportion of the variance in the pay gap than the radical feminists claim'. This again is more nuanced than his original Motte-grade claim that the pay gap does not exist.

## The Perfect Is the Enemy of the Good

Related to all these discussions is a point sometimes made by Heather Heying and Jordan Peterson: 'the perfect is the enemy of the good'. Even if we know that a system unfairly produces inequalities in outcomes, sometimes what we do to remedy this is worse than the inequalities themselves. I see such problems every day within the university administration. In an attempt to systematise extensions for student assignments, a vast bureaucracy has been established. Navigating this is difficult for academics, and can be even more challenging for students who are often already distressed – there is nothing like battling a faceless bureaucracy to lift your spirits. Better to just let the academics give extensions as they see fit, even if this results in some inconsistencies.

But it goes further than systems. For the IDW, problems in our world derive not just from bad systems or structures – an idea that has its roots in the Marxist tradition – but from human nature. Objecting to utopianism, and supporting the idea that there is a human nature that is imperfect, Francis Foster, speaking on Rogan in July 2022, says:

> They [the far-left] are all utopians, Joe. They believe that if they get everything – if we do all of these things – we are going to reach this magical utopia, where everything is free, where everybody lives in perfect harmony, we are going to perfect the human race. But the problem is, humans can't be perfected. I was talking about Shakespeare earlier. Why does Shakespeare still resonate? Because it deals with the human condition. Ambition. Greed. Lust. Fragility. All of these different things. If we were able to perfect humanity, do you think people would still read *Hamlet* or *Macbeth*? … We are never going to reach utopia.

Konstantin Kisin, who grew up in the Soviet Union, adds, 'And every time you try, people die in the fucking millions'. He also says, 'The only way to achieve equality is a huge amount of tyranny'.[18]

While I am wary of alarmism (earlier I objected to Peterson's comparison of Transgender activism and Maoism), these are important points. Recall again that for Postmodernists, problems stem from discourse – there is no human nature. Thus, for them it is legitimate to take control of culture or indeed all communication, to transform bad discourse into good discourse. But if there is such a thing as human nature, then this is a fool's errand. In contrast to the Postmodern approach, the Liberal approach is to believe that the worst aspects of human nature can be blunted through education (exposure to, not indoctrination with, ideas), political systems, and prosperity. But for Liberals, there will always be problems, and this is why we retain the rule of law. Liberalism is the middle path.

## Notes

1   Enlightainment 2018 August 1.
2   Freethinkers of PSU 2018 February 26: 10:24.
3   Damore 2017.
4   Freethinkers of PSU 2018 February 26: 18:10.
5   Freethinkers of PSU 2018 February 26: 24:42.
6   Freethinkers of PSU 2018 February 26: 23:34.
7   Freethinkers of PSU 2018 February 26: 24:49.
8   Freethinkers of PSU 2018 February 26: 20:46.
9   Freethinkers of PSU 2018 February 26: 0:25:51.
10   Freethinkers of PSU 2018 February 26: 0:33:18.
11   Freethinkers of PSU 2018 February 26: 0:33:26.
12   Freethinkers of PSU 2018 February 26: 0:35:36.
13   Covert 2017.
14   Freethinkers of PSU 2018 February 26: 0:23:41.
15   Freethinkers of PSU 2018 February 26: 0:28:47.
16   Freethinkers of PSU 2018 February 26: 0:36:16.
17   Channel 4 News 2018 January 17: 0:05:16.
18   The Joe Rogan Experience 2022 July 27: 1:40:09.

## 11

# Individuals and Populations 2
## Race and Police Violence

In May 2020 in the United States, Derek Chauvin, a white police officer, killed George Floyd, a black man, by kneeling on his neck for over nine minutes. This led to a resurgence in the Black Lives Matter movement. Several people in the IDW voiced opinions about the murder of Floyd, and whether police violence against black Americans is indicative of racism, as was the dominant – even hegemonic – opinion at the time. I've included this chapter within the broader discussion of individuals and populations because much of what the IDW has to say can be seen as attempts to understand the causes of poor outcomes for the black population.

### Glenn Loury and John McWhorter and the Causes of Racial Inequality

Economist Glenn Loury and Linguist John McWhorter are IDW associates who appear together on The Glenn Show. Neither has appeared on Rogan, but both have appeared on Jordan Peterson's and Bret Weinstein's podcasts, and Loury has appeared on Fridman's podcast. They are often mentioned within the IDW. They suggest that we need to consider causes in addition to racism to explain some of the outcomes experienced by black people in the United States. This is not easy to say.

But the challenge is that we should, to use Peterson's language, remain open to a multivariate analysis rather than assume single causes. And we should do this because, as Damore suggests, we won't solve our problems if we misrepresent the problems' causes.

On The Glenn Show in April 2021, McWhorter suggests two possible causes other than racism of the elevated black deaths at the hands of the police. The first is class. He says

> yes, Black people are killed [by police] two and a half times more than our representation in the population. But black people are also two and a half times more likely to be poor, and being poor attracts the cops to you. That's not fair, but it's also true.

He goes on to say that such things are 'just considered to be unsayable outside of certain circles'. And, 'I'm not saying that I'm censored. I can say whatever I want. Fine. But it's not the way respectable people are allowed to talk about this sort of thing'. Echoing Mearsheimer's claim that for post-Cold War idealists, the point is not to have the better argument, but the only argument, McWhorter says that to make the kinds of claims that he just made about class 'is considered heretical. It's treated as heresy. It's not treated as a fact that's refutable,' and that because of this, discussions about police violence, which attribute the violence to racism, are 'a fake conversation'.[1]

The second cause that McWhorter suggests for there being more Police killings of black people is even harder to stomach: culture. He says:

> In the Black community, there is a value placed on being a badass motherfucker. Some of this is that a critical mass of people salute these men for the resistance. The idea being that that's the black thing. You don't put up with any shit. I don't know what to do with that.

He then says, 'I don't know whether there's any point in saying that something should change'. Loury describes how he used to hang out in the hood while he was a tenured professor at Harvard, just so that he could be a badass motherfucker. He says that in acting the way he did, he was convincing himself that he was 'authentically black'. He asks,

'How fucked up was that?' and says, 'I am familiar with the syndrome' and asserts that 'it is a deep and profound problem in our culture', and 'there's no glory in it. You think this is politics? You think you are representing your ... enslaved ancestors?' McWhorter, talking specifically about deaths at the hands of the police, says, 'We agree folks, I'm human, I know the person shouldn't have died. But the point is, if only he hadn't resisted, he would still be alive. But there's no room for that point'. He finishes by saying:

> We are heard, and I'm very gratified by it – by a great many people. And it is not just white Conservatives. But every time you have this mob out on the street, and the *New York Times* writing the usual piece, I just think to myself: this is never going to change.[2]

In another discussion with McWhorter, and in relation to the ideas of Thomas Sowell, Glenn Loury makes a broader point about culture that echoes Pinker's remarks from the beginning of the previous chapter. 'Disparity does not prove discrimination. There's no reason to expect equality between groups, or to take inequality between them ... to be evidence of discrimination. Culture matters'.[3]

I myself do not know what to do with these claims. Surely cultural differences do lead to differences in outcomes between populations. But how do we talk about such things with precision, especially when current problems in cultures have been caused by horrific events in the past, or indeed, when racism and sexism do persist?

But regardless of whether McWhorter and Lowry are correct, the point, which is part of the way of the IDW, is that we should keep an open mind when considering what causes differences in outcomes between populations. We do this not just because we have a regard for truth, but, once again, for the practical reason that problems won't get solved if they are mischaracterised. And if the left wants to solve problems, not just signal group membership, then keeping an open mind is surely axiomatic.

**Sam Harris on whether racism can be inferred from police violence**

On 13 June 2020 Sam Harris released 'Can We Pull Back from the Brink?' on his Making Sense podcast. This was during some of the darkest days of the COVID pandemic. Protests and riots in response to the murder of George Floyd had spread across the US, and the racial tension could be felt around the world, including here in Australia. In the podcast, Harris explores several topics, including the problem of making population-wide generalisations about police violence based on individual videos, and also, once again, the problem of determining whether police violence is caused by racism, which sees Harris exploring statistics that describe different populations.

The episode begins with Harris delivering a long and careful preamble. It deserves our attention because it is indicative of the way of the IDW. He starts with familiar IDW points: 'Conversation is the only tool we have for making progress. I firmly believe that. But many of the things we most need to talk about seem impossible to talk about', and later, 'All that we have between us and the total break-down of civilisation is a series of successful conversations'. He criticises social media, saying, 'all information has been weaponised; all communication has become performative'. This is yet another instance of truth slipping into corrupt power. He also makes the broader point that 'most people are behaving as though every important question was answered a long time ago'.[4] This is consistent with Peter Boghossian's remarks in Chapter 4 that 'They [certain academics] think they've found the truth, there's no need to seek it, they are activists. But your epistemology has to come before your activism. Why you are doing activism matters'.

With respect to policing in general, Harris says that wanting to abolish the police is foolish (at the time 'defund the police' was a common slogan) and that giving the state a monopoly on violence is just about the best thing humans have ever done – along with keeping their shit out of their food. But he also suggests that policing needs to be greatly improved, and he criticises the enduring racism in the United States and the inequalities that exist that are a consequence of slavery and the colonisation of America.

Later, Harris addresses the issue of whether the colour of his skin disqualifies him from speaking about race:

I could have invited any number of great black intellectuals onto this podcast to make these points for me. But that struck me as a form of cowardice. Glenn Lowry, John McWhorter, Thomas Chatterton Williams, Coleman Hughes, Kmele Foster. These guys might not agree with what I'm about to say. But any one of them could walk the tightrope I'm now stepping out on far more credibly than I can. But you see, that's part of the problem. The perception that the colour of a person's skin, or even his life experience, matters for this discussion, is a pernicious illusion … We have to break the spell that the politics of identity has cast over everything.[5]

It is worth lingering on this point. Identity does matter for some questions. Thinking about the previous discussion, if we want to know what it's like to be a woman in the technology sector, we should ask women. But many questions about women in the technology sector do not need to be answered by women. For example, one does not need to be a woman to make Heather Heying's point that the proximate cause of there being fewer female than male software engineers is that fewer females graduate with related degrees.

Moving to the main discussion: police violence against black people, Harris asks:

Do the dozen or so other videos [other than the George Floyd video] that have emerged in recent years of black men being killed by cops – do they prove or even suggest that there is an epidemic of lethal police violence directed especially at black men, and that this violence is motivated by racism? Now most people seem to think that the answer to these questions are so obvious that even to pose them as I just did is obscene.[6]

He says, 'Many of the things you think you know about crime and violence in our society are almost certainly wrong. And that should matter to you'. Harris discusses several videos of police murders, including murders of white people and asks us again and again to consider what we know based on the videos. He says that some of the videos are easy to interpret, while others aren't. His broad points are that we often have simplistic interpretations of police videos and that we incorrectly generalise from individual videos about what happens across the population of the United States. He makes many difficult points such as, 'The media is not showing us videos of white people being killed by cops; activists are not demanding that they do this'. To this he adds, 'I'm sure white supremacists talk about this stuff a lot'.[7]

Harris then states his main point: 'In terms of the story we're telling ourselves in the mainstream, we're not actually talking about the data on lethal police violence'.[8] He points out that African Americans make up 13% of the US population but are 25% of police homicides. He mentions the familiar interpretation that this difference must be due to racism. He then says, 'blacks are 13% of the population, but they commit at least 50% of the murders and other violent crimes'. He asks, 'what percent of police attention should it [the African American population] attract?' and replies, 'I honestly don't know. But I'm pretty sure it's not just 13%. And given that the overwhelming majority of their [the killers'] victims are black, I'm pretty sure most black people wouldn't set the dial at 13% either'.[9] He then makes his most significant point: 'But as far as I know, the best data we have, suggests that for whatever reason, whites are more likely to be killed by cops once an arrest is attempted'.[10] Harris provides many more such details and analyses. Notably, he mentions a study that found that 'there is a 25% greater likelihood that the police would go "hands on" with black suspects than white ones. Cuffing them or forcing them to the ground or using other non-lethal force'.[11] I cannot guarantee the veracity of Harris's claims. However, there is an annotated transcript of the podcast with links to the supporting evidence.[12]

All of this feeds into Harris's broader argument that regardless of what we think about policing in the United States, the generalisations we often make about the causes of police violence are not necessarily accurate. Police violence against black people is not necessarily indicative of racism.

Towards the end, Harris returns to familiar IDW criticisms of Identity Politics. He says:

> We have to vote Trump out of office to restore the integrity of our institutions. And we have to make the political case for major reforms to deal with the problem of inequality – a problem which affects the black community most of all.

He goes on to say, 'But it's not at all clear that progress … primarily entails us finding and eradicating more racism in our society',[13] and that race has become a 'fetish' and a 'sacred object' and that it is 'ringed on all sides by taboos'.[14] In these remarks, we see Harris aligning his version of left-wing politics with Enlightenment values (making a 'political case') and also shifting the focus from race to class. We see further reference to class concerns in the following:

> [T]he path to success and power for historically disadvantaged groups isn't generally barred by white racists who won't vote for them or hire them or celebrate their achievements or buy their products. And it isn't generally barred by laws and policies and norms that are unfair. Now, there's surely still some of that but there must be less of it now than there ever was. The real burden on the black community is the continued legacy of inequality with respect to wealth and education and health and social order, levels of crime in particular, and the resulting levels of incarceration and single parent families and it seems very unlikely that these disparities, whatever their origin in the past, can be solved by focusing on the problem of lingering racism, especially where it doesn't exist. And the current problem of police violence seems a perfect case in point. And yet now we are inundated with messages from every well-intentioned company and organisation singing from the same book of hymns. Black Lives Matter is everywhere. Of course black lives matter. But the messaging of this movement around the reality of police violence is wrong and is creating a public hysteria.[15]

In finishing, Harris talks about the fear of the 'other'. The other is a person or group who we believe is different from us – who does not value what we value. When we object to 'othering' someone, we are often implying that the person doing the othering is fabricating the characteristics of the other, as typically occurs with racism, sexism, or homophobia – all of which Harris mentions. Harris's twist on this concept is that sometimes the other should be feared, and, in IDW fashion, he says the following:

> [T]he fear of the other that does seem warranted – everywhere, right now – it is the other who has rendered him or herself incapable of dialogue. It's the other who will not listen to reason. Who has no interest in facts. Who can't join a conversation that converges on the truth because he knows in advance what the truth must be. We should fear the other who thinks that dogmatism and cognitive bias aren't something to be corrected for because they are the very foundations

of his epistemology. We should fear the other who can't distinguish activism from journalism, or politics from science. Or worse, can make these distinctions but refuses to. And we are all capable of becoming this person … And this is a bug in our operating system. Not a feature. And we have to continually correct for it.[16]

These comments are reminiscent of a quotation from Aleksandr Solzhenitsyn's *The Gulag Archipelago* that was popularised by Jordan Peterson:

It was granted me to carry away from my prison years on my bent back, which nearly broke beneath its load, this essential experience: how a human being becomes evil and how good. In the intoxication of youthful successes I had felt myself to be infallible, and I was therefore cruel. In the surfeit of power I was a murderer, and an oppressor. In my most evil moments I was convinced that I was doing good, and I was well supplied with systematic arguments. And it was only when I lay there on rotting prison straw that I sensed within myself the first stirrings of good. Gradually it was disclosed to me that the line separating good and evil passes not through states, nor between classes, nor between political parties either – but right through every human heart – and through all human hearts. This line shifts. Inside us, it oscillates with the years. And even within hearts overwhelmed by evil, one small bridgehead of good is retained. And even in the best of all hearts, there remains … an unuprooted small corner of evil.[17]

## Notes

1   The Glenn Show 2021 April 27.
2   Nonzero 2021 April 22.
3   Nonzero 2021 February 24: 0:05:35.
4   Sam Harris 2020 June 13: 0:00:40.
5   Sam Harris 2020 June 13: 0:33:30.
6   Sam Harris 2020 June 13: 0:44:13.
7   Sam Harris 2020 June 13: 0:47:44.
8   Sam Harris 2020 June 13: 1:14:49.
9   Sam Harris 2020 June 13: 1:16:35.
10   Sam Harris 2020 June 13: 1:23:25.
11   Sam Harris 2020 June 13: 1:19:46.

12   Sam Harris 2020 June 19.
13   Sam Harris 2020 June 13: 1:39:43.
14   Sam Harris 2020 June 13: 1:44:40.
15   Sam Harris 2020 June 13: 1:47:05.
16   Sam Harris 2020 June 13: 1:51:55.
17   Solzhenitsyn 1998: 614–5.

12

# Individuals and Populations 3
## Intersectionality

In the Culture Wars, one of the great battles in relation to individuals and populations that straddles nearly every other battle involves 'Intersectionality'. Intersectionality has two components. The first is the somewhat innocuous idea that an individual is the outcome of the interaction or *intersection* of various social forces. The second, which is where the teeth come from, is that some individuals experience multiple forms of discrimination because of their 'identities'; for example, being a woman, Asian, and disabled.

I encounter the concept of Intersectionality regularly at university. Students (albeit a minority) often use the term 'privilege' to object to certain identities: one is privileged if one's identity has fewer components that are associated with disadvantage than someone else's identity. So, a gay white man would probably be more privileged than a straight Asian woman – though it depends on which theoretical framework you are using. Several of my colleagues continue to invoke Intersectionality. At a recent (early 2023) school-level meeting (in my university it goes Faculty > School > Department), there was a discussion about 'Intersectionality and the Ideal Workplace'. The first bullet point was: 'Compounded discrimination due to multiple marginalising and interlinked characteristics'. Here, we get to the heart of the problem with Intersectionality. The aim of an Intersectionalist is not to identify instances of discrimination and redress them (such as people using the concept of Intersectionality to transform staff meetings into struggle sessions, where the men are denounced and also rewarded for admitting and apologising for their privilege). This would be the intuitive Platonic approach. Rather, the aim is to assume that discrimination in certain forms already exists and that by instituting policies underpinned by the concept of Intersectionality, discrimination will be eradicated and, I suppose, the tyrants of the university will be brought to heel. Note that this is another instance of the abuse of 'theory' or 'theoretical frameworks' within the university: Rather than beginning by observing what occurs in reality, you begin by assuming that reality functions in a certain way. And this is permissible because of the Postmodern sleight of hand that I mentioned in Chapter 4; that is, because there is, for the Postmodernists, no truth, you can say whatever you want – so long as you have a theoretical framework. The IDW has had a lot to say about Intersectionality.

## Trying to Understand Intersectionality

Helen Pluckrose and James Lindsay in their book *Cynical Theories* provide the following account of Intersectionality by Patricia Hill Collins and Sirma Bilge; it is deceptively anodyne:

> Intersectionality is a way of understanding and analyzing the complexity in the world, in people, and in human experiences. The events and conditions of social and political life and the self can seldom be understood as shaped by one factor. They are generally shaped by many factors in diverse and mutually influencing ways. When it comes to social inequality, people's lives and the organization of power in a given society are better understood as being shaped not by a single axis of social division be it race or gender or class, but by many axes that work together and influence each other. Intersectionality as an analytic tool gives people better access to the complexity of the world and of themselves.[1]

Yes, people's lives are affected by numerous factors, and if we are to understand a person, it would be helpful to understand all the factors – if this is possible. Funnily enough, the first three sentences are reminiscent of Jordan Peterson's remarks to Cathy Newman when he stresses the need for a 'multivariate analysis' of the gender pay gap – again, according to Peterson the gender pay gap is affected by around 18 variables, not the single variable of discrimination on the grounds of sex.

Peterson himself identifies the benign, even banal, aspects of Intersectionality in a conversation with Jonathan Haidt and Greg Lukianoff:

> I was thinking about Intersectionality, which I think, by the way, is a painfully obvious idea – the idea that you can be classified among many group dimensions and that there are social status consequences to all of those and that they interact. But Intersectionality is actually the discovery of the fatal flaw of Identity Politics, because if you fragment people down, if you allow their group identities to multiply and interact, then you get to the point where each individual is a unique nexus of group identities, and I actually think that that's what Western culture discovered over the last several thousand years.[2]

To continue Peterson's observation: How many group – or population – level dimensions ought we to consider before we are able to map an individual? We can consider the usual suspects of sex, sexuality, race, and class. But there are many other candidates, such as intelligence, attractiveness, personality, and height. And within each of these, as with class, and race, there is considerable variance. But then we should also consider life experiences: how one was parented, the type of education one received, whether one has experienced violence, and so on. Yet even if we can identify all the dimensions that constitute a person, what do we know about how the dimensions interact? Does being intelligent and attractive with just the right amount of assertiveness and ambition nullify being short and being born into a poor family with an alcoholic father? Who the fuck knows. We are rapidly moving towards one of those 'there are more combinations than there are atoms in the universe' scenarios.

However, this is a little glib. I don't agree with Peterson that Intersectionality reveals the fatal flaw of Identity Politics because it leads us away from collective identity and to the individual. Sometimes, it is valuable to consider individuals as members of a group. In Australia, Aboriginal males are overrepresented in the prison population.[3] This statistic is useful because by considering the intersection of two categories – Aboriginal and male – we are in a better place to devise solutions to this problem of overrepresentation. And we might do even better if we considered other dimensions such as class and age. There are many such examples. Making a similar point, Jonathan Haidt, in the same conversation with Peterson, speaks about justice and argues that many low-wage workers in the United States are cheated by the companies they work for. He explains when we should be concerned about Social Justice in relation to identity:

> If [a failure in distributive fairness] is disproportionately affecting one race, or if people are being cheated because they are members of any identity group, that is a violation, I would say, of Social Justice – or of justice applied to identities.[4]

So, Intersectionality, Identity Politics, and Social Justice do well when they observe differences in outcomes for different populations. And they do even better when they establish the causes of different outcomes and suggest genuine solutions.

Interestingly, if we do use Intersectionality to identify differences in outcome, we sometimes come across unexpected outcomes. Consider the case of GCSE success in the United Kingdom – the GCSE is a high-school academic qualification. When performances are mapped according to sex and ethnicity, it turns out that the best performers are ethnically Chinese females, followed by ethnically Indian females.[5] This is not to say that such people do not experience racism or sexism, but rather that it is not obvious how a person's membership of various populations will affect their opportunities and outcomes.

With all this in mind, the fatal flaw within Intersectionality is that in its weaponised – corrupted – form, it does not encourage careful observation and analysis. Rather, it assumes the existence of a caste system. It begins by selecting a number of expedient dimensions and ascribing to each a 'privileged' and 'oppressed' position. White males are the most privileged, and all who belong to this category must carry with them this original sin. As Greg Lukianoff says, the more privilege I have, the more I must experience 'a permanent situation of guilt and shame about an identity that I have no control over'.[6]

Here it is worth quoting Stephen Fry who, in the older Liberal tradition, is a great lover of connecting with people as individuals. He is talking about a passage from a *Sherlock Holmes* novel:

[Sherlock Holmes] says, you know, Watson, the statistician has shown that we can predict to an extraordinary order of accuracy the behavior of the average man … The average man, we can absolutely predict how they will behave, but no one has yet and probably never will be able to predict how an individual will behave. So we can be talked about as a mass and advertisers and politicians and psephologists and all kinds of other people are very good at knowing how we behave as a group. But as individuals we are unknowable without face-to-face conversation and the [individual's] history and so on.[7]

Returning to Peterson, Haidt, and Lukianoff, in the remainder of the conversation, they continue to explore the problems with Intersectionality, making further familiar points about populations and individuals.

Peterson, discussing how we should understand populations, reminds us that there is great variability within populations:

[If] on average, straight white men are doing well or have done relatively well economically, it's also very much worth pointing out that it's a tiny minority of straight white men who have been doing spectacularly well. So you have a Pareto distribution problem within each ethnic identity group. And so, to say that because on average the socio-economic status of a given group is higher than the status of another group, all the people who are members of that group are disproportionately benefiting, is actually a rather motivated and resentful analysis.[8]

In a Pareto distribution, a small percentage of individuals have a high score on some variable, while most have a low score. Thus, all individuals within a population cannot be judged as being the same even when there are inequalities of outcome at the population level.

Peterson then makes an important additional point:

It is always a tiny proportion of people in a group that are doing spectacularly well. Then you have to do something else. Which is, you have to look at the proportion that are doing spectacularly well and you have to decide about how many of them are doing well because they actually deserve it, and how many of them are doing well because they are inappropriate rent seekers. And I would say because our culture is pretty damn functional, and because we do generate a lot of wealth along with the inequality, there's a fair number of people who are doing disproportionately well who are doing that by benefiting everyone else, and we are not very careful about making those sorts of distinctions. And they are actually crucial.

The point here is that even if individual white males are overrepresented at the extremes of income, it does not follow that they should be condemned. It is one thing to want to lift up people at the bottom. It is another to want to pull down the competent people at the top.

## Resentment

This brings us to the idea of 'resentment' that Peterson mentions. Earlier, Haidt had said the following: 'the world is not perfectly equal across all categories' and conceded that straight white males have a disproportionate amount of the wealth – Haidt is politically to the left of Peterson. But he then quotes Bret Weinstein, 'There are some people who see inequality and want to end it. There are other people who see inequality and want to reverse it'.[9] His point is that Intersectionality is not merely concerned with ending inequality, but with something far darker: revenge or even cruelty.

While resentment, revenge, and cruelty are likely as old as humanity itself, we can return to Foucault to get a sense of how they have been sanctified in their Woke incarnation (we could go back further to Hegel's Master/Slave dialectic). Recall Foucault's claim that power produces truth. By this account, truth is not something we get to by drawing on reasoning and evidence. Foucault's claim can be used to strike at powerful people who create so-called truths to suit their interests, and we do see such people all the time in everything from corrupt governments, to cults, to bad relationships. But in the Postmodern realm, there are two dangerous twists. First, for the Postmodernist, it is enough to identify someone as powerful to dismiss them. Second – and this is far more interesting – if, indeed, a person's claims are diminished by his or her putative high status, then the claims of a person with a putative low status are necessarily enhanced. James Lindsay when he was on Rogan in October 2018 describes this phenomenon as 'Competitive Victimhood'.[10] In short, in the universe of Intersectionality, the value of what one says or does is inversely proportional to the power one has, where this power

– or lack of power – is determined by the identity groups one belongs to.

Once again, this is a little glib. We ought to listen to people with less power. Democracy and a free press are brilliant because they help societies listen to those with less power. Having said this, those with less power must still make their case using reasoning and evidence.

Nietzsche provides the best account of the problem with Intersectionality with his concept 'Slave Morality':

> [In Slave Morality] the miserable alone are the good; the poor, powerless, lowly alone are the good; the suffering, deprived, sick, ugly are also the only pious, the only blessed in God, for them alone is there blessedness, – whereas you, you noble and powerful ones, you are in all eternity the evil, the cruel, the lustful, the insatiable, the godless, you will eternally be the wretched, accursed, and damned.[11]

And a little later, and even more to the point he writes:

> The slave revolt in morality begins when *ressentiment* itself becomes creative and gives birth to values: the *ressentiment* of beings denied the true reaction, that of the deed, who recover their losses only through an imaginary revenge. Whereas all noble morality grows out of a triumphant yes-saying to oneself, from the outset slave morality says 'no' to an 'outside', to a 'different', to a 'not-self': and *this* 'no' is its creative deed.[12]

Such ideas can lead us to dangerous places, such as hating the poor, or anyone who is struggling. But when used thoughtfully, they help us elucidate the vital distinction that many in the IDW circle around. Again, as Heidt, quoting Bret Weinstein says, some people want to end inequality, others want to reverse it. **It is one thing to want to help the disadvantaged; it is another to say that the disadvantaged are good, or have a special access to truth, by virtue of being disadvantaged. Similarly, it is one thing to want to reform corrupt power, but it is another to say that those who live better lives – the 'privileged' – are necessarily bad, and do not have access to the truth.**

Consider this thought experiment. If I am poor, but somehow manage to give my children a good education and instill in them good values, there is a fair chance they will be successful in life. They will then be amongst the ranks of the privileged. Thus, if we dislike privilege, an excellent way to prevent it is to be a bad parent. The unavoidable conclusion is that privilege is good. The problem is that not everyone is able to purse it. Thus, our focus should be on improving opportunities.

A theme that runs through human history is that humans are always finding new ways to license cruelty. Rogan and Lindsay pithily summarise the problem. Rogan says, 'It's so funny how racist you can be as long as you are racist against white people'. Lindsay replies, 'That's what we saw. As long as you are going up the river against privilege then you can really just get away with some nasty stuff'.[13] This is why Peterson often talks about the brutal treatment of the Kulaks – the more successful peasants – in the early Soviet Union. We could also add that the Jews in Hitler's Germany dominated the professional classes prior to the Second World War, where their success was a source of resentment amongst non-Jews.[14] Rogan, objecting to judging people based on their ascribed group identity says:

> And you can generalise. Gross generalisations. Do not treat people as individuals. It's very strange. It's very strange that this is the left. You know, I was a kid, in San Francisco in the 1970s. We lived in the hippie times … It kind of formed a lot of my opinions about people – like the 'who gives a shit' part of my appreciation for any group – whatever it is, whether it's race or gender or sexual orientation. I don't understand it from either way. I certainly don't understand it from a racist perspective. But I really don't understand it from racism that's condoned because it's racism against white people. This is the left. These are the people that are preaching against hate. And these are the people that used to be the people that are supposedly so open minded and so open to ideas and now they're trying to stifle creativity, stifle dissent, stifle anything that doesn't fit inside that very narrow paradigm they're trying to push.

Lindsay's deeper analysis, which I touched on earlier, is, 'They [the Woke left] co-opted the civil rights movement. The good name of the civil rights movement, is kind of the brand that they ride on'.[15] Here again we have the slip from truth to corrupt power mentioned in Chapter 7.

Lex Fridman and Douglas Murray talk at some length about such matters on Fridman's podcast. Fridman, who is the IDW archetype because he is so wary of polarisation, pushes Murray to understand the position of those who seek to silence those with alleged privilege. He says:

> I'm just saying there's a few of those folks listening to this [podcast] with that real raw emotion, and one argument they say is you Douglas Murray, you Lex Friedman don't have the *right* to talk about race and racism in America, it is our struggle. You are from a privileged class of people that don't know what it's like to be a black man or woman in America walking down the street. Can you steel man in that case?

Murray, whose flawless erudition and urbane manner make him the archetypical Peter O'Toole-grade Englishman, replies:

> First of all, fuck that … I really resent that form of argumentation. I really resent it. I have the right to talk about whatever the hell I want. And no one's going to stop me or try to intimidate me or tell me that I can't simply because of my skin colour.

He then says:

> But seriously, is that a reasonable form of argument? You haven't been through everything I've been through in my life. Therefore, you can't comment. No. In that case, nobody can talk about anything. We might as well pack up, go home and isolate ourselves.[16]

As Harris says, Identity Politics, at its extreme, precludes any form of genuine communication.

Fridman continues to push Murray, and they begin to explore the nuances of the problem – the cases where knowledge is attached to identity, or at least to experience. They consider the example of Holocaust survivors having authoritative knowledge about the Holocaust. Murray gives ground here but refines his position in an interesting way. In relation to people who have suffered, he says:

> in terms of wanting to listen to another person who has experienced something. Yes, yes. But not endlessly. Not endlessly. There are people who have written about the Holocaust who didn't experience the Ho-

locaust, and have written about it better than people who did.[17]

We should listen to people who have suffered, but suffering does not guarantee authority.

To finish, for the IDW, Intersectionality is dangerous because it is a psychological weapon born of resentment rather than a tool for analysis. This being the case, the deeper question is: when we are suffering how do we recover our losses when, as Douglas Murray himself says, 'there are very good reasons that some people in their lives might feel resentment?'[18] For some in the IDW, the antidote to resentment is gratitude. Murry and Fridman, in their broader discussion of Identity Politics, consider Dostoyevsky's *The Brothers Karamazov*. Murry mentions that in the novel the devil appears, and that the defining characteristic of the devil is that he is incapable of gratitude – Murray marvels at this insight, which is indeed impressive. Fridman draws together all they have been saying: 'I think it's a really powerful idea. That with gratitude you don't get the resentment that rots you from the core'.[19] We all must struggle with resentment. God knows, I struggle with it.

## Notes

1   Bilge cited in Pluckrose and Lindsay 2021: 127.
2   PhilosophyInsights 2019 November 30: 0:00:00.
3   Australian Bureau of Statistics 2022.
4   PhilosophyInsights 2019 November 30: 0:06:07.
5   GOV.UK 2022 March 18.
6   PhilosophyInsights 2019 November 30: 0:03:46.
7   Jordan B Peterson 2021 May 18: 1:08:36.
8   PhilosophyInsights 2019 November 30: 0:03:59.
9   PhilosophyInsights 2019 November 30: 0:01:51.
10  The Joe Rogan Experience 2018 October 31: 0:38:34.
11  Nietzsche 1998 [1887]: 16–17.
12  Nietzsche 1998 [1887]: 19.
13  The Joe Rogan Experience 2018 October 31: 0:10:12.
14  This is covered in many books, such as Evans' *The coming of the Third Reich* (2005) and Friedländer's *Nazi Germany and the Jews, 1933-1945* (2009).
15  The Joe Rogan Experience 2018 October 31: 0:11:45.
16  Lex Fridman 2022 June 21: 0:26:22.

17  Lex Fridman 2022 June 21: 0:28:45.
18  Lex Fridman 2022 June 21: 0:40:35.
19  Lex Fridman 2022 June 21: 0:44:08.

# 13

## Individuals and Populations 4
## Rick and Morty

I must be careful not to claim too many people and bits of culture as IDW. It is important to maintain that to be in the IDW you need to both follow the IDW way *and* associate with the IDW. However, there are some recent cultural works that lean heavily in the IDW direction. Perhaps the early *Simpsons*, unquestionably *South Park*, and probably also *Rick and Morty*. *Rick and Morty's* Season 3 Episode 7 'The Ricklantis Mixup' (aired 10 September 2017)[1] is the apex of the show – much of what we had already seen feeds into it, and the show was never quite as good after it. The episode does not explicitly refer to Identity Politics, but it appeared at a moment when Identity Politics was in the ascendency. The episode makes the point that even when there are marked differences between populations, the immense variance that usually exists within populations means that we cannot judge an individual drawn from a population based on the characteristics of the population.

Some background. In *Rick and Morty*, genius Libertarian alcoholic Rick Sanchez has adventures in the multiverse – he uses a 'portal gun' to travel between universes. In the multiverse, every possible variation of our own universe exists. Rick's partner is his grandson Morty. The power between them is something like 90/10 or 80/20. This is part of the attraction of the show: Rick is dominant, at times monstrous, but he is not all-powerful – he needs Morty. As Rick and Morty travel the multiverse, they sometimes encounter versions of themselves. Within the show, many Ricks from across the multiverse have come together and created the 'Citadel', a space city where Ricks (and their Mortys) can live their lives free from interference from government – The Galactic Federation. The great irony is that in the Citadel a class system has developed, which includes the 'Council of Ricks', which rules the Citadel. Reflecting the inequality in the relationship between the main Rick and Morty of the show, Mortys form the bulk of the underclass within the Citadel – what Marxists would call the lumpenproletariat. Amongst the working class – the proletariat – there are both Ricks and Mortys. The upper echelons – the capitalists and politicians – are dominated by Ricks (see Figure 5).

However, within the various storylines of the episode, we see that many individual relationships do not conform to the population-level inequalities between Ricks and Mortys, nor indeed to the power relationship between the Rick and Morty that the show follows. In one storyline, one Morty is a corrupt cop who persecutes the lumpenproletariat Mortys and bullies his partner: an inexperienced, but morally upright Rick. In another storyline, a downtrodden Rick works on the soul-destroying production line of a factory run by other Ricks. But the standout storyline is that even though the ruling class is composed of Ricks, the most powerful and corrupt figure in the citadel is Evil Morty, who seizes power through a violent coup.

The episode's point is that to understand reality we must do two things: we must acknowledge population-wide inequalities, but at the same time, we must continue to judge individuals on their merits. This is far from a radical idea – it's almost banal – but in the world of Identity

**Figure 5. The Respective Power of Ricks and Mortys in the Citadel**

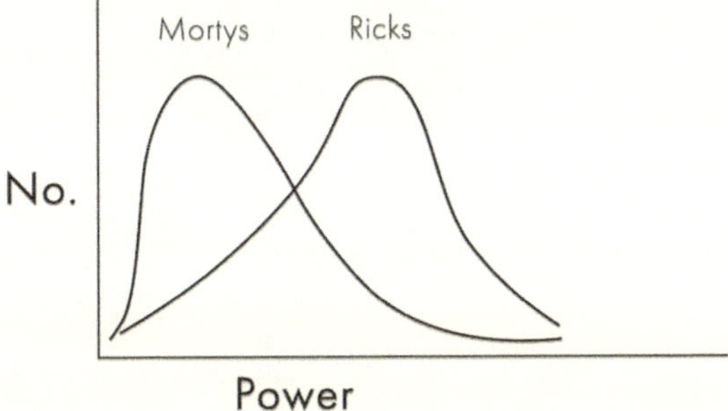

Politics, this does not happen. When we play Identity Politics, individuals are judged based on what populations they belong to.

Why is it that we struggle to balance a recognition of population-level differences with a respect for individual differences? This might be yet another Dunbar Number problem. In small communities, when everyone is known, people are very much judged on their individual characteristics. But in our world of eight billion people, we use heuristics derived from our knowledge of populations. And these heuristics are themselves corrupted by in-group/out-group dynamics and the ever-present resentment.

## Note

1    Guterman and Ridley 2017.

# 14

# IDW Views toward Masculinity and Responsibility

The IDW is on reasonably firm ground for many of its talking points, such as its championing of Enlightenment values and free speech and its ideas about populations and individuals. When I discuss such things with my students, familiar student positions, which the IDW typically opposes, such as 'my truth is as good as your truth', or 'white males are privileged' don't hold up very well – at least not in their strong or 'Bailey' forms. However, on sex and gender matters, IDW claims are a touch harder to adjudicate. This is particularly true for IDW ideas about masculinity.

Consider the 1999 movie *Fight Club*, which is in the ballpark of IDW ideas about masculinity. In *Fight Club*, the nameless protagonist is depressed because of his mundane white-collar life. He finds meaning when he establishes Fight Club – a club where men fight each other – with the charismatic and mysterious Tyler Durden. Writing for *The Times*, James Christopher said *Fight Club* 'touched a nerve in the male psyche'.[1] *Fight Club* certainly did touch a nerve. But what nerve did it touch? Did *Fight Club* reveal that contemporary men have lost something vital – something which their natures urge them towards, and without which they are diminished? Or was *Fight Club* a reactionary movie that encouraged the resentful perception amongst men that they have been robbed of some power that used to be their birthright? Such questions again take us to the heart of the Culture Wars.

Like *Fight Club*, the IDW has certainly touched a nerve in the male psyche, and similar questions come to mind. Does the IDW point the way for men to better align with their natures and thus be more fulfilled? Or does it fuel reactionary male resentment? Recall Henry Farrell's remarks in Chapter 5: 'It's hard for erstwhile hegemons to feel happy about their fall'. Joe Rogan himself is a *Fight Club* kinda guy. He commentates for Mixed Martial Arts, loves hunting, and works out. And there are several IDW associates like him; for example, ex-Navy SEALs David Goggins and Jocko Willink.[2]

There is much that I could cover in this chapter. However, first I will briefly revisit the question of whether gender is a social construction. Then, for the main event, I will present some of the IDW's concerns about how masculinity is currently viewed and manifested. This leads to the question of how men ought to be in the world, but also to identifying links between IDW ideas about masculinity and IDW concerns about Identity Politics.

## Again: Gender Isn't a Social Construction

The orthodox, Postmodernism position that the IDW opposes is that gender is a social construction. This means that no aspect of our personalities, abilities, or interests is influenced by our biological sex; thus, any differences that we see between men and women at the population level are the result of cultural forces. A typical remark is the following from a book chapter titled 'Gender and Sexuality as a Social Construct':

> Gender is so pervasive that in our society we assume it is bred into our genes. Most people find it hard to believe that gender is constantly created and recreated out of human interaction, out of social life, and is the texture and order of that social life. Yet gender, like culture, is a human production that depends on everyone constantly 'doing gender'.[3]

The IDW position, which we saw in Chapter 10, is that population-level differences between men and women with respect to personality and especially interests derive to some extent from biology.

While the origins of the Postmodern position are several, speaking on Rogan, IDW associate Debra Soh, who has a PhD in neuroscience, explains one fear that lies behind the claim that gender is a social construction:

> *Soh:* If you read the scientific studies, you cannot come away from them saying gender is a social construct.
>
> *Rogan:* What's the argument for it?
>
> *Soh:* The idea is that women should be equal. And obviously as a woman I believe that. And so any sort of subjugation of women must somehow be imposed by society, because if we acknowledge that women are different biologically in any way, that's going to be used as justification for why they don't deserve to be treated the same as men, or they are not as capable as men.
>
> *Rogan:* But why is different 'subjugation', why is different 'incapable', why is different 'inferior'?
>
> *Soh:* Because I guess there has been a history of sexism. So with the whole Google memo thing, and this idea that women are biologically – we are different – not to say we are not as capable; but if there are any sort of biological correlates to what women find interesting, could that be extrapolated to capability, extrapolated to women should go back to the kitchen, and women aren't good at math, and things like that. I mean I get why people don't like biological explanations for things. It's a lot easier – it's a lazy way to dismiss the whole thing and say, we don't need to think about it: nothing to see here.[4]

In short, Soh argues that some people do not want to acknowledge certain biological differences between men and women at the population level because to do so would be to license further discrimination against women. However, no such grounds exist for discrimination against women because even if there are population-level differences between men and women, there is substantial overlap between the populations for most traits and inclinations.[5] But because such nuances can be hard to express in the public sphere, some use the blunt weapon of arguing that gender is a social construction.

Yet many questions remain: If we have certain natures, how ought we to live in relation to these? Ought we to try to live closer to our natures? And if we don't, will we suffer? And, given the variability within populations, how do we know what our individual natures are – to what extent can we take our cues from population-level differences? I shall return to these challenging questions at the end of this chapter.

## A Crisis of Masculinity

### *The Castrated Male*

The following account is familiar: Humanity is finally extricating itself from thousands of years of patriarchy: war, rape, harassment, dueling and dodgy or absent property and political rights for women. Much has had to change. The IDW agrees with this. For example, Rogan, when talking with Soh about sexual harassment at work, says, 'There's clearly, without doubt, been a lot of unchecked sexual harassment in the workplace'. He also says, 'men are gross'.[6] Yet the sense in the IDW is that a baby has been thrown out with the bathwater: there has been an overcorrection in how we think about masculinity such that we now have a 'crisis of masculinity'. (Crisis is a funny old word. It always sounds great when you append it to your own cause, but it tends to make your cause look a little desperate to the other side.)

Some within the IDW have also made the meta observation that IDW opponents think it is suspect that the likes of Peterson even want to talk to men in the first place. Ben Shapiro, in conversation with Peterson, says, 'You've literally been asked why you are even bothering to speak to men'.[7] Along these lines, in the Cathy Newman interview, Newman asks Peterson: 'Does it bother you that your audience is predominantly male? Isn't that a bit divisive?'[8]

If indeed the trajectory of humanity involves reducing the horrors that women have been experiencing for millennia, then speaking about a crisis of masculinity can come across as tone deaf. And yet insofar as men have been a problem for women, it is axiomatic that if males find better ways to be men, women will benefit. The battle, then, is over what is meant by 'better'. As I will discuss, the IDW seeks a middle path between the extirpation of masculinity and its excesses. The perceived crisis in masculinity was discussed by Bret Weinstein and actor, director and author Greg Ellis on Weinstein's *DarkHorse Podcast* in August 2020. Ellis says, 'We are bombarded by messages about the deeply corrosive effects of toxic masculinity. And confronted with institutions, psychologically conditioned now to think that masculinity is toxic. That men are bad'.[9]

Similarly, Debra Soh says, 'It's acceptable to hate on men now'. To which Rogan replies: 'Nobody criticizes misandry … I've never even said that word before … Male pride is not ok. But girl pride is fine; girl power is ok'.[10]

Jordan Peterson in his conversation with Ben Shapiro echoes this, and adds some analysis about the consequences:

> What I see happening to young men in particular, boys as well … we have [society has] this sense … that human beings live in antagonism to nature and that we are actually a malevolent force and that our social structures which are clearly capable of the commission of atrocity, are fundamentally oppressive – patriarchal in their nature. And so then if you're a male in a society with that ethos, the motive force that drives you into the world to live is associated with rapaciousness and despoliation on the natural front and oppression and atrocity on the social front, it's like well then, if you're the least bit conscientious because this sort of accusation hurts conscientious young men the most, then the best you can do is – well let's say, castrate yourself. How would that be? And that would be real comical, except that it's also happening. So I guess that's why I think there's a crisis.[11]

So, for Peterson, people have a 'motive force' – an instinctual ambition – that inclines them to leave the hearth and make something of themselves in the world. But if this instinct becomes associated with doing wrong, and people repress the instinct, they will suffer negative consequences. And while women can unquestionably suffer from hobbling their ambitions (Peterson is talking about 'young men in particular', not *only* men), Peterson's concern is not only that worldly ambition is, on average, more important for males (I'll return to this shortly), but that currently males also carry the guilt of being toxic.

Weinstein makes a comparable point while also giving us a sense of the IDW's middle path when he says:

> It's not like I want to go back to the 50s, right, and that's how sometimes it's portrayed. At the same time, I think we are doing a tragic

disservice, especially to our boys, in telling them that masculinity is a hazard or is inherently bad, or something like this, because among other things … the fact is, straight women do not like weak men. And so if you induce your boys to become weak, you're setting them up for a tragic romantic failure.[12]

Anyone who has had any experience with courtship, including dating apps, in recent years knows that women continue not to find weak men attractive. On this point, Peterson asks Cathy Newman: 'What sort of partner do you want? Do you want an overgrown child? Or do you want someone to contend with that's going to help you? And that you can rely on?'

These points are also interesting because they indicate that there is, for the IDW, a mixed message, or even a paradox, that originates from the female world. On the one hand, masculinity is derided. On the other, weak men are unattractive and also derided (what are INCELS if not weak men?). This paradox is not the sort of thing that can be discussed in polite society.

### The Toxic Male and the Sexual Revolution

But the IDW's discussion of the crisis of masculinity does not just focus on the castration of males, to use Peterson's term. It also explores how the dark side of masculinity is a part of the current crisis. Bret Weinstein, in his discussion with Greg Ellis, says:

[W]e are very complex creatures … and what that means is the way things are hooked together is often not obvious. And so there's this tendency – this Chesterton's Fence problem – where something, the purpose of which is not totally obvious, gets removed, because a strong argument can be made that it's somehow antiquated. And that very frequently we are living the harm that arises from having eliminated something vital without realizing we were doing it … We have renegotiated the rules of sex – basically we are told that any resistance to just getting laid and not thinking about the consequences is somehow oppressive … There's no reason even to give a damn about the person that you're having sex with. The consequences of this are many. And one of them is that it puts males in one of two modes, and it's not the one we should want to flourish. Men have always had the opportunity to spread their seed without taking responsibility for the consequences, and that is not men at their best, that's men at their worst. The problem, the reason we are now hearing about toxic masculinity, is that in a world where men have been told that that part of them is just fine and they should activate it, is a world that is dangerous to women, because the men are viewing them as targets, rather than as partners … In a world where sex had not been demystified and where it was therefore difficult to come by, and required real investment by men in order to persuade women to go to bed with them, men moved mountains in order to impress the women they were most interested in, and that was a process that was tremendously powerful. And the fact that these things are now frequently satisfiable with a kind of junk level of sex is resulting, I think, in a great deal of potential just being absolutely squandered, because there is no motivation to follow it.[13]

In short: our newish culture of easy sex, which has been made possible by contraception, has rewarded the less-admirable aspects of masculinity.

(To digress for a moment, all this is so interesting for me, because, as I have mentioned, I was trying to explore such things 20 years ago when I first ran afoul of the Postmodernists and Identity Politics. I despise the way men use women. But what troubles me even more is the way some women champion the system which seems so clearly not to support their interests. I'll deal with this in the next book.)

Peterson made similar remarks in January 2018 in his first interview after the Cathy Newman interview. Peterson begins by telling a story about a world-class athlete who, at parties, would be presented with several attractive young women from whom he could take his pick. Peterson says, 'That is appealing to the Hugh Heffner, playboy, 14-year-old fantasy, that's sort of gripped our culture from the 1960s onwards'. Then, he makes his main point, which is subtle:

Imagine that you sleep casually with 100 women in a six month period … And you're ecstatic with yourself because you've been validated by this opportunity. And I'm not making light of that. It's not nothing to be attractive to women like that. It's really something to be attractive to women like that. But it isn't obvious to me that your choice to conduct yourself in that manner enriches your life and the life of other people

more in any way than picking one person and actually having a relationship with them. It's only true that that promiscuous pathway, let's
say, is better if you can actually divorce sexuality from all the other elements of life – say, well, it's about variety and it's about impulsive pleasure. Or maybe it can be even slightly deeper, than merely impulsive
pleasure: it could be shared impulsive pleasure. But I don't think you
can do that. Because sexuality isn't divorceable from family and from
morality and from all the other elements of your life. And if you're ma-
ture, you know that, and so you make a decision. You make a decision
not to capitalize on your opportunity – not to misuse your opportunity.
And you know, a huge part of the 'me too' phenomenon – a huge part
of this battle that's being played out in our culture is a consequence of
the failure of men to recognize that. Now it's not only the failure of
men. [Peterson goes on to mention the complicity of women in 'this
pathological game'.][14]

The most weighty claim here – and it is a big one – is that sexuality
cannot be divorced from the rest of one's life, in particular from morality.
Returning to Postmodernism, if the human mind is a blank slate, then of
course, all things are possible – sexuality can just be a stand-alone mod-
ule, especially now that we have effective contraception (though God
knows how sexuality even exists if it is a social construction). But if sexuality is, say, evolutionarily connected with other facets of our life, then
the stakes shift. There are immense depths to be explored here.

In *Disgrace* by J. M. Coetzee we read that the protagonist, who is a
lothario, 'is all for double lives, triple lives, lives lived in compartments'.[15]
If we have to wall-off parts of our lives from, say, our sense of morality,
clearly something is wrong. Such considerations take us all the way to
Kant's 'categorical imperative': 'I am never to act otherwise than so that
I could also will that my maxim should become a universal law'.[16] Are
we satisfied with our sexuality, such that we would wish that all people
would act as we do?

Peterson develops his ideas in his conversation with Ben Shapiro:

We know, for example, that younger women are more likely to be attracted to men who show dark triad traits: narcissistic, Machiavellian
and psychopathic. And people who have those traits are characterized
by the mimicry of competence and so what women want in men more

than anything else is competent generosity and the data on that are very clear, but you can mimic that if you are narcissistic, and if you are a young woman you can be deluded by that. It's partly because it points to the problem of dissociating competent confidence from the expression of power per se. So we could call power – I'll define that as the willingness and ability to use compulsion to attain your aim. So if you are someone who has a proclivity to manifest power, then that looks like the manifestation of both ambition and will, and if you haven't had a positive relationship with anyone masculine in your life, and maybe not even with your own internal masculinity, you can't discriminate between power and the ambition that serves competence.[17]

The challenging word here is 'deluded'. Is it true that women – young women in particular – are deluded? Do they mistake narcissistic displays of power for competent generosity? Or is it more that in a world of contraception and endlessly replaceable partners, narcissistic displays of power are enough – just as for many men beauty (or even just having female anatomy) is enough. More depths.

To summarise – in reverse order: for some in the IDW, the crisis of masculinity has two dimensions. On the one hand, narcissistic, Machiavellian, and psychopathic males are rewarded by the newish sexual norms for treating women as targets not as partners because such males can be sexually successful by imitating the confidence that ought to be derived from genuine ambition and competence. On the other hand, other males are retreating from a masculinity that is characterised by 'competent confidence' because they fear that if they follow this path, they will be being narcissistic, Machiavellian, and psychopathic. We could say that conscientious males retreat from their masculinity because they don't want to be assholes. Nice guys finish last.

To what extent does this crisis exist? I'm not certain. A large book would be needed even to begin to get to the bottom of it all. Ultimately, I think that on these tougher questions, it comes back to the question of whether a nerve is touched within each of us. Peterson, in his conversation with Shapiro, says:

I never really set out to talk to men specifically, but I did set out at least in part to make a case for the utility of both the feminine and the masculine spirit, and it turned out that making the case for the masculine spirit was something that was more demanded by the culture …[18]

And in a video I will discuss further in the next section, he says: 'Well, what's really cool … when I talked to these crowds about this [responsibility], the men's eyes light up … Young men are so hungry for that, it is unbelievable …. For men there is nothing but responsibility'.

## Responsibility and Merit

While I could finish this chapter here, I want to present a few more IDW ideas about responsibility. Not only will these help to clarify the IDW position on masculinity, they will help to link the current discussion with material from the previous chapters.

Jordan Peterson and Bret Weinstein spoke about responsibility in March 2021 on Weinstein's *Dark Horse* podcast.[19] Weinstein says to Peterson, 'You are sometimes taken to task for being overly focused on personal responsibility and neglecting the collective well-being, functioning of society, level'.[20] This is a familiar objection. If we focus too much on personal responsibility, then it is easy to ignore structural forces that generate inequality – or even just bad luck – and to blame individuals for their own misfortunes.

After making this observation, Weinstein (who describes himself as a 'lifelong Liberal who has now gotten to an age where wisdom is beginning to dawn'[21]), speaking in support of taking personal responsibility, says:

> If you're going to advise somebody or some small group of people on how to approach life, it [taking personal responsibility] is the slam-dunk winner … It actually works. You do have power over yourself and how you interact with the world. So if you encounter a system that is very unfair you can complain about the unfairness. And you have a very low chance of affecting it at all. Or you can say well, it may be unfair, but I'm going to play the cards I've been delt as well as I can, and that's something over which you have a tremendous amount of control. So I think … in terms of return on investment, there's almost no return on the investment in complaining about a broken system.[22]

The value in this point is that Weinstein is not denying that unfair systems exist. But rather, he is thinking probabilistically about where success can be achieved. However, this is a difficult calculus.

Peterson then argues that transforming the system is more likely if you are competent: 'Maybe you have some ghost of a chance of changing things if you are competent and are seen to be competent …. But before then, you can break things, but building them is pretty damn hard'.[23] This is a familiar criticism of those who would tear down the current system.

Peterson's position becomes more nuanced when he says:

> There are systems that are completely unplayable, and there are systems that are relatively playable, but the idea that your conscience should be bothered by the corruption of the system is like absolutely true, but that doesn't mean you should go making incautious changes as a consequence of resentment.[24]

Weinstein picks up on this and says:

> Now the present looks so insane from this perspective that you and I appear to share, where we are now educating children ever younger in obsessing about defects of the system, many of them imaginary, rather than giving them competence. In fact we are demonizing the very acquisition of competence.

Peterson jumps in here:

> There, perfect. That's something that needs to be broadcast everywhere. I think the pathology that's at the core of the Culture War is an attack on competence itself – it's an attack on competence, the idea of competence as well …. Do you rise according to your merit? It's like, partly. Ok. Partly. And corruption reduces the correlation. But to say 'partly' and to admit to the existence of some corruption is not the same thing at all as to say 'merit itself is a corrupt idea' … Competence presupposes value, and value presupposes a hierarchy, so if you admit to competence, you admit to a value hierarchy and differential ability, and that flies in the face of equality.[25]

As Peterson himself identifies, this gets us to the heart of the matter; namely, to the Postmodern devaluing of merit. However, as with so much in this book, a book would be needed to determine the extent to which merit as a concept is derided, and the extent to which, for example, our education systems are failing students by not prioritising the acquisition of knowledge and skills.

Now let us return to responsibility and masculinity. Peterson's position about the two is most clearly and controversially stated in the following (I am quoting from a video of one of his lectures that was uploaded in 2017 – 11,059,641 views as of 12 October 2023):

> Women have their sets of responsibilities. They're not the same. Right. Because they're complicated. Because women of course have to take primary responsibility for having infants at least, then also for caring for them. They're structured differently than men. For biological necessity, even if it's not a psychological issue, and it's also partly a psychological issue. Women know what they have to do. Men have to figure out what they have to do. And if they have nothing worth living for, then they stay Peter Pan, and why the hell not? Because the alternative to valued responsibility is impulsive, low-class, pleasure.[26]

And then there are some of the most powerful words Peterson has ever spoken:

> I've been talking a lot to the crowds that I've been talking to, not about rights but about responsibility. Because you can't have the bloody conversation about rights without the conversation about responsibility … And we are only having half that discussion … And then the question is, well what are you leaving out if you are leaving out responsibility? And the answer might be, well maybe you are leaving out the meaning of life … Here you are suffering away. What makes it worthwhile? Rights? … It's almost impossible to describe how bad an idea that is. Responsibility. That's what gives life meaning … It's like, lift a load. Then you can tolerate yourself. Cause look at you. You're useless. Easily hurt. Easily killed. Why should you have any self-respect? … Pick something up and carry it. Make it heavy enough so that you can think, yeah well, useless as I am, at least I could move that from there to there.[27]

We can see now that the IDW championing responsibility and a middle path of masculinity dovetails with the IDW's critique of resentment within Identity Politics and ultimately Nietzsche's concept of Slave Morality. Recall that Nietzsche speaks about the '*ressentiment* of beings denied the true reaction, that of the deed'. The point is that if we focus too heavily on objecting to the state of the world and not enough on making something of ourselves – on taking responsibility – our mental health will suffer. But the kicker is that for Peterson, this problem is more marked for men. Men, in order to dispel the worst of negative emotions, must pursue competence in the world – they must take responsibility. And by doing this, they will thread a path between castration and cheap, destructive, pleasure – both of which are, paradoxically, championed by our decadent society.

Many would see this as a Conservative vision. However, it is also a Liberal vision in that the person who adopts it charts a path between being subsumed by a tyrannical group identity (whether this be from the far-left or far-right) and the tyranny of biology. All of this is articulated by Peterson in his appearance with Bret Weinstein on Rogan in September 2017 (this is one of the most important IDW podcasts):

> I've been trying to agitate for the adoption of personal responsibility as an alternative to political ideology. It's like: get your act together, have a vision, straighten out your life, say what you think. Stay away from the ideological idiocies and oversimplifications and try to put yourself together. I do believe at the most fundamental level, and I think this is the remarkable realization of Western Civilisation, is that the well-developed individual is the antidote to the tyranny of society and biology. I think that's our great discovery in the West. It's not like other cultures haven't had that idea in nascent form, but it's been hyperdeveloped in the West. And I think it's right. And so we abandon that pathway of divine individuality and revert to ideological identification of race or sex, we're going to tear each other apart. And I think part of the reason we are motivated to do that, Joe, is because many people don't want to bear the responsibility of developing themselves as individuals. So they'll shuffle off the responsibility. And if that means that we're dancing in the streets because everything's on fire, that'll be just fine.[28]

Later in the same conversation, Peterson entrenches his IDW identity when he says that his position represents a third way:

> You could make a case that there isn't [an alternative to ideological conflict]. There's right and there's left and there's a war. But there is a third way, and I think that is the **way** of the heroic individual. And I mean that technically. That involves the development of individual character so that you can say what it is that you think – that you can articulate your experience properly, and that you can bring what it is that is unique to you into the collective landscape, and that is what updates the collective landscape. It's absolutely vital.[29]

The immense tragedy of universities today, and also parts of the media, is that the heroic individual is increasingly despised. But if the values of the collective cannot be properly updated, then we are in great danger. The point is that for society to be healthy, there must be a dialectic between the Conservatism of the collective and that which transforms the collective. It is the eternal tension between Nietzsche's Apollonian and Dionysian. Or, in more familiar terms, it is what happens in science. And yes, because those who champion Identity Politics close themselves off, they are deeply Conservative. They are far from being the radicals they present themselves as being.

It is not entirely clear how our natures feature in all of this. Peterson talks about finding a middle path or third way between the tyranny of the collective and the tyranny of biology. And yet throughout all the discussions there is also the sense that men ought to adhere to their natures and adopt responsibility, and that by doing so they will gain self-respect and ultimately unite sexual attractiveness and morality.

Perhaps we can make sense of it all by drawing on Pinker. One of Pinker's many books is *The Better Angels of our Nature*.[30] The implication of the title is that, in the Liberal tradition, we can blunt the less desirable aspects of our natures which, in modern society, have become bugs in the system, and we can amplify the more desirable aspects of our natures. This allows us to avoid the 'naturalistic fallacy' which Bret Weinstein mentions from time to time: 'just because something is, doesn't mean it ought to be'.[31] So, it is not that complicated in the end. Yes, we have natures, but by making good individual and also collective decisions (for example, by having a strong education system), we can make the most of our natures. And in a world which reels between rewarding the worst aspects of masculinity and castrating masculinity, this is a salutary message.

## Notes

1   Christopher 2001.

2   Goggins has appeared on Rogan three times and Willink has appeared five times.

3   Lorber 2017: 348.

4   The Joe Rogan Experience 2018 July 26: 0:29:22.

5   We see such claims regularly. For example: Terracciano et al. 2005.

6   The Joe Rogan Experience 2018 July 26: 1:22:40.

7   Jordan B Peterson 2022 July 20: 0:03:18.

8   Channel 4 News 2018 January 17: 0:02:26.

9   Bret Weinstein 2020 August 15: 0:28:19.

10  The Joe Rogan Experience 2018 July 26: 0:21:45.

11  Jordan B Peterson 2022 July 20: 0:01:08.

12  Bret Weinstein 2020 August 15: 0:30:18.

13  Bret Weinstein 2020 August 15: 0:34:55.

14  GeenStijl 2018 January 23: 0:51:15.

15  Coetzee 1999: Chapter 1.

16  Kant 2002 [1785]: 30.

17  Jordan B Peterson 2022 July 20: 0:04:53.

18  Jordan B Peterson 2022 July 20: 0:03:48.

19  The discussion comes from DarkHorse Podcast Clips 2021 March 23.

20  DarkHorse Podcast Clips 2021 March 23: 0:00:00.

21  DarkHorse Podcast Clips 2021 March 23: 0:00:26.

22  DarkHorse Podcast Clips 2021 March 23: 0:00:58. Weinstein also talks about this on his third Rogan appearance in December 2017. There he says that following the Evergreen State College incident he had met a number of black Conservatives and that these people changed his thinking to a degree:

> They [black Conservatives] are very sensitive to the issue of what happens when you focus on the unfairness of how the cards are dealt, which is that – what Progressives typically miss – is that it really does create a culture of dependency. If you focus on the fact that the cards are unfairly dealt, and that that's why you are facing a disadvantage, which is largely true. Nonetheless, it demotivates you from pursuing success (2017 December 20: 0:25:56).

23  DarkHorse Podcast Clips 2021 March 23: 0:01:51.

24  DarkHorse Podcast Clips 2021 March 23: 0:06:56.

25  DarkHorse Podcast Clips 2021 March 23: 0:07:16 DarkHorse Podcast Clips 2021 March 23.

26  Alex Swan 2017 November 5: 0:07:37.
27  Alex Swan 2017 November 5: 0:04:19.
28  The Joe Rogan Experience 2017 September 1: 0:50:12.
29  The Joe Rogan Experience 2017 September 1: 0:58:59.
30  Pinker 2012.
31  Pangburn 2018 November 29: 0:32:49.

15

# IDW Views toward the Trans Issue

The Trans issue is small from the point of view of how many people are Transgender, yet it has become the defining battleground of the Culture Wars. Dictionary.com's word of the year for 2022 was 'woman', which reflects the immense interest in the now notorious question, 'What is a woman?'[1] – this question is asked because of the often-heard claims 'Transwomen are women' and 'A woman is someone who identifies as a woman'.

Trans looms large not just because there is a tension between wanting people to live their best lives and issues such as children transitioning and Trans women using women's spaces and competing in women's sports, but because a powerful taboo has been established against dissenting perspectives (as of August 2024 this is weakening a little). And as is so often the case, it is the taboo that causes the trouble: if people are in good faith, then surely there ought not to be a taboo against discussing an issue. Or maybe there should be a taboo, because in the Postmodern universe, where language constructs reality, taboos are necessary for bringing about a better world because they silence harmful discourse. *Sigh*. The terrain is almost impossible to navigate.

In our Postmodern world, 'Trans women are women' has taken on something of the Orwellian '2 + 2 = 5': people have to say it even if they don't believe it to show their allegiance to the orthodoxy. We saw this in an interview with Scottish First Minister Nicola Sturgeon. Sturgeon awkwardly affirms that Trans women are women but says that there is no automatic right for a Trans woman, such as a rapist, to be housed in a woman's prison. The interviewer asks: 'so there are contexts in which a Trans woman is not a woman'. Sturgeon struggles to respond.[2] The episode contributed to Sturgeon stepping down as Scottish First Minister.[3] Several figures in the IDW such as Joe Rogan and Jordan Peterson gained notoriety over their opinions about Trans issues. And Trans continues to be regularly discussed in IDW circles, notably on the UK show, Triggernometry, which has interviewed many of the TERFs (Trans Exclusionary Radical Feminists) from so-called TERF Island (England).

## The Big Question: Is Trans Genuine?

Within the IDW, the question of whether Trans is genuine sits above all the others. As distant IDW associate Camille Paglia states, 'I question whether the Transgender choice is indeed genuine in every single case'. Why is this question so important? Because, as Douglas Murray says in *The Madness of Crowds*, 'A gay person who goes straight or a straight person who goes gay is doing nothing that is permanent or irreversible. Whereas the end-point of Trans advocates is irreversible and life-altering'.[4]

But what is meant by 'genuine'? While its meaning will become clearer – though never clear – in what follows, a good place to start is to distinguish between problems and solutions. We can say that a person's suffering is genuine: angst is angst. But what causes someone's angst? If we are unclear about the cause, then we will struggle to provide an effective solution. As we have seen, this point arises again and again for the IDW. Ultimately, the IDW strongly doubts that the Woke left actually wants to solve problems.

Several figures in the IDW do say that being Trans is genuine; although we hear this more from IDW figures on the left than on the right, and less so these days. In 2013, early in the debate, Joe Rogan objected to a Transwoman competing against women in mixed martial arts. But in discussing this, he says, 'I want everyone to know that if you really feel like you are supposed to be a woman and you are a man, I will still be friends with you, like I have zero issue with that'.[5]

A similar perspective is expressed in the following remarks by Rogan and Abigail Shrier, author of *Irreversible Damage: The Trans Craze Seducing our Daughters*, during their July 2020 conversation:

> *Rogan:* I think we should probably establish some things up front. Some people surely as adults are Trans.
>
> *Shrier:* Of course. I interviewed a lot of them.
>
> *Rogan:* And we fully support that.
>
> *Shrier:* Absolutely. I have friends who fall into that category.[6]

However, as we might expect, we get a different opinion from Ben Shapiro. In a 2015 discussion about Caitlyn Jenner, who had recently transitioned, and who had received a woman of the year award, he asks, 'why are we mainstreaming delusion?'[7] Yet there is some nuance in his perspective, which we see in another video. In this video we see one of Shapiro's more sympathetic performances; in fact, we feel his humanity, as does the woman in the audience whose question he is responding to. He says:

> I have said and I will continue to maintain that Gender Dysphoria or Gender Identity Disorder – whichever DSM you choose to use – is a mental illness. God forbid that it should be said with any animus, because this is not said with animus. When people are suffering – these are clearly folks who are suffering – when people are suffering, you shouldn't be saying stuff with animus. I'm not saying that as a 'got you' to people who are Trans. The point that I am making is that when a society begins treating folks who have mental illness as though they are representing an objective reality, they are doing no service to the people who actually suffer from mental illness … Now I'm not saying there's even a great solution for folks who have Gender Identity Disorder, or Gender Dysphoria. Because the solutions that I've seen, including Trans surgery, are not intensively effective, from all the studies I've seen. It's a tragic, tragic situation. But the solution is not to redefine as a society what sex means along anti-biological lines.[8]

So, for Shapiro, the suffering is genuine, but he is not convinced by the solutions to the suffering, whether this be transitioning or, on a society-wide level, transforming how we understand biological sex.

Returning to Rogan, we see a similar perspective:

What I keep going to is: If you are a woman, and you know you're a woman, why do you need to get these hormones injected into your body. Why can't you just be a woman? I'll call you a woman. What are we doing with all these hormones ... Imagine you're a person who says 'I need to transition to be a woman and I know that I need a chemical that I've never had in my body before, and if I get that chemical injected, then I'm going to be happy. And if I get surgery, then I'm going to be happy'.[9]

For Rogan, as for Shapiro, the problem is genuine, but the solution is not convincing. Or at least, it is not clear to Rogan how transitioning medically, in its current form, is a solution. Later, in a discussion with Tulsi Gabbard, he says:

It's [transitioning medically] not a cut and dried thing. Look, if there was a way, where we had some sort of genetic engineering ... where I could just decide, I want to be a woman now, then bam, now I have a XX chromosome, I have a vagina, I'm an actual woman, 100%. Not surgery.[10]

The deeper issue to which Rogan alludes is that if, in the Postmodern tradition, gender, and even biological sex, are social constructions, then surely it is enough to believe you are a woman to be a woman. The constructedness of sex is implied by Trans activists when they speak about people being 'assigned' a sex a birth – 'assigned' implies that something arbitrary or capricious has occurred.[11] Rogan and Peterson talked about this in November 2016. Peterson was discussing a colleague of his, Nicholas Matte, from the University of Toronto who, on Canadian television, said, 'It's not correct that there is such a thing as biological sex'.[12] Later, when explaining what is meant by 'cisnormative', Matte says, 'Cisnormative is basically the very popular idea and assumption that most people probably have, and definitely that our structures convey [i.e. it's a part of dominant discourse, not reality] that there is such a thing as male and female'.[13] About this, Rogan says, 'It's such an insane thing to say. If there's no biological difference, then why are they taking hormones?' Peterson says, 'That's a good question. Why bother with the surgery and especially the hormones. You could argue with the surgery that that's cosmetic'. [14]

It's confusing. It seems that the function of calling something a social construction is to discredit it: it becomes discourse – a manifestation of power – not truth. The effect of this ought to be to cause the construction to melt away. A century ago, we recognised that the idea that women did not have the capacity to participate meaningfully in politics was a dodgy social construction, and it melted away. Now women vote, lead countries, and so on. But insofar as transitioning involves taking hormones and having surgery, the Trans world seems to be upholding the biological categories of male and female it discredits. But the problem is not only questionable logic (is questionable logic a problem?). It is, as Rogan says, that the medical alteration of the body does not actually alter someone's sex. The paradoxes pile up.

In amongst it all, there seems to be something of the Postmodern sleight-of-hand that I mentioned in Chapter 4, combined, once again, with Nietzsche's idea of Slave Morality that I discussed in Chapter 12. The claim that gender is a social construction can be used to strike at the likes of James Damore for suggesting that biological differences between men and women might to some extent account for different preferences at the population level. A Postmodernist might say that Damore is not trying to get to the truth; rather, he is just trying to maintain male power by presenting a social construction as truth. But then, once a Postmodern-aligned group, such as Trans activists, is in the ascendency, a social construction can be elevated to the level of truth, and nothing can be done about it because truth is a property of Identity, **at least when the Identity putatively has no power**. This is why the paradoxical statement 'Transwomen are women' has such staying power.

Helen Joyce, Konstantin Kisin, and Francis Foster discussed such confusions on Triggernometry in January 2023. Joyce has a PhD in Mathematics and worked for nearly 20 years as a journalist for *The Economist*. She is the author of *Trans: When Ideology Meets Reality*.

Foster says, 'Let's talk a little bit about the ideology, because – I mean – it's just weird.

Joyce replies, 'Isn't it just'.

Foster says, 'I wish I could be more articulate, and erudite, but it is weird … The leaps of logic … I've sat down and I've read this stuff, but I can't get my head around it. What's going on?'

Joyce, making the same sort of comment that John McWhorter has made about race politics, especially as they play out in America, says: 'Partly I think it's because it's basically a new religion. And you're not meant to get your head around religions. Specifically, you're not meant to. Any attempt to get around it is showing that you don't have faith'.[15] So here we have the implication that to the extent that Trans is a new religion, it is not genuine. Kathleen Stock makes the same point.[16]

The IDW has questioned the genuineness of Trans in a number of other related ways.

## Trans as Fashion

This is a straightforward point. Bill Maher, in May 2022, says: 'part of the rise in LGBT numbers is from people feeling free enough to tell it to a pollster, and that's all to the good. But some of it is, it's trendy'.[17]

Rogan, in his conversation with Debra Soh in July 2018, makes a complementary point:

> I absolutely believe that there are women who really are wired the wrong way and they should be men, and there's men that are wired the wrong – it only makes sense … But I do also believe there are people that are crazy. There's people who have legit mental illness. They're delusional. And they are also very susceptible to influence.[18]

In a world where Trans is strongly, even unquestionably, supported in some circles, the danger is that some people will permanently alter themselves because they are susceptible to influence, not because they are applying a genuine solution to their genuine problem.

Rogan makes a subtler point in his later discussion with Shrier:

> This is where I'm torn. On the one hand, if you are Trans, and you, and you do feel better about this, but you are confused about how people will react, and all of a sudden people are celebrating you, like yes, this is great: I love the idea of an accepting society, and people are open and loving and happy that someone is making this transition. But on the other hand, I'm very aware of the influence of the masses and of people's love and praise. It can shift you one way or another.[19]

This puts a more positive angle on the Trans phenomenon. It is great that people are being accepting. But the danger is that this is skewing people's assessment of how they ought to address their problems. The saying, 'The road to hell is paved with good intentions' comes to mind.

## The Issue of Children and Young – Especially Female – Adults Transitioning

A main concern with Trans within the IDW is children transitioning. The key issue is consent. In one of his many Q&As with students, Ben Shapiro, in November 2019, is asked: 'If somebody is going to be a happier person because they say they are a man or a woman, what's the harm in just letting them do it?' Shapiro replies:

> I'm not in favour of government banning people who are adults – children I'm in favour of banning because now you are talking about someone who is not capable of consent, and all of our laws are based on the ability of people to consent – if you're a child, you can't consent. So I'm very much in favour of banning gender transition for kids. I think that it's frankly evil. I think you are making decisions for people who are not capable of making decisions for themselves that are permanent – that have long lasting and significant and severe impact.[20]

Related to this is the question of the extent to which Gender Dysphoria passes in children. Rogan in his 2018 conversation with Soh says:

> I'm 100% for freedom. So I'm 100% for you being able to do whatever you want. The real question becomes when people are Trans and young, how much of this is going to pass, and how much of this are you going to stop from ever passing because you are going to inject your body filled with hormones?[21]

Echoing his earlier comments, Rogan, in November 2022, in a discussion with Matt Walsh (producer of the documentary *What Is a Woman*) also raises the possibility that by heavily praising children for making identity decisions, rather than focusing on their worldly achievements (note the link here again with the IDW's championing merit), we risk creating perverse incentives. He says, 'You're giving them [children] an opportunity to be special. And to get special treatment without any special act'.[22]

Another aspect of this discussion that arises within the IDW is the concern that homosexual children are being treated as Trans. This reflects a fault line that exists to some extent between homosexuals and Transgender people – however, as with much within the Culture Wars, I am not sure of the magnitude of this tension. Rogan, in his discussion with Shrier, says: 'There was a study done on men who experience gender dysphoria at a young age, and then transition to become gay – and just became gay. And they realise like this was just a part of their process and they're happy as a gay man, and they didn't transition'.

Shrier replies: 'So that's very typical. Most of these kids would emerge as homosexual adults'.

Rogan goes on to struggle with the complexities of this – he doesn't fall heavily on one side or the other. He says, 'Are they happier this way or that way [not transitioning and being gay, or transitioning]? This is a very human problem. By "human problem" I mean there's not really a good answer'. [23]

More stridently, Debra Soh, in response to Rogan objecting to children transitioning, says: 'But you can't even have that conversation now, because that's considered Transphobic. What it is, is Homophobic, though, that you can't consider that some of these kids might just be gay children'.[24]

Even more stridently are some remarks by Helen Joyce. Joyce tells a story about a woman she interviewed who had suffered from bulimia and who had believed herself to be Trans. The woman had been encouraged to transition by a gender clinic. Having gone through much of the process, the woman realised it was a mistake. Joyce concludes by saying, 'Oh fucking hell, they are sterilising gay kids'.[25]

This issue does not just involve children, but also young adults. Shrier says:

> So we have a hundred year diagnostic history of Gender Dysphoria. We know what it is. It's not guesswork. We know that it has in this whole history, it typically presents in early childhood ages 2 to 4 is when we see it starting, and it was overwhelmingly boys. Little boys, who say, no Mommy, I'm not a boy, I'm a girl. Call me a girl. I only want to play

with other girls, only want to do, you know, play with girl toys and they sometimes they hate their sexual organ. I mean, sometimes, you know, it's a severe persistent insistent, consistent feeling. And then a lot of them would grow out of it. And some of them wouldn't and they would become what we used to call Transsexuals. Now, we're seeing an explosion of young women, you know, suddenly deciding they're Trans with their friends and they are doing it in friend groups.[26]

Debra Soh makes the same point in her discussion with Rogan in July 2018:

*Rogan:* Explain 'Rapid Onset Gender Dysphoria', because I'm not really aware of that.

*Soh:* So it's this phenomenon. That's been growing more recently – probably say in the last 10 years. There's been a switch. So before referrals to gender clinics of kids, who are feeling that they were born the opposite sex is predominantly boys, and then suddenly there's been this explosion of girls. And so when you talk to the parents and it's interesting when you listen to the episode that we did, their stories are so similar, they're literally identical. Their daughters have always been gender typical. So they're always very girly girls. They've never been gender dysphoric. They go through puberty. They develop, you know, there's no problem there. And then usually what happens is there's some sort of – I don't know educational session at school or one of these girls, their friends come out as Trans. And then the daughter says, oh, I want to be a boy. And so if you take that child to a professional – like a therapist, the therapist has to affirm – the therapist can't question that. So, you have these girls. A lot of them have autism, or they have other mental health issues. They're not getting treated for those issues instead, they're being told okay, if you want to transition, we'll help you. And like I said, I'm not against adults transitioning. I don't think it's anyone's place to tell an adult what to do and I think transitioning can be beneficial. But if someone transitions you want this to actually help them feel better. And for these girls, if the issue is not even about gender, it doesn't make sense for them to transition. [27]

So even when consent, in a legal sense, is not an issue, there is an enduring concern that young women in particular are becoming Trans because of 'social contagion'.

Similar concerns were raised in relation to The Tavistock Centre in the UK, which assisted people, including children, to transition. It has recently been shut down. Marcus Evans, who worked at Tavistock and was a whistleblower, described, on Triggernometry, how, from his point of view, the culture at Tavistock in relation to transitioning, became increasingly activist in that there was 'a shutting down of any dissent or wish to examine what was going on beneath the surface of the kid'.[27] Jamie Reed, who worked for four years at the Washington University Trans Center in the United States makes similar observations; she says that in the Center 'there was an actual directive that we were no longer allowed to use the phrase, "I have concerns about a patient"'. She also mentions the problem of social contagion.[29]

In support of transitioning, the point is often made that children and young people's beliefs about their gender identity should be affirmed lest they harm themselves. About this Debbie Hayton says, 'Why was this not picked up 40 years ago – 30 years ago – whenever, when there wasn't a spate of children committing suicide because their identities were not recognized?'[30]

## Autogynephilia

We see very different concerns when we move to men and the phenomenon of autogynephilia. Autogynephilia refers to a male who is sexually aroused by thinking of himself as a woman. This is a deep issue. If a man is autogynephilic, then this is, surely, genuine. But many questions arise: Ought a sexual fantasy be the basis for transitioning? And how widespread is this? I really don't know. However, as Douglas Murray writes in *The Madness of Crowds*, the phenomenon of autogynephilia does not sit well with many in the Trans community:

> One of the most striking trends as the Trans debate has picked up in recent years is that autogynephilia has come to be severely out of favour. Or to put it another way, the suggestion that people who identify as Trans are in actual fact merely going through the ultimate extreme of a sexual kink has become so hateful to many Trans individuals that

it is one of a number of things now decried as hate speech.[31]

Autogynephilia becomes a particularly serious issue when autogynephilic Trans women commit sex crimes and want to be housed in female prisons.

## Narcissism

While women are just as capable of narcissism as men, for some in the IDW, the issue of male narcissism has a special quality. The concern is that for some men who have transitioned, we see not just a continuation, but a licensing of the worst aspects of the Patriarchy – what in other contexts might be referred to as 'toxic masculinity'.

Dave Chappelle has a bit where he makes fun of Caitlyn Jenner for winning the woman of the year award after having only been a woman for one year. He jokes that the women in the audience, who have been working on being a woman their whole lives, must be annoyed.[32] Joe Rogan has also done a bit about Jenner. Rogan's point is that Jenner's transition could not be separated from the narcissistic desire for immense amounts of attention.[33]

We see what looks like toxic masculinity in a famous encounter between Ben Shapiro and Trans woman and reporter, Zoe Tur (Murray also mentions this incident in *Madness of Crowds*). Ben Shapiro is involved in a debate with several people, including Tur, about whether Jenner should have received a woman of the year award. This is where Shapiro asks, 'Why are we mainstreaming delusion?' Later he refers to Tur as 'sir'. Perhaps he is being rude. But my sense is that he believes that Tur is motivated by narcissism and is thus a bad faith actor – not genuine. As if to confirm Shapiro's suspicions, Tur threateningly puts a hand on Shapiro's neck and says, 'You cut that out now, or you'll go home in an ambulance,' to which Shapiro replies: 'That seems mildly inappropriate for a political discussion'.[33] No one cares about Tur's threat: the monster in the room is Shapiro.

Feminist Posie Parker tells a similar story on Triggernometry about a Trans woman who, along with a number of other Trans women, attended an online women's political group:

This one man, and he told like a Bernard Manning type joke [i.e.

coarse], and the essence of which – I think the punchline was – a feminist tied to my radiator in a basement after a beating. Some sort of male violence type thing – that generally women don't tell jokes like that. And I just [thought] are you sure you identify as a woman? … And he went absolutely nuts at me. But that was bad. But all the women joined in. Saying that I was hateful, disgusting, Transphobic, how could I question this man, or woman, they would say – he knows better than I do how he identifies. And so then I was switched on to: actually, if I'm not allowed to talk about this and this is obviously very serious, then I need to talk about it as much as I possibly can.[35]

'Narcissism' is a tricky concept. Most of us have a strong regard for ourselves – this is how existence works. I'd even say that ambition makes the world go around. But the point of narcissism is that this self-regard is excessive to the point that it comes at the expense of others, and perhaps more abstract values such as truth. Yet it's very hard to be certain when someone is being narcissistic – there's always plausible deniability. However, if some Trans people are dangerous narcissists (or even just seduced by trends), the hegemonic endorsement of all things Trans becomes impossible to sustain. But I suspect that if nuance were introduced into the Trans debate, then the Trans edifice may well collapse – it depends upon being hegemonic.

## Women's Spaces and Language

Another concern for some associated with the IDW is Trans women using women's spaces, such as bathrooms, and using or changing women's language. About women's spaces, Posie Parker says:

What are those [Trans] rights? Because as a man or a woman in this country, you're allowed to pretty much do the same sort of things … But generally speaking, I don't know what rights they don't have. Except to invade women's spaces. That seems to be the beginning and end of the demand.

Kathleen Stock covers similar territory, arguing that in a society where women are on average weaker than men and are much more likely to be sexually assaulted by men than men are by women, it makes sense that women have their own spaces, and it's not enough for a man to say that he identifies as a woman to gain access to these spaces.[36]

Ricky Gervais addressed the issue of using women's spaces in a recent comedy special on *Netflix*:

Ahh women … not all women. I mean the old-fashioned ones. The old-fashioned women. Oh God! You know, the ones with wombs. Oh. Those fucking dinosaurs. No, I love the new women. They're great, aren't they? The new ones we've been seeing lately. The ones with beards and cocks. They're as good as gold. I love them.

And now the old-fashioned, they go, 'Ooh, they want to use our toilets!'

'Why shouldn't they use your toilets?'

'For ladies!'

'They are ladies. Look at their pronouns. What about this person isn't a lady?'

'Well, his penis'.

'Her penis, you fucking bigot!'

'What if he rapes me?'

'What if she rapes you? You fucking TERF whore'.[37]

With respect to language, for some in the Trans universe, women are no longer women. They are 'nonTrans women', or 'ciswomen', or 'people who menstruate'. It was by objecting to the last that JK Rowling got in trouble. But she's not an easy woman to cancel.

IDW figure Ayaan Hirsi Ali supported Rowling and received blowback because of this. She struggled to find anyone in the mainstream media who would promote her 2021 book, *Prey: Immigration, Islam, and the Erosion of Women's Rights;* whereas she'd received extensive support for her 2015 book *Heretic: Why Islam Must Change to Join the Modern World*. Hirsi Ali, speaking on Rogan in March 2021, talked about how *Bust* magazine cancelled a promotional piece on her book. *Bust,* which describes itself as 'the groundbreaking, original feminist lifestyle brand'[38] claimed, according to Hirsi Ali, that her support of Rowling made the people that read *Bust* 'unsafe'. Hirsi Ali says that in her view, 'J K Rowling came out in support of women'. After comparing the absence of women's rights in Somalia with the standards achieved in the West, Hirsi Ali says:

In the advanced world, you can't even be called by your own name [woman] – people who menstruate – when I heard that first I thought it was a joke. And I thought I could laugh it off. And then I came round and I thought this is not a laughing matter, we are going to have to stand up for at least what we've achieved in the West … Our name as 'woman' – plural 'women' – is not going to be taken away. And I admire J K Rowling for taking that fight on.

She then says:

I want to make it very clear that I think that people who identify as Trans – Trans – whatever they want to call themselves – I'm a proponent of them getting their dignity, their freedom, live as they please … But it must not be zero sum. It cannot be that Trans people can only thrive and flourish only if they put down women.[39]

Making a similar point about language, Posie Parker, on Triggernometry in November 2019, says:

We couldn't talk about being women anymore. We couldn't use female language … Women were beginning to be told that we had to put 'cis' in front of our name. Or that Transwomen are women. And so, I wanted to get this word [woman] back.[40]

Then there is the already-mentioned issue of Transwomen in women's sports, about which Rogan first commented in 2013.

## Detransitioning

In Rogan's July 2020 conversation with Abigail Shrier, Shrier says: 'I talked to one detransitioner. So, she had gone on testosterone and regretted it'. Rogan says, 'detransitioner?' with a tone that indicates this term is new to him, but noteworthy.[41]

Obviously, if people transition and then regret it, the certainty that surrounds Trans activism cannot endure. Transitioning must in the least become a matter of weighing probabilities. But then much is lost once certainty is lost. Would someone working in a gender clinic say: 'Look, there is a cultish element to Trans, and if you are caught up in this, then you might regret transitioning'. In the same conversation, Rogan says: 'It makes you feel like there's a lot of lawsuits coming'.[42] We shall see.

## The Question of Proportion

Across all of this, proportion is difficult. On several occasions IDW figures point out that Trans activists are not representative of all Trans people. For example, Debra Soh says: 'I think the majority of Trans people are not on board with the whole across the board everyone should just transition. But it's another case of the vocal minority shutting down anyone who dares to disagree'.[43] But again, to what extent would the Transgender movement be able to continue in its current form if there was a robust public discussion about issues such as children transitioning and autogynephilia? And by 'robust' I mean that people can speak their mind without fearing or indeed experiencing repercussions.

## A Timeline of IDW Trans Events

### 1979: Monty Python

Monty Python was around long before the IDW. However, its critiques of all types of extremism and cultish behaviour gives it a strong IDW flavour. Monty Python's 1979 *Life of Brian*, which satirises both religion and politics, was ahead of its time when it critiqued Trans. At a meeting of the People's Front of Judea, one of the members, Stan, says he wants to be a woman so he can have babies.

Reg, the group's leader says, 'But you can't have babies'.

Stan replies, 'Don't you oppress me'.

Reg says, 'I'm not oppressing you, Stan, you haven't got a womb. Where's the foetus going to gestate? You going to keep it in a box?'

Judith says, 'Here, I've got an idea. Suppose you agree that he can't actually have babies, not having a womb, which is nobody's fault, not even the Romans, but that he can have the right to have babies'.[44]

This is a contribution to the 'Transwomen are not women' side of the debate and is consistent with Shapiro's question, 'Why are we mainstreaming delusion?'

### March 2013: Rogan objects to Trans women fighting women in mixed martial arts.

On episode #338 of his podcast, Rogan says, 'I don't care what the Olympic Committee says, there's a different mechanical advantage to being a man'.[45]

### July 2015: Trans reporter Zoe Tur threatens Ben Shapiro

Ben Shapiro is argumentative, asking 'Why are we mainstreaming delusion?' After calling Tur 'sur', Tur says, 'You cut that out now, or you'll go home in an ambulance'.[46]

### September 2016: Peterson opposes Bill C-16 in Canada

Jordan Peterson uploaded to YouTube three wide-ranging videos[47] which are primarily concerned with opposing Political Correctness, but which also critique Bill C-16 which, he believed, would compel people to use other people's preferred pronouns. Even though the videos are concerned with the familiar IDW talking point of free speech, the fault line runs through Trans. Later, a student uploaded a video to YouTube in which several students confronted Peterson about Trans issues. The students do a much better job of arguing with Peterson than the students at Evergreen did when arguing with Bret Weinstein: Peterson does ok, but the students have him on a few occasions.[48] Peterson also spoke at length to the Canadian Senate about Bill C-16.[49]

### July 2018: Debra Soh appears on Rogan

Rogan and Soh discuss a range of issues, including the problem of children transitioning and also the meta problem of there being a taboo against discussing the problem of children transitioning.[50] Soh returned in August 2020.[51]

### September 2019: Douglas Murray publishes The Madness of Crowds

In *The Madness of Crowds* Murray dedicates a part to Trans. He covers many of the issues mentioned in this chapter.

### December 2019: JK Rowling supports Maya Forstater

JK Rowling, author of the *Harry Potter* series, isn't in the IDW. But her views are consistent with IDW views. Further, Rowling's support of

Forstater was a substantial moment given Rowling's fame. In response to Maya Forstater losing her job for Tweeting that 'men cannot change into women', Rowling Tweeted:

> Dress however you please.
> Call yourself whatever you like.
> Sleep with any consenting adult who'll have you. Live your best life in peace and security.
> But force women out of their jobs for stating that sex is real?[52]

Six months later, in response to an article titled, 'Opinion: Creating a more equal post-COVID-19 world for people who menstruate' Rowling wrote: '"People who menstruate." I'm sure there used to be a word for those people. Someone help me out. Wumben? Wimpund? Woomud?'

It was around this time that many of us became familiar with the acronym TERF.[53] A heavily liked response to Rowling's Tweet was: 'I actually appreciate how much you are honest about being a huge fucking TERF so that no one is confused about whether or not you're awful'.[54] We can hear echoes of this Tweet in Ricky Gervais' bit about Trans that I mentioned earlier.

In June 2020 Rowling published a defence of her position on her website. It's worth reading.[55]

### July 2020: Abigail Shrier appears on Rogan

Shrier talks about her book, *Irreversible Damage: The Trans Craze Seducing our Daughters*.[56]

### October 2021: Dave Chappelle's Netflix special: The Closer

As Dave Chappelle observes in his comedy set, *The Closer*, he is often called Transphobic. Early in the set, Chappelle, having said that he is addressing the LGBTQ community, brings up the musician DaBaby. DaBaby had recently caused controversy for a series of comments he made about HIV/AIDS and gay people at a concert. Chappelle then says:

> He [DaBaby] once shot a nigger and killed him, in Walmart … Nothing bad happened to his career. Do you see where I'm going with this? In our country, you can shoot and kill a nigger. But you better not hurt

a gay person's feelings. And this is precisely the disparity that I wish to discuss.

The show takes many turns. It comes to a head when he says:

> They've canceled people that are more powerful than me. They cancelled JK Rowling … And they cancelled her because she said in an interview … gender was a fact. And then the Trans community got mad as shit. They started calling her a TERF. I don't even know what the fuck that was. But I know that Trans people make up words to win arguments. I looked it up. TERF is an acronym. Stands for Trans Exclusionary Radical Feminist. This is a real thing. This is a group of women that hate Trans women – they don't hate Trans women – but they look at Trans women, the way we Blacks might look at blackface. It offends them. Like, ooh, this bitch is doing an impression of me … I'm team TERF. I agree. Gender is a fact … Every human being in this room. Every human being on earth, had to pass through the legs of a woman to be on earth. That is a fact.[57]

Chappelle then tells a long story about a Trans friend of his whom he got to open one of his shows. She stuck up for Chappelle in a Tweet and, as Chappelle tells it, 'The Trans community dragged that bitch all over Twitter'.[58] She killed herself several days later – though as Chappelle says, he doesn't know if the dragging did it. The point Chappelle is making is that if he were transphobic, he would hate all Trans people. (In *The Closer* he also says: 'Apparently, they dragged me on Twitter. I don't give a fuck because Twitter is not a real place'.)[59]

### May 2022: Ricky Gervais's Netflix special SuperNature

Ricky Gervais, in his May 2022 Netflix special, 'SuperNature' has a section on Trans that I quoted earlier.

### May 2022: Bill Maher addresses the Trans issue in his opening monologue.

In May 2022, Bill Maher, on his HBO show, Real Time, dedicated a 10-minute monologue to Trans. Within this he says:

I'm happy for LGBT folks that we now live in an age where they can live their authentic lives openly, and we should always be mindful of respecting and protecting. But someone needs to say it. Not everything's about you. And it's ok to ask questions about something that's very new, and involves children. The answer can't always be that anyone from a marginalized community is automatically right … Because we are literally experimenting on children … Weighing tradeoffs is not bigotry … Yes, part of the rise in LGBT numbers is from people feeling free enough to tell it to a pollster, and that's all to the good. But some of it is, it's trendy.[60]

## June 2022: Peterson is suspended from Twitter for Ellen/Elliot Page tweet.

In a tweet, Peterson criticises Ellen Page who had recently transitioned and publicised this in Esquire Magazine. He also refers to the doctor who performed the surgery as 'criminal'. In a subsequent video, Peterson spends some time objecting to pronouns and name changes before saying:

Ellen slash Elliot … is also a ritual model for emulation. Being a star with all the privileges and let us point out the responsibilities that go along with that. So by acquiescing to this surgery, and by publicizing it by insisting upon the sanctity and the moral virtue of his her their new expensive dangerous and medically enhanced identity and by participating in the whole identity charade,

Ellen slash Elliot has undoubtedly with his her their so-called courage – and remember the white house itself has tweeted out every indication of believing in the courage of those who transition enticed many a poor confused adolescent girl most likely to blame her emergent pubescent self-consciousness confusion and discomfort on being born in the wrong body and believing that the courageous self-affirming and morally admirable route is hormonal treatment, sterilization, subjugation to a lifetime of expensive medical complication – how delightfully profitable is that – and misery … And I believe Ellen/Eliot … bears moral culpability for that.[61]

## June 2022: Peterson publishes an article in the UK's The Telegraph titled 'We are sacrificing our children on the altar of a brutal, far-Left ideology'[62]

In a YouTube discussion of the article[63] uploaded shortly after, Peterson says that his preferred title for the article was 'Doctors and psychotherapists: butchers and liars'. What is interesting is that he says that the backlash against the article was rather small, and that the piece received very positive feedback, despite the fact that he was, as he says: 'calling out the casual, pathetic and cringing compliance of the psychotherapeutic community, and suggesting, again, somewhat bluntly, that the sadistic and greedy surgeons, masked by an appalling moral self-righteousness, should be jailed for practicing their fiendish and ghoulish craft on children'.[64] Peterson says that even his editor was shocked that there was such a positive response – both had expected an immense backlash. Peterson asks: 'Why are we butchering children if no one thinks it's a good idea?'[65] Later he answers this, saying, 'A very tiny minority, left unchecked, can exert a disproportionate and deadly influence on an entire society'.[66]

### June 2022 Matt Walsh releases his documentary What Is a Woman

Matt Walsh isn't IDW; he's a typical online Conservative figure. However, it's significant that he appeared on Rogan. The documentary *What Is a Woman* shows numerous people defining a woman as 'Someone who identifies as a woman'. The sense is that women have no definable characteristics. One of many questions that arise from this is: if a woman has no characteristics, what are men transitioning into? But also, why is it that of all the nouns, 'woman' is undefinable. We do just fine in defining 'cat' or 'tree' or 'government' or anything else for that matter.

### October 2022 Tulsi Gabbard appears on Rogan

Rogan and Gabbard spend some time discussing Trans issues. Gabbard says:

> The women's march when Trump got elected, right? … And the irony is here we are sitting now with a lot of these same people who like: 'Ooh, I don't know how to define a woman' and 'there is no such thing as a woman'. All of these examples point to the hypocrisy – the fact that they don't believe in truth, and that whatever their cause of the moment is whatever they decide is the truth – and the thing that must be measured against for you: you're either with us or you're against us.[67]

## Notes

1   In 2022 YouTube personality Matt Walsh released the documentary *What is a Woman?*

2   Daily Mail 2023 January 31.

3   Jackson 2023 February 16.

4   Murray 2019: 203.

5   The Joe Rogan Experience 2013 March 13: 0:59:18.

6   The Joe Rogan Experience 2020 July 16: 0:00:22.

7   HLN 2015 July 18: 0:00:31.

8   DailyWire+ 2018 October 6: 0:05:12.

9   The Joe Rogan Experience 2020 July 16: 0:37:26.

10   The Joe Rogan Experience 2022 October 11: 0:22:27.

11   The idea that people are assigned a sex at birth is present not just in political discourse, but in the scientific literature. See for example Burke, Manzouri & Savic (2017) in the journal *Nature*.

12   The Agenda | TVO Today 2016 October 27: 0:11:21.

13   The Agenda | TVO Today 2016 October 27: 0:12:10.

14   The Joe Rogan Experience 2016 November 28: 0:31:52.

15   Triggernometry 2023 January 9: 0:43:25.

16   Triggernometry 2021 November 22: 0:08:24.

17   Real Time with Bill Maher 2022 May 21: 0:04:22.

18   The Joe Rogan Experience 2018 July 26: 0:20:58.

19   The Joe Rogan Experience 2020 July 16: 0:17:32.

20   DailyWire+ 2019 November 9: 0:00:00.

21   The Joe Rogan Experience 2018 July 26: 0:11:22.

22   The Joe Rogan Experience 2022 November 7: 0:32:49.

23   The Joe Rogan Experience 2020 July 16: 0:33:38.

24   The Joe Rogan Experience 2018 July 26: 0:11:22.

25   Triggernometry 2023 January 9: 0:00:00.

26   The Joe Rogan Experience 2020 July 16: 0:31:42.

27   The Joe Rogan Experience 2018 July 26: 1:01:24.

28   Triggernometry 2021 January 14: 0:07:46.

29   Triggernometry 2023 April 17: 0:00:32.

30   Triggernometry 2021 April 1: 0:36:42.

31   Murray 2019: 196.

32   Chappelle 2021: 0:53:54.

33   Rogan 2016: 0:59:53.

34   HLN 2015 July 18: 0:02:07.

35   Triggernometry 2019 November 18: 0:01:21.

36  Triggernometry 2021 November 222: 0:05:00.

37  Gervais 2022 0:04:17.

38  Bust 2023.

39  The Joe Rogan Experience 2021 March 2: 0:02:21.

40  Triggernometry 2019 November 18: 0:8:17.

41  The Joe Rogan Experience 2020 July 16: 0:24:53.

42  The Joe Rogan Experience 2020 July 16: 0:40:05.

43  The Joe Rogan Experience 2018 July 26: 1:07:46.

44  PkLugia 2007 April 21.

45  The Joe Rogan Experience 2018 July 26: 1:50:48.

46  HLN 2015 July 18: 0:2:07.

47  Jordan B Peterson 2016 September 27; Jordan B Peterson 2016 October 4; Jordan B Peterson 2016 October 6.

48  Aerial View 2021 August 17.

49  Jordan B Peterson 2017 May 19.

50  The Joe Rogan Experience 2018 July 26.

51  The Joe Rogan Experience 2020 August 5.

52  Rowling 2019 December 19.

53  Rowling 2020 June 7.

54  Chirico 2020 June 7.

55  Rowling 2020 June 10.

56  The Joe Rogan Experience 2020 July 16.

57  Chappelle 2021 October 5: 0:52:23.

58  Chappelle 2021 October 5: 1:05:00.

59  Chappelle 2021 October 5: 1:03:56.

60  Real Time with Bill Maher 2022 May 21: 0:02:01.

61  Jordan B Peterson 2022 July 2: 0:10:06.

62  Peterson 2022 June 16.

63  Jordan B Peterson 2022 July 16.

64  Jordan B Peterson 2022 July 16 Timestamp: 1:09.

65  Jordan B Peterson 2022 July 16 Timestamp: 4:18.

66  Jordan B Peterson 2022 July 16 Timestamp: 8:04.

67  The Joe Rogan Experience 2022 October 11: 0:18:24.

16

# The IDW, New Atheism, and Religion

As mentioned, the IDW has links with the New Atheist movement that was prominent from the 2000s to the early 2010s. The obvious link is the continuity of personnel. Sam Harris was present in both, as was Ayaan Hirsi Ali. Richard Dawkins has appeared on several IDW podcasts and has spoken strongly against the culture of silencing speech that became prominent in the mid-2010s. It is easy to think of Christopher Hitchens as IDW material – I am confident he would have been at the heart of the IDW if he hadn't died, and Stephen Fry has associate status in both. Other links include the fact that New Atheism and the IDW are characterised by charismatic public intellectuals using reasoning to debunk dogmas. However, a key difference is the status of religion. Obviously, the New Atheists did not think highly of religion. However, religion often has a positive status within the IDW; this is clearly the case for religious IDW figures Jordan Peterson and Ben Shapiro. Or at least religion is seen in a more neutral light. Eric Weinstein, speaking on Rogan in November 2018, discusses his brother Bret's beliefs about religion in comparison with Richard Dawkin's beliefs. Rogan says: 'I thought your brother was an atheist as well [like Dawkins]'. Eric Weinstein replies: 'Yeah. But Bret doesn't think that religion is a virus. It's not parasitising you. He believes that religion is actually an adaptation'.[1] In other words, religion is a social technology.

In this shorter chapter, I will detail the continuities and discontinuities between New Atheism and the IDW. However, before I get to this, I want to say a few general words about how times have changed between the 90s and 00s and now. Being anti-Christianity was very much a part of counter-culture in the 90s. 'Heresy' on Nine Inch Nails' *The Downward Spiral*, which was released in 1994, and Marilyn Manson's album *Antichrist Superstar*, released in 1996, stand out, as does *South Park* (first episode aired August 1997), which, not unlike the New Atheists, was embattled against Conservative Christian forces in its early years.[2] My sense is that in the 90s and into the 00s we saw the following opposition: 'Progressive, rational, truth-seeking, free, atheist' versus 'Conservative, dogmatic, truth-denying, constrained, Christian'. The 90s now feels a bit like another 1960s. Since then, the pack has been shuffled. Quentin Tarantino, one of the greatest movie makers of our time, who could be given IDW associate status (*Once Upon a Time in Hollywood* was an anti-Woke movie, but with considerable nuance), helps to shed light on this in a comment he made on Rogan in June 2021: 'And by the way, we are going through the 80s part two. Right now. Except there's more of a McCarthyesque black list aspect to it, than was in the 80s. The 80s seemed very – people were doing it to themselves. Whereas here, people are doing it to you'.[3] To a degree, we now see the following opposition: 'Conservative, rational, truth-seeking, free, Christian' and 'Progressive, dogmatic, truth-denying, constrained, atheist'. *South Park* itself reflects this shuffled pack. Where once it was embattled against the Conservative Christian world, now its main target is Progressive Woke culture.

## Continuity 1: Enlightenment values

The first continuity between New Atheism and the IDW is the championing of Enlightenment values in the form of the scientific method, which includes drawing upon reasoning and evidence to pursue the truth. In 2013, at the tail end of the New Atheist era, we see Dawkins in full flight when he responds to a clever-dick question from the audience about how the scientific method can be justified. He says, 'It [science] works. Planes fly. Cars drive. Computers compute. If you base medicine on science, you cure people … It works. Bitches'.[4]

## Discontinuity 1: A new secular opponent: Wokeness

The first discontinuity is that the IDW's primary opponent is not traditional religion – the religious right – but rather, the Woke left.

## Continuity 2: New foe, same problem: religiosity

However, for the IDW, the Woke left is driven by a religious zeal. Thus, in a broader sense, the New Atheists and the IDW have the same foe: a pious, tribal dogmatism, replete with blasphemies and confessions. We see this in several IDW-aligned books: John McWhorter's *Woke Racism: How a New Religion has Betrayed Black America* (2021), Andrew Doyle's: *The New Puritans: How the Religion of Social Justice Captured the Western World* (2022) and Michael Shellenberger's *Apocalypse Never* (2020), in which he claims environmentalism is like a secular religion. However, the point that Wokeness or Social Justice is like a religion is made again and again in IDW circles. Keri Smith, the host of the podcast *Deprogrammed*, describes herself as 'A Liberal who spent twenty years in the SJW Cult'.[5] She says she was indoctrinated during her time at Duke University in the early 2000s. Speaking on Triggernometry in December 2020 she says:

> For me it became a kind of religion. And I think it operates that way for a lot of people … It's a way of feeling like you are doing good in the world. And it gives you a moral plan for how to operate in the world.[6]

About Woke academics James Lindsay says, 'I think they're the people that are trying to build the kingdom of God on the planet Earth. To draw a religious metaphor. They are people that see an evil and they want to purge the world of that evil by any means necessary'. Rogan asks, 'And the evil being …?' Lindsay says, 'Privilege. Hate. White supremacy. Patriarchy'. Peter Boghossian says:

> It's the new religion. Christianity goes down. It's game of thrones. The only reason you need new gods is because people don't believe in the old gods. And so we have these religious modules in our brain. And the new religion is Intersectionality … Political correctness is paralleled with blasphemy.[7]

Shortly after, Lindsay is talking about the word 'sacred'. Defining sacred he says, 'What it really means is that it [the sacred thing] has taken on so much moral importance to somebody that they no longer will allow it to be questioned. When something's sacred, it's now been removed from the sphere of being doubted, questioned, or whatever'.[8] Lindsay again gives the example of the concept of 'privilege'.

## Discontinuity 2: Religiosity is unavoidable (therefore pick a good one!)

The second discontinuity is that for some in the IDW – not so much Sam Harris – there is a greater regard for religion; this partly derives from the conviction that humans are by nature religious, at least insofar as we cannot help but belong to something. The question then becomes: to what do we wish to belong? Perhaps some traditional religions or even just cultural traditions do better than the new secular religion of Wokeness (I am not religious, but I have a devoutly Jewish friend, and I am always impressed by the moral subtlety of the Jewish faith). Such points were raised in a conversation between Jordan Peterson, Douglas Murray and Sam Harris:

*Murray:* We may be in the midst of the discovery that the only thing worse than religion is its absence.

*Harris:* Where are we discovering that?

*Murray:* Look at the religions that people are making up as we speak. I mean, every day there's a new dogma. And you and I and Jordan have repeatedly tripped over those dogmas. Usually survived, it has to be said. They're stampeding to create new religion all the time … Every new heresy that's invented. And they're not as well thought through as past heresies. They don't always have the bloody repercussions yet. But you can easily foresee a situation in which they do. A new religion is being created as we speak by a new generation of people who think they are non-ideological, who think they are very rational, who think they are past myth, who think they are past story, who think they are better than any of their ancestors, and have never bothered to even study their ancestors.

*Harris:* Can't you say that dogmatism is the problem … [F]irm belief in the absence of good argument and good evidence.

*Murray:* Absolutely. We can agree that dogmatism of any kind has that danger … But the void also has a danger. The void that you can create if you throw out all the stories that helped get you to where you are. Also has this danger.

*Peterson:* What's flown in to fill the gap seems to be something like a new tribalism. Which is exactly what you'd expect in some sense. If you demolish the superordinate system – you know, religion divides people, no doubt, but it also unites people. And so one of the things that – arguably – unites people above their mere tribalism is their union in an abstract religious superstructure. And then if you demolish that, well then one of the things that does seem to happen is the emergence of a reflexive tribalism because people need a group identity of sorts. And the easiest thing to do seems to be to revert to ethnicity, and race and gender and sex, etcetera, etcetera. And then we do end up and have ended up in this situation that Douglas outlines.[9]

To reiterate Peterson's point: in the absence of a religious superstructure, we turn to religion-like tribalisms based on familiar identities; though the university has provided us with a religion-like superstructure for this Identitarianism with its so-called 'theory'. But these new religious touchstones are unworthy because they incline us towards a shallow us-versus-them mindset and insofar as they are dogmatic, and even anti-truth, they don't help us solve our problems.

Most interesting for me is what Murray says. For the atheist Murray, an equivalent for religion in our more secular age is having a reverence for our ancestors who brought us to our current point: the various Enlightened philosophers, artists, scientists and leaders who were, and often still are, the focus of education. Much of this turns on what we make of 'our current point'. Do we value modern Western democracies and the many benefits brought about by technological innovation? Or do we think that the West is rapacious and must be demolished? I shall return to these questions in the final chapter.

Interestingly, Peterson attempts to unify Western religion and the secular Enlightenment tradition (this is a major point). In another discussion with Sam Harris in June 2018 he says: 'Part of the conception of God that underlies the Western ethos is the notion that whatever God is, is expressed in the truthful speech that rectifies pathological hierarchies'.[10] This is remarkably Platonic. In *The Republic*, Plato writes:

> till philosophers [those who pursue truth] become kings in this world, or till those we now call kings and rulers really and truly become philosophers, and political power and philosophy thus come into the same hands ... there is no other road to real happiness either for society or the individual.[11]

Peterson's remarks are also surprisingly Progressive. He is talking about speaking truth to corrupt power.

To finish, if, once again, we cannot help but be creatures of faith, we must ask ourselves: What type of faith shall we belong to, one that is founded on truth, or one that is founded on corrupt power, resentment, and ultimately cruelty? James Lindsay makes some memorable remarks about this in August 2020 on Rogan:

> And so religions can kind of do one of two things ... I used to be hard arsed about religion ... And um what I realise is that some religions look up – they are like looking at God and they are afraid of sin but they are paying attention to God: they are thinking about renewal, they are thinking about redemption, they are thinking about forgiveness. Then some religions look down and all they do is look at the sin and they focus on the sin and that's where the witch hunts come from ... Next thing you know, they're killing witches ... If you look up, you know, then religion can be great; it can actually lead people [in their] spiritual development, community, so on. But if you are looking down you are going to start obsessing about ... if you're obsessing about sin, you're going to start obsessing about everybody else's sin too.[12]

## Notes

1   The Joe Rogan Experience 2018 November 16: 3:26:10.
2   Fagin 2000.
3   The Joe Rogan Experience 2021 June 29: 0:14:29.
4   Fahad 2013 March 17.

5   Smith n.d.

6   Triggernometry 2020 December 10: 0:2:28.

7   The Joe Rogan Experience 2018 October 31: 0:55:36.

8   The Joe Rogan Experience 2018 October 31: Timestamp 58:24.

9   Pangburn 2018 September 14: 1:20:57.

10   Pangburn 2018 August 31: 1:26:10.

11   Plato 2003 [380BC]: 473d-e.

12   The Joe Rogan Experience 2020 July 2: 0:11:05.

17

# The IDW as Champion of the West

As ought to be clear by now, the IDW, like many political enterprises, sees itself as being engaged in a civilisation-level battle. Beyond all the smaller skirmishes, the battle is over the status and trajectory of the West itself.

### The War on the West

Alongside, or maybe even encompassing, Postmodernism, Identity Politics, Wokeness, Social Justice, and so on, is an antipathy for the West. This antipathy is directed towards Western intellectual and cultural traditions, historical political figures, and much besides. For example, we hear from time to time about buildings being renamed – The David Hume tower at the University of Edinburgh is now 40 George Square,[1] and Woodrow Wilson's name has been removed from a school within Princeton University.[2] It was deemed that both were racists. Historical cancellation is complex, but it often involves judging people or countries or cultures based on the worst things they have done or even just said according to our current standards. The logical fallacy involved is something like this: 'Because X has done something bad, all things done by X are bad'. But there is a Slave Morality aspect to it as well. When considering non-Western countries, people or cultures, the fallacy is: 'If country X has suffered because of the West, X is good'. Or sometimes the fallacy is as simple as: 'Because country X is not Western, it is good'.

Anti-West sentiment continues to be strong in the universities I have been associated with. This spans everything from my supervisor 20 years ago wrinkling her nose in disgust when a student mentioned the ancient Greeks – why would you even bother to read them? – to the regular denunciations of the West by my students and colleagues. However, my best anti-West story comes from 2008. I was near the end of my PhD, and having finally got a sense of the lie of the land, and feeling ashamed for having remained silent for so long, I decided that I needed to call a spade a spade. I presented a paper at one of the weekly School seminars and argued, in Eric Weinstein fashion, that the university was a corrupt hierarchy in which PhD students and younger academics submitted to the dogmas of the older academics and, by doing so, were rewarded by being allowed to climb the hierarchy, and that all of this occurred at the expense of truth. I called that paper 'To submit or not to submit'. I expected an angry response from the academics and some of the students in the room, many of whom were exemplars of what I was talking about. However, no one even touched my arguments. Instead, my paper was unanimously dismissed for being Western. It's so often the case: whenever you try to get to the heart of the matter, you are dismissed on Identitarian grounds, or because of obscure technicalities, or you are met with silence. You never get to have a genuine discussion.

The IDW often addresses such matters. The IDW itself is pro-West; however, this is not a blind sort of nationalism – it's not a 'my country, right or wrong' thing. Rather, it is the conviction that the Western Enlightenment tradition, which spans the Sciences and Arts, Politics, rights, and the market, despite its numerous failings and unfinished business, has delivered remarkable benefits to humanity. Steven Pinker's books, *The Better Angels of Our Nature, Enlightenment Now*, and *Rationality* make such points. Recently – April 2023 – IDW associate Heather Mac Donald, in conversation with Jordan Peterson, delivered the most strident defence of the successes of the West that I have ever heard – she is speaking in opposition to the growing imposition of diversity, equity, and inclusion requirements on American academics:

> The only obligation of a scientist is to use his intellectual capacity to push back the boundaries of ignorance and to continue this stunning evolution out of poverty, penury, disease, want, vulnerability, that has

given us lives that would have been unimaginable 200 years ago. We live like no God on Olympus ever had a hope of living.[3]

Within the core of the IDW, Douglas Murray has most strongly taken up the anti-anti-West cause. He did this in his book *The War on the West* (2022). The blurb on the dust jacket of the book covers most of it:

> It's become perfectly acceptable to celebrate the contributions of non-Western cultures, but discussing their flaws and crimes is called hate speech. What's more it has become acceptable to discuss the flaws and crimes of Western culture, but celebrating their contributions is also called hate speech. Some of this is a much-needed reckoning; however, some is part of a larger international attack on reason, democracy, science, progress and the citizens of the West by dishonest scholars, hatemongers, hostile nations and human-rights abusers hoping to distract from their ongoing villainy.[4]

We read that the anti-West sentiment includes not just attacks on reason and science – such attacks are common in Postmodern thinking – but also progress. Anyone who has spent some time within universities will know that many there are sceptical that humanity has progressed (to be fair, it is a long and interesting discussion). Steven Pinker, in *Enlightenment Now*, makes a similar observation:

> Intellectuals hate progress. Intellectuals who call themselves 'Progressive' *really* hate progress. It's not that they hate the *fruits* of progress, mind you: most pundits, critics, and their *bien-pensant* readers use computers rather than quills and inkwells, and they prefer to have their surgery with anesthesia rather than without it. It's the *idea* of progress that rankles the chattering class – the Enlightenment belief that by understanding the world we can improve the human condition.[5]

I won't say much more here about why so many don't like the idea of progress – it's complicated; however, my sense is that as with Identity Politics, it is partly due to genuine concerns about ongoing inequalities, and partly due to baggage inherited from the long Marxist tradition, and the ever-present Slave Morality. The Marxist tradition is collectivist and revolutionary. Collectivism clearly stands against the individualism of the Liberal tradition which has arguably driven progress. So, if you don't like individualism, you better be sceptical about progress. Even harsher, collectivism can be attractive to the incompetent (Pinker's 'chattering class'); thus, again, the alignment between industrious Liberals and progress makes progress suspect. Finally, being revolutionary is attractive because its 'ends justifies the means' ethos allows resentment, destruction, and cruelty to be sanctified by utopianism – such affects and actions are harder to come by through a Liberalism that achieves progress incrementally (though Liberalism does have its own cruelties; there is the familiar 'I worked hard and made something of myself, so if you didn't, you must be lesser').

Moving to other IDW figures, Sam Harris has been a strong advocate of Western Enlightenment values for decades. It was this advocacy that lay behind the criticisms of Islam that antagonised Ben Affleck on Bill Maher's show (Chapter 6).

Ayaan Hirsi Ali is another IDW figure who is pro-West and who addresses anti-Westernism. On Rogan in March 2021 she says:

> Where I come from [Somalia], most women [are] actually fighting for the most basic rights – rights to be safe, not to be killed, where I come from, people – women [this is a reference to the Transgender debate about using the word 'women' to refer to biological females] – are subjected to femicide. They don't like you, they kill you. You violate their honour, they kill you. They take away your genitals … We are going to have to stand up for at least what we've achieved in the West. And hope to drag people in the developing world to come to where we are.[6]

Hirsi Ali's views can be criticised. The word 'drag' could be seen as being too paternalistic. As Abu-Lughod, author of *Do Muslim Women Need Saving*, writes:

> A moral crusade to rescue oppressed Muslim women from their cultures and their religion has swept the public sphere, dissolving distinctions between Conservatives ind Liberals, sexists and feminists. The crusade has justified all manner of intervention from the legal to the military, the humanitarian to the sartorial.[7]

But this is another case of having to find a middle path. Truth can always slip into corrupt power, but the solution is not to abandon the truth.

## The Individual (and the American) Spirit and Risk

As much as the IDW is a story of championing open discussion or battling Wokeness, it is, in the Western Liberal tradition, and as we have seen, a story of championing the individual spirit. Whence its endless veneration of Elon Musk. Whence its strong support of equality of opportunity, but its suspicion of enforcing equality of outcome. Whence the fact that the IDW is something of a self-help movement that preaches pushing on in the face of adversity and taking responsibility for one's life. Whence the fact that many IDW shows, such as The Joe Rogan Experience and The Lex Fridman Podcast, spend much more time speaking with remarkable people from all parts of life than they do complaining about Wokeness (Fridman, unlike Rogan, barely says a word about Wokeness these days – as mentioned, he thinks it is destructive to speak too much about it. [Yes, this book you are reading is not healthy! If I did not have several other creative projects in my life, I would be in serious trouble – as it stands, I'm just in trouble.]).

I have already mentioned Eric Weinstein's thesis that since the early 1970s there has been a broad stagnation in the West. For Weinstein, part of the problem is a devaluing of the individual spirit. Speaking on Rogan in February 2023, Weinstein says:

[In 1973 a] guy named Mike Mansfield ... passes something called the Mansfield amendment, which discontinues army – or department of defense – military funding for blue sky research inside of our universities. [Rogan asks, 'What is "blue-sky research"?'] Hey, you're a young person, you're super smart, here's a pile of money. Don't even tell us what you're working on. We just believe in you. Go to it. This is what caused us [The USA] to be the envy of the f-ing world. Cowboy science. We were wild, ok. We had skirt-chasing, hard drinking, charismatic, brilliant human beings, and we answered to no one. And walked around with swagger, with their shoulders back and their chests puffed out. Because around Sputnik, we wanted the best of the best to go into science ... You [the new system] turned the world's most vital people into Castrati [again the castration metaphor]. And you did it by accounting for their dollars; making them say how everything they did had a practical application, defending the purpose of blue-sky research, as if they were wasting tax-payer dollars. They got called 'welfare queens in white lab coats'. The whole thing is completely ridiculous. But we have been in the process of dismantling the world's most productive, powerful scientific enterprise, from really 1965 or 73 to the present day … So right now, if you go into a science department, the whole question is, 'well, what have you done for diversity, inclusion and equity? Let's agree that there's no lone geniuses in the world'. As if we didn't have Einstein and Von Neumann and Teller and all these people. Everything is communal … Nobody wants to work in this environment. Nobody good.[8]

Beyond the world of podcasts, such things are not often said.

Two things come to mind. First, we are back with Nietzsche's remarks: 'Carefree, mocking, violent—thus wisdom wants us: she is a woman, she always loves only a warrior'. Second, and more to the point, there is the concept of 'risk'. Here, I again think of the darkly compelling Rick Sanchez from the cartoon series *Rick and Morty*. In the show Rick is old; he came from a different era – before 1973 – but he remains a skirt-chasing, hard drinking, charismatic, brilliant human being who answers to no one (he is also deeply damaged – his skirt-chasing and hard drinking are aspects of this). One of his greatest remarks is: 'To live is to risk it all. Otherwise, you're just an inert chunk of randomly assembled molecules drifting wherever the universe blows you'.[9]

There is an eternal tension within the human condition between risk and security. Security is often desirable: War is horrible, as is not having necessities like food and shelter. And yet if individuals or even a society lean too far towards security, a certain elan is lost. But more than this, if we do not expose ourselves to a degree of risk and instead pursue safety, we can become psychologically weakened, even mentally ill, and, ironically, less safe. In the IDW realm, such issues are explored in *The Coddling of the American Mind: How Good Intentions and Bad Ideas are Setting Up a Generation for Failure* by Jonathan Haidt and Greg Lukianoff.[10] As we would expect, the book argues that American universities in particular have been driving risk aversion. The tension between risk and security is at the core of the already mentioned ultimate IDW moment: Jordan Peterson's remark to Cathy Newman: 'in order to be able to think you have to risk being offensive'.

Back to Elon Musk. As mentioned, within the IDW Musk is universally admired for his enterprising spirit, which includes taking immense risks. On Lex Fridman's podcast, Eric Weinstein says, 'You [Lex] probably have never seen an adult. Sometimes I think Elon looks like an adult. I know that he has a wild lifestyle, but I also see him looking like an adult'. Fridman asks, 'What does an adult look like exactly?' Weinstein replies:

> Oh, you know, somebody who weighs things, speaks carefully, thinks about the future beyond their own life span; somebody who has a pretty good idea of how to get things done, isn't wildly caught up in punitive actions, is more focused on breaking new ground than playing rent-seeking games.[11]

An important point is that this championing of brilliant individuals need not come at the expense of those who struggle in life. Eric Weinstein is himself a Progressive. And Elon Musk said he voted for Joe Biden in 2020.[12] We push for equality of opportunity so that we can produce more brilliant individuals (we push for equality of outcome so that we can castrate brilliant individuals).

I ponder whether it is hard for those further to the left to compute successful individuals; that is, whether they cannot help but see such individuals as merely riding on the back of a corrupt system. I have several times mentioned Foucault's famous position that power produces truth. If you believe this, then it makes no sense that someone might become powerful – or at least wealthy – because they did good things for the world, where good things are a form of truth. But also, there is the foundational Marxist idea that individuals are products of historical structures; the name for Marxist philosophy, 'historical materialism', reflects this belief. Marx himself wrote:

> Men make their own history, but they do not make it as they please; they do not make it under circumstances chosen by themselves, but under circumstances directly encountered, given and transmitted from the past. The tradition of all the dead generations weighs like a nightmare on the brain of the living.[13]

Here, Marx is talking about politics, but the point remains that there is not a lot of space within Marxist thinking – or at least in the caricature of it that simmers beneath some Progressive values – for individuals doing remarkable things off their own bats. So when a successful person like Musk is encountered he must be denounced. Along with anti-West sentiment, anti-Musk sentiment is strong amongst my students; although he has as many fans as he has detractors.

## The West's Slide into Decadence?

In the 16th century, Niccolò Machiavelli considered the question of how a city – a state – preserves itself against other cities. He identifies the familiar problem that we now call the 'security dilemma': Weak cities try to become strong so that they are not defeated, but they themselves come to be feared; alas, no balance is possible and conflict is inevitable. He then makes a more interesting observation: 'on the other hand, if heaven were so kind that it [the city] did not have to make war, from that would arise the idleness to make it either effeminate or divided; these two things together, or each by itself, would be the cause of its ruin'.[14] From the perspective of our modern pacifist sensibilities, this is a bleak, fatalistic vision. And yet it does encourage us to consider the question of whether cultures, even civilisations, move through stages or cycles. This movement could be a macro version of the process that I have mentioned throughout this book of truth slipping into corrupt power.

The broad opinion within the IDW is that many aspects of the Culture Wars are indicative of the West having entered a 'decadent' phase. In Chapter 4, we saw Bret Weinstein's concern that the problems within universities – Postmodern epistemology – are 'about a breakdown in the basic logic of civilisation'. In Chapter 12, we saw James Lindsay arguing that Wokeness has co-opted the civil rights movement. Steven Pinker talked about such things in response to a question about trigger warnings and microagressions, probably in 2017. Having talked about the odious bigotries of the recent past that afflicted women, black people, and homosexuals, he says:

> There was a legitimate movement to remove these crude barriers to full participation of these stigmatized groups … But often movements reach their decadent phase where they, having achieved the majority of their goals – having picked the low hanging fruit – they don't go out of business. But they need to find increasingly obscure grievances and

causes to maintain their moral franchise. And I suspect that's what happened to what we now call Political Correctness. Many aspects of which, in their original moderate form, were completely reasonable … Time after time you see what starts out as an understandable and defensible and desirable moral movement just go completely overboard.[15]

Andrew Doyle, on Triggernometry in December 2022, made a more specific version of this observation which incorporated some of Machiavelli's thinking:

We were at a point where no one cared – no one cared how you identified, or who you slept with, or whether you wanted to be called 'he' or 'she' – I don't remember knowing anyone who ever had a problem with any of that. Now I know a lot of gay people who won't use pronouns that people prefer on a matter of principle.[16]

Success is largely achieved. Then a decadent phase is entered which is characterised by conflict between groups between whom there was once little animosity.

Academic Camille Paglia sees the current focus on Trans, as well as the denigration of masculinity, as being indicative of the West having entered a decadent phase. She discusses this in a video posted in December 2016:

I think that a lot of it [the wide interest in Trans] – that the collaboration of the bureaucratic machinery with it – has to do with the assault on masculinity. 'Ahh, gender doesn't really exist. It's not really polarity'. Everything's all about expanding women's rights. But also terminating men. And defining men out of existence. Masculinity is by definition toxic. Masculinity doesn't exist. 'This is the proof of it' … The more I explored it [Paglia is now talking about her research into androgyny], I realized that historically the movement toward androgany occurs in late phases of culture. As a civilisation is starting to unravel. You find it again and again and again throughout history. In Greek Art, you can see it happening. All of a sudden the sculptures of handsome nude young men athletes that used to be robust in the archaic period suddenly began to seem like wet noodles towards the end. And the people who live in such periods of [the] late phase of culture, whether it's the Hellenistic era, whether it's the Roman Empire, whether it's the Mauve decade of Oscar Wilde in the 1890s, whether it's Weimer Germany, people who live in such times feel that they are very sophisticated, they are very cosmopolitan – homosexuality, heterosexuality, so what, anything goes. But from the perspective of historical distance, you can see that it's a culture that no longer believes in itself. And what you invariably get are people who are convinced of the power of heroic masculinity on the edges, whether they're the Vandals and the Huns, or whether they're the barbarians of ISIS, you see them starting to mass on the outsides of the culture, and that's what we have right now. There is a tremendous and rather terrifying disconnect between the infatuation with the Transgender movement in our own culture and what's going on out there.[17]

There are many more related discussions. The most intense remarks again come from Heather Mac Donald in her April 2023 discussion with Jordan Peterson. In it, Mac Donald speaks about the problem of the feminisation of universities in a way that also reminds us of Machiavelli. First, Peterson says:

And the universities, as Greg Lukianoff has pointed out, the universities couldn't be making people anxious and depressed at a more rapid rate, than they are, if they had planned, using the help of expert psychologists, to do precisely that. To produce this narcissistic emphasis on subjective feeling … and this corrosive nihilism in relationship to anything approximating a unifying identity [Peterson here is talking about the Western artistic tradition as a basis for a unifying identity] … That's exemplified by the proclivity of modern institutions of higher endeavour to immolate themselves on the pyre of an idiot reflexive guilt [that is, anti-West sentiment]. They're not doing anyone any favours by doing that. Including themselves. And they're certainly dooming an entire generation, especially of women as it turns out, to something like an abysmal hopelessness.

Mac Donald replies:

Well, let's face it. The feminization of the university is a complete disaster. It explains a heck of a lot that we're seeing now that we regard as pathological. Especially the shutdown of freedom of discourse, of inquiry, of speech, because females overwhelmingly embrace safety as values over those of rationality and freedom of intellectual inquiries.[18]

I'm not certain that the problem is embracing safety over rationality and freedom; perhaps this is part of it. I ponder whether there are other all the more unspeakable drivers, such as differences in how men and women relate to the power of institutions.

You can see how it all comes together – at least for some in the IDW. The West has entered a decadent phase, which is characterised by a self-loathing that is manifested in a degradation of all things Western, but also of what is noble in the masculine: a proclivity for risk, and a drive to get to the truth. Is the IDW onto something? It is easy to claim that one phenomenon or another is a sign of impending doom. Millenarianism is immensely attractive: it makes life much more exciting and it imbues our petty concerns with historical gravitas. Yet even if we dismiss the grand and polarising framings of some within the IDW, there is still a strong case to be made that we ought to be concerned that speech is not as free within our institutions as it ought to be and that the same institutions are undermining so much that we once considered to be valuable, whether this be individual works of philosophy or literature, or truth itself.

## Notes

1   Sharp 2020 September 15.
2   BBC 2020 June 28.
3   Jordan B Peterson 2023 April 21: 0:01:04.
4   Murray 2022.
5   Pinker 2019: 39.
6   The Joe Rogan Experience 2021 March 2: 0:04:30.
7   Abu-Lughod 2013 November 1.
8   The Joe Rogan Experience 2023 February 22: 1:07:16.
9   Becker 2017: 0:00:24.
10   Haidt & Lukianoff 2018.
11   Lex Fridman 2021 February 23: 0:30:55.
12   Feinberg 2023 April 18.
13   Marx 1969 [1852].
14   Machiavelli 1996 [early 16th century]: 1.6.4.
15   Gravitahn 2016 December 29.

16  Triggernometry 2022 December 26: 0:17:46.
17  Gravitahn 2016 December 15: 0:03:35.
18  Jordan B Peterson 2023 April 21: 1:42:27.

# Conclusion

Neuroscientist Jeff Hawkins has twice appeared on Lex Fridman's podcast. Hawkins is the author of *A Thousand Brains: A New Theory of Intelligence*. In the book, Hawkins writes: 'Independent of what other things the neocortex might do, we can say for certain that it learns an incredibly complex model of the world. This model is the basis of our predictions, perceptions, and actions'.[1] We humans are far from being able to grasp the totality of reality. And yet the fact that the human brain has evolved such that it is capable of producing a complex model of the world indicates that reality is to some degree knowable – evolution would not have selected for the capacity to model the world if the models we hold in our brains did not in some way correspond with reality, and indeed, help guide our actions.

There are, in fact, several sources of the models in our brains. The first, which is not specific to humans, is genetics: most life ships with the ability to identify certain patterns in the world and the inclination to respond in certain ways to these patterns, whether this be growing towards the light (if you are a plant) or something more complex like the fight or flight response in animals. The second, which is also not specific to humans, although humans do it very well, is interacting with the world – moving around in it and poking at it. The third, which is also not specific to humans, but at which humans excel, is using language to develop and transmit knowledge (reasoning arguably belongs in this category).

When I consider such things, I inevitably return to Plato, and I marvel that two and a half thousand years ago Plato was articulating something similar despite having no understanding of Neuroscience: the (Platonic) Form. I have mentioned the Platonic Form earlier in this book, and it is mentioned from time to time by the IDW, usually by Lex Fridman. Several of Fridman's more philosophically inclined guests also circle around the Platonic Form (the most kick-ass remarks I have ever heard on any podcast were made by Sara Walker and were Form-related[2]). As Plato argues in *The Republic*, things that occur in reality are imperfect echoes or shadows of forms that exist in a realm beyond reality. These quasi-religious forms intoxicate philosophers. A circle is a good example: there are no perfect circles in reality, yet we have knowledge of the form of the circle. But what's really interesting is that for Plato, forms extend to the moral and aesthetic realms, which include things such as justice and beauty. My point is that in describing the Form, Plato was in some ways identifying the brain's ability to model reality (though I would say that sometimes a model is reality perfected [the circle] and sometimes it is reality simplified [a map]). And his veneration of philosophers is effectively his veneration of individuals who have a greater proclivity for perceiving the patterns in reality.

The point is simple but profound. We humans – *Homo sapiens*, Wise Men – are fundamentally and uniquely constructed, and indeed driven, to perceive the complexities of reality and to communicate our thoughts about these complexities. But critically, power is inseparable from this process. A parent directs the knowledge acquisition of his or her child. An expert makes decisions that affect others. And those who are masterful at recognising the patterns in reality are often rewarded for their competence with prestige and money. But this is where the trouble starts.

Thinking again about Plato and his desire for philosophers to be rulers: when power is founded on knowledge, and along with this, some sense of the good beyond, let us say, narcissistic self-interest, it is itself good. But when power is founded on lies and/or is motivated by narcissistic self-interest, it is corrupt.

Let me return once more to Hawkins' account of how the brain functions before I bring this conclusion around to the IDW. He says:

The brain creates a predictive model. This just means that the brain continuously predicts what its inputs will be. Prediction isn't something that the brain does every now and then; it is an intrinsic property that never stops, and it serves an essential role in learning. When the brain's predictions are verified, that means the brain's model of the world is accurate. A misprediction causes you to attend to the error and update the model.[3]

The key assertion is: 'A mis-prediction causes you to attend to the error and update the model'.

You can probably see where I am going with all this. While Hawkins is talking about how a brain functions, there are broader implications. Healthy societies, institutions, and even relationships – which are healthy because the power within them is founded on knowledge and some sense of the good beyond narcissistic self-interest – are supple enough to allow the models of reality they endorse to be updated when they are found to be in error. Genuine power – non-corrupt power – has little to fear from this updating process because having an ever more accurate model of reality is almost always good.

However, in corrupt societies, institutions, and relationships, people lie about their knowledge and their motivations because of the benefits that come from power: things like prestige and money. The updating process is thus a fundamental threat to their existence. Corrupt power must use techniques to ensure that the models of reality it articulates are not challenged. In the most barbaric societies, institutions, and relationships, dissenters are killed, tortured, beaten, and imprisoned. In more moderate societies, institutions, and relationships, it is enough to be a bully and to establish taboos that, when breached, can cost people their livelihoods or public standing, or their time and mental health, or their friends.

While there is no shortage of corruption on the right, whether this be corporate greed, climate change denial or jingoistic nationalism, the left has, in recent decades, developed its own form of corruption and ringed this with taboos. This corruption typically surrounds ideas about sex, sexuality, and race (though notably, not class, which doesn't interest the left quite as much as it used to), but also the West itself and the nature of knowledge. This corruption is a unique tragedy because it runs counter to what has so often been a strength of the left: Liberal values such as free speech, treating people as individuals, and basing claims on reasoning and evidence.

It is in opposition to this corruption that the IDW arose. In the realm of Cyberspace – on YouTube – it challenged the models of the world that were becoming increasingly dominant, but that couldn't be challenged within traditional institutions like universities and the media. Joe Rogan, who is at the heart of the IDW, and who time and again gets to the point using plain and efficient language, said the following about the IDW: 'People are starved for controversial opinions' and 'they are starved for an actual conversation'.[4] These words appear innocuous but behind them lies the deepest yearnings of the human brain: **when the received claims do not conform to people's own models of reality, people want to talk about this.** The IDW has been a prosthetic conversation for tens of millions of people who have been unable to talk. None of this is to say that the IDW is always right, or even that the IDW has not itself been corrupted, but it does account for the immense success of the many figures associated with the IDW.

For the IDW, the corruption on the left can partly be understood as the civil rights movements from the second half of the twentieth century having entered a decadent phase. This itself has many causes: (i) the necessity for academics to keep publishing even if there is not much to say; (ii) the arrival in the academy and the adult world of a generation of young people who grew up on social media; (iii) legacy media's increasing dependence on polarisation following the collapse of traditional revenue streams; (iv) the corporate world's championing of costless left-wing concerns (race and sexuality as opposed to class). But perhaps, as Machiavelli argues, it also derives from the easy life; though I am wary of such a bleak assessment.

As the IDW discusses, this decadence is, at its worst, characterised not just by resentment and a love of revenge and cruelty, but a Slave Morality in which victimhood confers virtue and rightness upon the victim and through which people can gain power without doing anything. And it is underpinned by an epistemology which is typically called 'Postmodernism' that allows criticisms to be dismissed on the grounds of identity without recourse to reasoning and evidence. Indeed, Postmodern epistemology is foundational to establishing taboos. It encourages silencing speech because in a world where reality is conjured into being by language, the way to purge the world of evil is to silence bad speech and replace it with your preferred speech. Over the last decade, we have seen that the Woke pursue their quarry with a McCarthyesque vigour, and those guilty of wrong think must engage in public Maoist struggle sessions in which they confess their guilt. Further, as I regularly see in my own university, mawkish praise is heaped on the mediocre or even just cowed individuals who have submitted to the dictates of Diversity Equity and Inclusion.

As I mentioned in Chapter 5, in October 2019 on an episode of Rebel Wisdom titled 'Fighting Postmodernism from the Left', Pluckrose says, 'I think there's going to be a big pushback against Social Justice and I want it to come from the Liberal left, rather than the populist right'. However, even though, as Jonathan Haidt said in 2019 (see Chapter 3), many on the left do not endorse the illiberalism on the left that we refer to as 'Woke', in the most recent years, the pushback against Social Justice has very much come from the right. This has been to such an extent that many of the ideas that the IDW has popularised are now a normal part of right-wing thinking, whether this be championing free speech, endorsing the good aspects of the Western tradition, or being concerned about the Transgender movement's encroachment on women's and children's wellbeing. It is strange times. Rogan himself has said that the left and the right have flipped. Perhaps this is as it should be: the right becomes Progressive when the left falls into decadence.

I don't know. Wokeness is real, but I continue to struggle with proportion. How much of a threat is Wokeness? And to what extent are many of us caught up in a futile Culture War? Alas, this alien has been in my life so long I can't remember anything else.

But I shall finish on positive note. More or less. What is the greatest lesson we learn from the IDW? It is as Matt Taibbi, quoting William Blake, says: we ought always to speak our mind. Not only will the base man avoid us (I don't know about this – maybe it was different before the internet), we will be engaged in the greatest adventure there is: the pursuit of truth. But there is an even more important benefit from speaking our mind. Every time we fail to speak our mind, we are diminished. The best depiction of this I have encountered is Philip Larkin's poem, 'Wires',[5] which describes how 'young steers', in search of 'purer water' blunder up against electric fences and become 'old cattle'. You really must look it up.

When I step back from the Woke enterprise and all of my university experiences, for the most part, I do not see people fighting for a better world, but lost souls trying to anaesthetise their pain by surrounding those who still have a spark in their eyes with the wires. Though, it is not just the Woke or universities that do this. Lost souls are everywhere.

I could stop here, but there is one more heavyweight from the Western tradition I would like to draw upon: Tolstoy, the Christian anarchist. Tolstoy's final novel was *Resurrection*. It presents a view of Russia's mad society at the end of the nineteenth century (Tolstoy was cancelled by the Russian Orthodox Church for it). Towards the end of the novel, we encounter an individual who has stepped beyond the wires: an old tramp. The scene occurs when the protagonist Nekhludoff is crossing a river on a barge:

> 'What is your faith, Dad?' asked a middle-aged man, who stood by his cart on the same side of the raft.
>
> 'I have no kind of faith, because I believe no one – no one but myself,' said the old man as quickly and decidedly as before.
>
> 'How can you believe yourself?' Nekhludoff asked, entering into a conversation with him. 'You might make a mistake'.
>
> 'Never in your life,' the old man said decidedly, with a toss of his head.
>
> 'Then why are there different faiths?' Nekhludoff asked.
>
> 'It's just because men believe others and do not believe themselves that there are different faiths. I also believed others, and lost myself as in a swamp, – lost myself so that I had no hope of finding my way out. Old believers and new believers and Judaisers and Khlysty and Popovitzy and Bespopovitzy and Avstriaks and Molokans and Skoptzy – every faith praises itself only, and so they all creep about like blind puppies. There are many faiths, but the spirit is one – in me and in you and in him. So that if every one believes himself all will be united. Every one be himself, and all will be as one'.[6]

## Notes

1   Hawkins 2021: 34.

2   Walker says:

> Abstractions do exist. They're real physical things … I think the thing we need to explain is what abstractions are, and what they are as physical things, because for all of human history we've thought that there were these properties that are disembodied – exist outside of the universe –

and really, they do exist in the universe, and we just don't understand what their physics is. So I think Mathematics is a really good example. We do theoretical physics with math, but imagine doing physics of math, and then think about math as a physical object. And math is super interesting, I think this is why we think it describes reality so well, because it is the most copyable kind of information – it retains its properties when you move it between physical media. So it seems to describe the universe really well, but it probably is because it's information that is very deep in our past. And it's just – we invented a way of communicating it very effectively between us (Lex Fridman 2022 April 25: 0:45:00).

3    Hawkins 2021: 32.
4    Weiss 2018.
5    Larkin 2012 [1950].
6    Tolstoy 1999.

# Appendix: IDW Figures

As mentioned earlier, I use four categories to organise the IDW: core, near core, near associate, and distant associate. Perhaps two would be enough: the core and everyone else. However, I do think a little more detail is useful. The core is largely agreed upon by those interested in the IDW. After that, the debate begins. All people included have some relationship with the core and are themselves IDW minded. I only mention books for the first two tiers.

## Tier 1: Core IDW figures

### Joe Rogan

Joe Rogan is a stand-up comedian, mixed martial arts commentator, and, of course, podcaster. He is the Godfather of the IDW. Not only has his immensely popular podcast, The Joe Rogan Experience, provided a platform for numerous IDW figures, Rogan's approach to knowledge and politics are metonymic of the way of the IDW. Rogan is open-minded and willing to explore diverse, often taboo, topics. His open-mindedness is mostly a strength, but sometimes a weakness. Politically, he is hard to pin down. He often endorses traditional left agendas, such as universal health care, good quality public education, and social safety nets, and yet his Libertarian, masculine edge, and strong criticisms of Wokeness put him at odds with parts of the left.

### Jordan Peterson

While Rogan is the Godfather of the IDW, Canadian academic and Psychologist Jordan Peterson is its most significant figure. In this book I have mentioned his views more than those of anyone else – sometimes I tried not to write about him and find some other IDW figure who said the same thing. No one has battled against Wokeness, Identity Politics, and Postmodernism with more vigour than Peterson. But also, Peterson's simple, down to earth, self-help message that for life to be meaningful we must shoulder a burden has resonated with legions of people, in particular, men. This perspective is Peterson's antidote to obsessing about Identity and the victim culture that is a part of this. Peterson has shown men the middle path between being narcissistic pickup artists and brow-beaten apologists for a now decadent Feminism. In a time when the noisy parts of the left appear to be intellectually, morally, and spiritually bankrupt, Peterson's moderate Conservatism and increasing religiosity have become appealing for many. However, Peterson does at times push too hard, and he lets himself be deranged by Twitter – now X. Peterson has interacted with numerous IDW figures within and beyond the core. Beyond-core figures include Steven Pinker, Jonathan Haidt, Lex Fridman, Dogulas Murray, and Stephen Fry. Peterson joined Ben Shapiro's *DailyWire+* in mid-2022.

*Books*
*Maps of Meaning: The Architecture of Belief* (1999), *12 Rules for Life: An Antidote to Chaos* (2018), *Beyond Order: 12 More Rules for Life* (2021)

**Ben Shapiro**
Ben Shapiro is a Conservative political commentator, author, lawyer, and public speaker. He co-founded The Daily Wire media empire. Shapiro advocates for limited government, free markets, and individual liberty. Shapiro was on stage with Sam Harris when the name 'Intellectual Dark Web' was introduced by Eric Weinstein in January 2018. In IDW fashion, he has showed that he is willing to go against his own side of politics by not endorsing Trump to be the US president in 2016. For this and other acts, he attracted immense ire from Trump supporters and numerous anti-Semitic attacks.[1] Though having said all this, some remarks by Cathy Young about Shapiro's place in the IDW have always stuck in my mind: 'As for Weiss's article, I have some quibbles with it; I'm not sure, for instance, that Ben Shapiro, who is not so much a "renegade" as a straight-up Conservative pundit, belongs with the others'.[2] However,

even if Shapiro is not a heterodox thinker like Rogan or Harris or the Weinstein brothers, he remains at the core of the IDW, not just by association but because of his strong criticisms of Identity Politics. Along with his Rogan appearances, he has appeared on Peterson's, Harris's, and Rubin's shows.

*Books (partial list)*
*Brainwashed: How Universities Indoctrinate America's Youth* (2004), *Porn Generation: How Social Liberalism Is Corrupting Our Future* (2005), *Primetime Propaganda: The True Hollywood Story of How the Left Took Over Your TV* (2011), *The Establishment Is Dead: The Rise and Election of Donald Trump* (2017), *Facts Don't Care About Your Feelings* (2019), *How to Destroy America in Three Easy Steps* (2020), *The Authoritarian Moment: How the Left Weaponized America's Institutions Against Dissent* (2021)

## Eric Weinstein

Eric Weinstein coined the name 'Intellectual Dark Web'. He has a PhD in Mathematics and has worked as an Economist and was the managing director of Thiel Capital. There is just about nothing more thrilling than hearing Weinstein teeing off about Mathematics and Physics and unfolding his hypotheses about the stagnation of society and the crumbling sense-making apparatuses of the Western world – the universities and media. He is a prodigious intellectual and free spirit. And while his mathematical theory of everything – 'Geometric Unity' – may not get off the ground (though who really knows), the fact that he is attempting to solve one of the greatest problems is impressive – all the more so because he is working outside academia. There is a populist edge to Weinstein; but in true IDW fashion, he walks a path between being critical of the expert-class and upholding the need for institutions. Weinstein developed many of his ideas on his somewhat short-lived podcast, The Portal, and also interviewed IDW figures such as Douglas Murray and irrepressible surfing legend, Kai Lenny. When Weinstein appeared on Rogan in February 2023, I had the vivid sense that the IDW would never really die.

## Sam Harris

Sam Harris has a PhD in neuroscience. He is known for his meticulous reasoning and also for his thoughts about religion, ethics, free will, and, of course, Woke politics. His involvement in the New Atheist movement made him famous long before the IDW appeared. His politics are centre-left, and of the central IDW figures, he is furthest from Populism. He has regularly interacted with all the other core IDW figures. Notable IDW events include a live debate in August 2018 with Jordan Peterson, mediated by Bret Weinstein.[3] Controversies surrounding the defeat of Trump and COVID led Harris to become estranged from some IDW figures; though not the great diplomat Lex Fridman. Harris first appeared on Rogan in 2012!

### *Books*

*The End of Faith: Religion, Terror, and the Future of Reason* (2004), *Letter to a Christian Nation* (2006), *The Moral Landscape: How Science Can Determine Human Values* (2010), *Free Will* (2012), *Lying* (2013), *Waking Up: A Guide to Spirituality Without Religion* (2014), and *Islam and the Future of Tolerance: A Dialogue* (2015) (with Maajid Nawaz)

### Bret Weinstein

Bret Weinstein, Eric's bother, has a PhD in Biology and is an Evolutionary Biologist. Of the central IDW figures, he had the most significant encounter with the Woke mob. His experiences at Evergreen State College in 2017 were indicative of the kind of Identity Politics that so many of us have struggled with for decades, albeit at a lower intensity. The most glorious aspect of what occurred at Evergreen is that Weinstein stood his ground and debated the mob – or at least the more moderate figures within it who were willing to speak with him. His first appearance on Rogan in June 2017, like Peterson's appearance in November 2016, was a major moment in bringing IDW values to wider attention. After leaving Evergreen, he started *The Dark Horse Podcast* with his wife and significant IDW figure, Heather Heying. Weinstein's politics are somewhere on the left.

### *Books*

*A Hunter-Gatherer's Guide to the 21st Century: Evolution and the Challenges of Modern Life* (2021) (with Heather Heying)

## Dave Rubin

Dave Rubin started out as a stand-up comedian and transitioned to being a YouTube personality. I haven't mentioned him much in this book. While he is affable, my sense is that others say what he says in a more convincing manner. Nonetheless, The Rubin Report has featured many IDW figures. Rubin is interesting because he began on the left but moved to the right following the explosion of Woke politics in the mid-2010s. You can even watch his conversion, which occurred in an interview with Conservative political commentator Larry Elder. Elder challenges Rubin to provide examples of systemic racism. Rubin talks about police shootings of black people. Elder responds with a range of facts that indicate that Rubin's point is weak. Elder then challenges Rubin to present further evidence. Rubin struggles. Rubin had portentously introduced the interview by saying:

> According to his biography, Larry uses facts and common sense to arrive at his conclusions. That sounds familiar, right. Now if I use those same precepts as a Liberal, can we both be right at the same time? Can we both be wrong? Is the answer somewhere in the middle?[4]

*Books*
*Don't Burn This Book: Thinking for Yourself in an Age of Unreason* (2020), *Don't Burn This Country: Surviving and Thriving in Our Woke Dystopia* (2022)

## Claire Lehmann

Alas, I have barely mentioned Claire Lehmann in this book. However, she is a special case. Lehmann is not known for her views, but for her publication: *Quillette*. Lehmann launched *Quillette* in 2015 with the aim of promoting discussion about ideas that were difficult to discuss within the mainstream, such as the possibility that the human mind is not a blank slate. *Quillette* is often thought of as the publication most closely associated with the IDW. Lehmann is an Australian.

## Tier 2: Near core IDW figures

## Steven Pinker

Canadian Steven Pinker is one of the world's most prominent public intellectuals. He received his PhD from Harvard in 1979 in Experimental Psychology. For decades, his popular books have championed Enlightenment values and have pushed back against Postmodern and Woke dogmas, including the beliefs that the human mind is a blank slate and that humanity is not progressing. Few make a better case than him for upholding moderate Liberal values (recall that Pinker championed the concept of the 'Radical Centre'). He has appeared on Rogan and has engaged with several IDW figures such as Jordan Peterson and Jonathan Haidt. He could be in the core of the IDW; however, he is so successful in his own right that he floats somewhere above it all.

*Books (partial list)*
*The Blank Slate: The Modern Denial of Human Nature* (2002), *The Stuff of Thought: Language as a Window into Human Nature* (2007), *The Better Angels of Our Nature: Why Violence Has Declined* (2011), *The Sense of Style: The Thinking Person's Guide to Writing in the 21st Century* (2014), *Enlightenment Now: The Case for Reason, Science, Humanism, and Progress* (2018), *Rationality: What it is, why it seems scarce, why it matters* (2021)

## Jonathan Haidt

Jonathan Haidt along with Peterson and Pinker makes up the triumvirate of prominent academic Psychologists in the IDW. Amongst other things, Haidt's research has explored the foundations of moral judgement and the recent problems on university campuses. Haidt co-founded the Heterodox Academy in 2015 to promote viewpoint diversity within universities. His politics are centre-left. He certainly could have gone down the Jordan Peterson mega-star path, but there is a 'nice guy' quality to him that mitigates against this, if you know what I mean: Peterson is a warrior; whereas Haidt is a conciliator. Haidt, Pinker, and Peterson appeared together on Peterson's podcast in June 2021.[5]

*Books (partial list)*
*The Righteous Mind: Why Good People Are Divided by Politics and Religion* (2012), *The Coddling of the American Mind: How Good Intentions and Bad Ideas Are Setting Up a Generation for Failure* (2018), *The Anxious Generation: How the Great Rewiring of Childhood is Causing an Epidemic of Mental Illness* (2024).

## Heather Heying

Heather Heying is the wife of Bret Weinstein and, like Weinstein, worked as an evolutionary biologist at Evergreen State College. She too became a public figure following the Evergreen State College incident and is co-host of *The Dark Horse* podcast. Heying's politics are somewhere on the left.

### Books

*A Hunter-Gatherer's Guide to the 21st Century: Evolution and the Challenges of Modern Life* (2021) (with Bret Weinstein).

## Douglas Murray

Douglas Murray is the great orator and prose stylist within the greater core of the IDW. He is a formidable figure. Born in Britain, he studied English Literature at the University of Oxford and works as a journalist and political commentator. He is Conservative, and within the IDW is the strongest defender of the Western tradition. For Eric Weinstein, Murray was IDW 'patient zero'. He has appeared on various IDW podcasts and on stage with Peterson and Harris.

### Books (partial list)

*Islamophilia: A Very Metropolitan Malady* (2013), *The Strange Death of Europe: Immigration, Identity, Islam* (2017), *The Madness of Crowds: Gender, Race and Identity* (2019), *The War on the West: How to Prevail in the Age of Unreason* (2022)

## Helen Pluckrose

Britain Helen Pluckrose, along with James Lindsay and Peter Boghossian, was responsible for the Grievance Studies Affair that broke in 2018, in which the three produced hoax academic articles to draw attention to the problems within academia, especially in relation to Identity Politics and Postmodernism. Pluckrose was the editor of *Quillette*-like publication *Areo*. She has not appeared on the main IDW podcasts; however, she has had many discussions with IDW figures. In comparison with the other superstars of the IDW, Pluckrose has a humble, down-to-earth quality. I read on Wikipedia that her husband is a fork-lift driver. She's an old-school Leftist. Her dedication within her book *Cynical Theories* says, 'To my husband, David, who makes all things possible, and my daughter, Lucy, who never wants to hear about Postmodernism again. My work there is done'. I always think of this and how painfully corrosive fighting these battles is.

*Books*
*Cynical Theories: How Activist Scholarship Made Everything about Race, Gender, and Identity—and Why This Harms Everybody* (2020) (with James Lindsay), *Social (In)justice: Why Many Popular Answers to Important Questions of Race, Gender, and Identity Are Wrong – and How to Know What's Right* (2022) (with James Lindsay), *The Counterweight Handboook: Principled Strategies for Surviving and Defeating Critical Social Justice – at Work, in Schools, and Beyond* (2024)

## James Lindsay

James Lindsay was part of the Grievance Studies Affair. He was a mathematician and a New Atheist before moving into the IDW realm. Lindsay has interacted with many IDW figures. He has put considerable energy into demystifying Woke academic jargon and revealing the older intellectual roots of Postmodernism and Identity Politics. Lindsay has slid to the right in recent times.

*Books (partial list)*
*God Doesn't; We Do: Only Humans Can Solve Human Challenges* (2012), *Dot, Dot, Dot: Infinity Plus God Equals Folly* (2013), *Everybody Is Wrong about God* (2015), *Life in Light of Death* (2016), *How to Have Impossible Conversations: A Very Practical Guide* (2019) (with Peter Boghossian), *Cynical Theories: How Activist Scholarship Made Everything about Race, Gender, and Identity—and Why This Harms Everybody* (2020) (with Helen Pluckrose), *The Marxification of Education: Paulo Freire's Critical Marxism and the Theft of Education* (2022), *Race Marxism: The Truth about Critical Race Theory and Praxis* (2022), *Social (In)justice: Why Many Popular Answers to Important Questions of Race, Gender, and Identity Are Wrong – and How to Know What's Right* (2022) (with Helen Pluckrose)

## Peter Boghossian

Philosopher Peter Boghossian was part of the Grievance Studies Affair.

He too was a New Atheist before becoming aligned with the IDW – Boghossian's first appearance on Rogan in 2015 is interesting because there is a discussion of atheism before there is a discussion of Woke politics. He worked as a philosopher at Portland State University before resigning in 2021; his resignation letter mentions many familiar problems within the university, such as subordinating the pursuit of truth to ideology.[6] He is an academic after my own heart. In his resignation letter he says:

> I never once believed – nor do I now – that the purpose of instruction was to lead my students to a particular conclusion. Rather, I sought to create the conditions for rigorous thought; to help them gain the tools to hunt and furrow for their own conclusions.

Boghossian's politics are centre-left.

*Books*
*A Manual for Creating Atheists* (2013), *How to Have Impossible Conversations: A Very Practical Guide* (2019) (with James Lindsay)

**Lex Fridman**
Russia-born artificial intelligence specialist Lex Fridman could just about be a core IDW figure. All that stops him is that he was a little late to the party: the first episode of The Lex Fridman Podcast aired in April 2018. But also, and ironically, he is the best embodiment of IDW values, and because of this, he is not as controversial as other IDW figures. He has had all the central IDW figures on his Podcast except Rubin and Lehmann, and while he does explore many IDW talking points, his podcast more frequently focuses on topics such as artificial intelligence and astronomy. He continues to interview many significant figures from all walks of life. Ultimately, and to his credit, he is not much of a Culture Warrior. Fridman is friends with Rogan – Rogan appeared on Fridman's 300th episode, and Fridman racked up 9 Rogan appearances in under 5 years. Fridman is a Centrist.

**Bari Weiss**
I include journalist Bari Weiss within this near-core bracket because she

wrote the article that popularised the name 'Intellectual Dark Web'. But besides this, she has had her own IDW adventures with the *New York Times*. As mentioned, her own resignation letter makes many familiar IDW points. Weiss describes herself as a Classical Liberal.

*Books*
*How to Fight Anti-Semitism* (2019), *The New Seven Dirty Words* (2019)

### Elon Musk

The world's sometimes richest man, Elon Musk, is close to the core of the IDW. He is regularly discussed and praised within the IDW, has appeared on Rogan's and Fridman's podcasts, and – I believe – coined the term 'Woke mind virus'. Musk is admired because he has a grand vision and an indomitable spirit. His 'first principles reasoning' is consistent with the 'think for yourself, don't just run with the crowd' approach of the IDW. And in a world of chatter, he makes things: cars, rockets, tunnels. Some memorable remarks from his second appearance on Rogan are:

> Some people have this absurd view that the economy is like some magic horn of plenty. It just makes stuff. There's a magic horn of plenty – the goods and services just come from this magic horn of plenty … Now let me just break it to ya – the fools out there. If you don't make stuff, there's no stuff.[7]

Musk's politics were centre-left, but in recent times (post 2022) his politics have been less clear; although this can be explained by a well-known cartoon produced by Colin Wright that Musk retweeted: 'My political journey in a nutshell'. As Wright describes it:

> At the outset [2008], I stand happily beside 'my fellow Liberal,' who is slightly to my left. In 2012 he sprints to the left, dragging out the left end of the political spectrum and pulling the political 'center' closer to me. By 2021 my fellow Liberal is a 'Woke "Progressive,"' so far to the left that I'm now right of centre, even though I haven't moved.[8]

Musk, for the sake of promoting free speech, purchased Twitter in 2022.

## Tier 3: Near Associates

### Gad Saad

Evolutionary Psychologist Gad Saad is very close to being a 'Near-core' IDW figure – it was a tossup. He has appeared on Rogan 11 times and was one of the earlier figures on the podcast to be talking about the problems in the academic world. He has his own podcast: the Saad Truth, and he tackled the Woke phenomenon in his recent book, *The Parasitic Mind: How Infectious Ideas Are Killing Common Sense.*

### Michael Shermer

Michael Shermer is a science writer and founder of The Skeptics Society. Like many who have had a keen interest in debunking pseudoscience, supernatural claims, and religion, the IDW was a natural place for him to end up in that so much that is associated with Wokeness is pseudo.

### Ayaan Hirsi Ali

Ayaan Hirsi Ali is another IDW figure who started out in the New Atheist realm. She is a unique figure in that she was born in Somalia and herself experienced the oppressiveness of radical Islam. She presents her experiences and perspectives in several books, including *Infidel* (2006) and *Prey: Immigration, Islam, and the Erosion of Women's Rights* (2021). She is an IDW figure because of her championing of Western Liberal values, especially as they relate to women, and her objection to the Postmodern cultural relativism that itself objects to elevating Western Liberal values over other value systems. She also defended JK Rowling after Rowling objected to the phrase 'people who menstruate'. Other IDW connections include that she is married to distant IDW associate, Historian Niall Ferguson.

### Matt Taibbi

Journalist Matt Taibbi is a Joe Rogan or Bret Weinstein–style IDW figure: an old-school Progressive. His politics is clearly identifiable in the title of his 2014 book: *The Divide: American Injustice in the Age of the Wealth Gap.* My sense is that in Taibbi we see someone whose politics has remained the same while the left has gone mad about him. He is a man of the people and calls out lies and corruption wherever he sees them – he grasps the Platonic Form of such things.

### John McWhorter

John McWhorter has a PhD in linguistics and has written numerous books. He hasn't been on Rogan, but he has associated with other IDW figures including Peterson, Harris, and Bret Weinstein. His book *Woke Racism: How a New Religion Has Betrayed Black America* (2021) has helped to cement the broad IDW belief that Wokeness is a new secular religion. McWhorter is sceptical that the problems experienced by Black Americans stem entirely or even largely from current racism. McWhorter appears on The Glenn Show alongside Glenn Loury.

### Glenn Loury

Glenn Loury has a PhD in Economics. Like – and with – McWhorter, he often speaks about race issues in America. Loury hasn't appeared on Rogan, but he has interacted with Peterson, Harris, Bret Weinstein, and Fridman. Loury has gravitas. The following remarks from when he was on Fridman's podcast about the problem of supporting equality of outcome have stuck with me:

> I hate affirmative action. I don't just disagree with it. I don't just think it's against the 14th Amendment, I hate it. The hatred comes from an understanding that it is a bandaid. That it is a substitute for the actual development of the capacities of our people to compete. They want to tell African Americans – to pat us on the head – we're going to have a separate program for you. We're going to give you a side door that you can come into. That doesn't make us any smarter. It doesn't make us any more creative. And it doesn't make us any more fit for the actual competition that's unfolding before us.[9]

### Debra Soh

Debra Soh has a PhD in neuroscience. She came to be associated with the IDW because of her anti-blank slate perspectives about gender, and in particular, her objection to children transitioning. In IDW fashion, Soh spoke about such things when many were too afraid to do so. She has appeared on Rogan and has her own podcast which has featured many IDW figures.

**Erika and Nicholas Christakis**

In October 2015 at Yale, Erika and Nicholas Christakis were involved in one of the earlier instances of outrage on US university campuses related to free speech. In response to an email sent to students advising them about how to dress for Halloween, Erika Christakis asked students whether they wanted to be instructed what to do by university administrators.[10] Many students objected that they were not being provided with a safe and inclusive environment and attempted to remove the two.[11] The footage of a student abusing Nicholas Christakis is one of the more grotesque pieces of footage of college outrage you will see and an excellent illustration of Slave Morality.[12] The two said very little publicly about the incident. Erika wrote an opinion piece about the event for the *Washington Post* a year later,[13] and it was not until 2019 that Nicholas appeared on Rogan. It is interesting, even laudable, that the two did not use the event to become more significant public figures; although Nicholas was already well known: in 2009, he was named one of *Time's* 100 most influential people. On Rogan, Nicholas says that he did not want to be defined by the event.[14] One of the deepest questions across all of this is whether it is best to move on or whether it is best to fight.

**Richard Dawkins**

Evolutionary biologist and public intellectual Richard Dawkins is another New Atheist figure who has more recently moved in IDW circles. He has appeared on Rogan's, Peterson's, Rubin's, and Fridman's podcasts, and on stage with Bret Weinstein. His particular interest has been championing free speech. On The Rubin Report in 2017, in relation to his own experience of being deplatformed in Berkely, he says:

> I lived in Berkeley – I lived there for two years – this was a Liberal beacon at a time in the late 60s when Berkeley was the home of free speech – the Free Speech Movement was 1963 [it was 1964]. How have the mighty fallen. Berkeley the home of free speech now the home of suppression of free speech.[15]

Interestingly, about the incident he says, 'The less said about it the better, really'.

### Russell Brand

Russell Brand, the loquacious British personality, is, like Fridman, a late-comer to my IDW list. I'm not even sure he belongs on it. For some time, he had struck me as being a left-wing populist figure but not strongly aligned with IDW concerns. However, as the politics of the left has shifted, Brand's Populism has taken on more of an IDW flavour, in that it is critical of corrupt elites on both sides of politics. And in IDW fashion, he is highly critical of the mainstream media. He does, however, remain an enigma to me. Like so many populist figures, he floats between charlatan and sage. He has been on Rogan four times, and his likeness, along with those of other IDW figures, is embroidered on the inside of one of Jordan Peterson's jackets.

### Christina Hoff Sommers

Christina Hoff Sommers has a PhD in philosophy. She was an early IDW figure who has been less active lately. She is a feminist but is critical of victim Feminism – 'fainting couch Feminism' as she calls it. She is also critical of 'female chauvinism' which is characterised by not wanting equality between the sexes, but a vengeful desire to reverse earlier inequalities – this echoes Bret Weinstein's broader objection to Identity Politics, that it doesn't seek equality but revenge (see Chapter 12). And, like Peterson, she has objected to simplistic interpretations of the gender pay gap. She has been the focus of several protests when speaking at universities. Her moderate politics as well as the broader politics of the IDW are well illustrated on an appearance on Real Time with Bill Maher in September 2019.[16]

### Andrew Doyle

Britain Andrew Doyle has a PhD in early Renaissance poetry (lol) and is a comedian and author. He became an IDW figure because of his satirical Twitter character, Titania McGrath. McGrath is a humourless, wealthy young white woman who pursues Social Justice causes with a religious fervour that is all too familiar. As Rogan says to Doyle, 'You do such a good job of blurring the line between outrageously Woke and satire'.[17] Doyle has also interacted with Douglas Murray and appeared on Peterson's podcast and several times on Triggernometry.

## Tulsi Gabbard

Tulsi Gabbard was a Democratic member of the US House of Representatives from 2013 until 2021. She was also a candidate for the Democratic nomination for the 2020 election and served in the US military. She has been critical of interventionist US foreign policy and the US military–industrial complex. In her, we see the growing disillusionment with the left-establishment that is characteristic of the IDW. While 2020 Democratic candidates Bernie Sanders and Andrew Yang both appeared on Rogan to promote their candidacies, Gabbard appeared on Rogan before she chose to run and returned four more times, establishing herself as a significant IDW figure.

## Bill Maher

US television personality Bill Maher was on the edge of the IDW for a long time – his talk show Politically Incorrect first aired in 1993. But more recently, in the context of his HBO show Real Time, he has fallen into the middle of the IDW by being strongly critical of Identity Politics and suggesting that being Transgender is trendy. Portentously, on The Rubin Report in June 2018 with Jordan Peterson and Eric Weinstein, Ben Shapiro says:

> I think that Maher is secretly one of us. Now maybe I'm wrong. But I think that Maher is tired of the – I mean, his show was called 'Politically Incorrect' – I mean I think that he is tired of the Identity Politics, I think he is tired of the Intersectional nonsense, I think that he wants to have some open conversations, I just think that he is tied politically to the left.[18]

As with Rogan's show, many IDW figures have appeared on Bill Maher's show. In an interview on Sam Harris's Making Sense podcast, he refers to colleges and universities as 'asshole factories' and brings up Helen Pluckrose and James Lindsay's *Cynical Theories,* which he describes as a 'dissection of where this – kind of crazy ... what we think of [as] old-school liberals basically – what we think of as the nutiness on the left'.[19]

## Konstantin Kisin and Francis Foster

Konstantin Kisin and Francis Foster host the British podcast Triggernometry. Like Lex Fridman, they are second-generation IDW figures: people who entered the IDW scene from 2018 onwards (the generations are short!). The first episode aired in April 2018. Since then, numerous IDW figures have appeared on Triggernometry. Kisin and Foster's appearance on Rogan in July 2022 was a walkthrough of IDW politics – it cemented for me that there is very much a 'way' of the IDW. Listening to it, I had the sense that the apprentices were repeating their lessons before the master. Kisin has become increasingly prominent over the last year or two.

### James Damore

James Damore had a short but powerful moment in the IDW sun – he was like an interstellar object passing through the IDW solar system. His memo – the 'Google memo' – brought to wider public attention the IDW belief that there are biological differences between male and female populations beyond the physical.

## Tier 4: Distant associates

### The Comedians: Dave Chappelle, Bill Burr, Ricky Gervais, and Louis CK

Dave Chappelle, Bill Burr, Ricky Gervais, and Louis CK are each immensely popular. I saw Chappelle in Sydney in early 2023, where he twice sold out a 15 000-seat arena (he opened by saying: 'so, this is what being cancelled looks like'). All four have a close relationship with the IDW. Chappelle, Burr, and CK have been on Rogan – Burr has been on 12 times, with his first appearance being in 2010 – and Gervais has interacted with Sam Harris – which makes sense given Gervais' atheist edge. They are all strongly anti-Woke. Gervais and Chappelle are notorious because of their bits on their respective *Netflix* specials about Trans issues.

### Stephen Fry

British public intellectual Stephen Fry is something of an unexpected figure amongst the ranks of the IDW, but I am confident he belongs there. Like other IDW figures, he was on the New Atheist wave before he began to promote IDW ideas. His most significant IDW moment was when he appeared alongside Jordan Peterson on the Munk Debate about Political Correctness in early 2018, which has several million You-Tube views across its various postings. His opening remarks were an excoriating attack on the failures of Political Correctness. Fry also appeared on Peterson's podcast in May 2021.

## Niall Ferguson

Historian Niall Ferguson is an academic heavyweight, comparable with Steven Pinker. He could have been much closer to the core of the IDW; however, he hasn't appeared on very many IDW podcasts. His appearance on Fridman's podcast is worth watching.[19] Ferguson is a strong critic of the current higher education system. In 2021, he announced that he is helping to start a new university – The University of Austin – because higher education in broken.[20] IDW figures associated with the university include Heather Heying, Peter Boghossian, and Kathleen Stock.[21] Ferguson is married to Ayaan Hirsi Ali.

## David Fuller

Britain David Fuller is the host of Rebel Wisdom, an independent UK 'media platform'. He has had conversations with several IDW figures, including Jordan Peterson, Eric Weinstein, Helen Pluckrose, and Peter Boghossian.

## Abigail Shrier

Like Debra Soh, Journalist Abigail Shrier is known in the IDW for writing about Transgender issues. Her book *Irreversible Damage: The Transgender Craze Seducing Our Daughters* (2020) raised concerns about the growing numbers of young women transitioning.

## Maajid Nawaz

Like Ayaan Hirsi Ali, Maajid Nawaz has a place within the IDW because of his willingness to critique Islamic excesses and champion Western values. Nawaz's 2015 book, *Islam and the Future of Tolerance: A Dialogue*, was co-authored with Sam Harris.

## Heather Mac Donald

Heather Mac Donald has a PhD in English. She belongs to the smaller node of Conservative IDW figures (as opposed to the larger node of disillusioned Liberals). She is Douglas Murray-like: an atheist Conservative who has an almost religious reverence for the Western cultural tradition. When she gets going, she is as formidable as Jordan Peterson – her breadth of knowledge about Western culture is staggering and she is brutally opinionated about what she sees as being the decline of universities and the scourge of Identity Politics. She hasn't appeared on Rogan; however, she was in devastating form on a recent Jordan Peterson podcast.[22]

### Andy Ngo

Andy Ngo is a Conservative journalist who is known for reporting on left-wing protests and violence in Portland and other US cities. His fame rose when he was attacked by left-wing protesters in 2019.

### Camille Paglia

Camille Paglia has a PhD in English Literature. Like Christina Hoff Sommers and Steven Pinker, she was an IDW-type figure long before the IDW reached critical mass. In the realm of Feminism, she has often been a contrarian and politically incorrect. Her great contribution to the IDW is the idea that civilisations, when they enter a decadent phase, prior to their collapse, become obsessed with gender identities and disparage masculinity.[23] Her conversation with Peterson on his podcast is significant – it really is worth listening to. She destroys Postmodernism. Paglia is even more intense than Heather Mac Donald. Paglia's position on Postmodernism, and one of its relatives, contemporary art, is reminiscent of Eric Weinstein's thesis that the West began to stagnate around 1970. She says: 'So we have been going on now for 50 years – the Postmodernism in academe, hand in hand with the stupidity and infantilism that masquerades as important art at galleries everywhere'.[24]

### Quentin Tarantino

Maybe I'm taking a liberty here, but what the heck. Quentin Tarantino's 'fuck you I won't do what you tell me' attitude to film making has always marked him as a free thinker who would not be cowed by Political Correctness. And his latest movie, *Once Upon a Time in Hollywood* (set in 1969), made a strong and subtle contribution to the Identity Politics debate. In the main plot, the Sharon Tate murdering Hippies stand for the Woke generation of our day. The Hippies are brutally defeated by the seemingly over-the-hill white male actors Rick Dalton (played by Leonardo Di Caprio) and Cliff Booth (played by Brad Pitt). However, the two are themselves flawed: Dalton suffers from crippling anxiety and Booth probably murdered his wife. Interestingly, in the movie, there is a rapprochement between Dalton and a seemingly Woke girl Trudy Frazer (Julia Butters) who is acting alongside Dalton. Dalton learns from Frazer to be less of a chauvinist, and Frazer demonstrates that unlike many who are seduced by Identity Politics, she is able to recognise merit – to judge an individual based on what he or she does, not his or her so-called identity – when she praises Dalton's stunning performance in a scene they share.

**The TERFs: Kathleen Stock, Helen Joyce, and Posie Parker**
Kathleen Stock (PhD in philosophy), Helen Joyce (PhD in Mathematics), and Posie Parker are all British women who have pushed back against Transgender issues, largely because they believe Transgender advocacy negatively impacts women. Because of this, along with JK Rowling and others, they have become known as 'TERFs': Trans Exclusionary Radical Feminists. None are close to the core of the IDW; although the three have appeared on Triggernometry, and Helen Joyce has been on Peterson's podcast. As mentioned, Stock has been associated with the University of Austin. Her star is rising.

**Coleman Hughes**
Hughes is a figure like John McWhorter and Glenn Loury: he has fact-based and nuanced discussions about topics such as race and policing in America.

**Greg Lukianoff**
Lukianoff is the President and CEO of Foundation for Individual Rights and Expression, an organisation that supports fundamental rights, such as free speech, on college campuses and beyond. He co-authored *The Coddling of the American Mind* with Jonathan Haidt.

**Peter Thiel**
Venture capitalist Thiel is the second billionaire, after Elon Musk, in the IDW. Thiel shares Eric Weinstein's thesis that since the early 1970s

much has stagnated, despite technological progress in communication.

### The List Goes On ...

There are several figures in this book, and quite a few others whom I have not mentioned, who might deserve a place in this final part. I have hesitated to include them for several reasons:

1)  The person does not have a strong enough association with the core of the IDW.
2)  The person is not prominent or only became prominent recently.
3)  Even if the person does have a strong association with the core and is prominent, he or she is not sufficiently concerned with IDW talking points.
4)  I ran out of words.

I included, for example, Paglia and Tarantino because even though their connection with the core is light, they are both prominent and are concerned with IDW talking points. Here are some more edge cases.

**Jocko Willink**: Willink, an ex-Navy SEAL, has appeared on Rogan 5 times and engaged with other IDW figures such as Peterson and Fridman. He represents an old-fashioned, upright type of masculinity that the IDW values.

**David Goggins**: Goggins, another ex-Navy SEAL, has appeared on Rogan 3 times. He represents the unrelenting determination that the IDW values.

**Mike Nayna**: Nayna has made IDW documentaries. His most well-known documentaries cover The Grievance Studies Affair and The Evergreen State College incident.

### ... and on

Then there is Andrew Sullivan, Chris Williamson, Gregg Hurwitz, Jonathan Pageau, David French, Daniel Schmachtenberger, Michael Shellenberger, Andrew Yang, Balaji Srinvasan, Cathy Young, Diane Fleischman, Geoffrey Miller, Toby Young, Jonathan Kay, Slavoj Žižek, Greg Ellis, Zuby, Ryan Long, John Cleese, Michael Malice, Stephen Kotkin, Andrew Gold, Neal Stephenson ...

## Notes

1  Chang 2019 March 28.
2  Young 2018 May 20.
3  Pangburn 2018 August 31.
4  The Rubin Report 2016 January 16.
5  Jordan B Peterson 2021 October 26.
6  Boghossian 2021 September 8.
7  PowerfulJRE 2020 May 8: 1:21:09.
8  Wright 2022 May 2.
9  Lex Fridman 2022 May 15: 0:00:00.
10  Christakis 2015.
11  Friedersdorf 2015 November 9.
12  Foundation for Individual Rights and Expression 2015 November 7.
13  Christakis 2016 October 28.
14  The Joe Rogan Experience 2019 March 28: 0:02:29.
15  The Rubin Report 2017 August 9: 0:01:53.
16  Real Time with Bill Maher 2019 September 7.
17  The Joe Rogan Experience 2020 February 5: 0:00:41.
18  The Rubin Report 2018 June 30: 0:01:02.
19  Making Sense 2024 June 14: 0:09:18
20  Lex Fridman 2021 November 9.
21  Ferguson 2021 November 9.
22  Kelleher 2021 November 8.
23  Jordan B Peterson 2023 April 21.
24  Gravitahn 2016 December 15.
25  Jordan B Peterson 2017 October 3: 0:11:17.

# References

Abu-Lughod, L. (2013, November 1). Do Muslim Women Need Saving?: The Western crusade to rescue Muslim women has reduced them to a simplistic stereotype. *Time*.

Aerial View. (2021, August 17). The Video That Made Jordan Peterson Famous. *YouTube*. The Agenda | TVO Today. (2016, October 27). Genders, Rights and Freedom of Speech [Video]. *YouTube*.

Alexander, S. (2014, November 3). All in All, Another Brick in the Motte. *Slate Star Codex*. slatestarcodex.com.

Alex Swan. (2017, November 5). Jordan Peterson on the Meaning of Life for Men. MUST WATCH [Video]. *YouTube*.

Arendt, H. (1968). *The Origins of Totalitarianism*. Harvest Books, Harcourt Brace Janovitch, San Diego, New York and London.

*Australian Bureau of Statistics*. (2022, November 3). Twenty-Seven Years of Prisoners in Australia. abs.gov.au.

The Babylon Bee. (2022, December 21). Elon Musk Sits Down with the Babylon Bee [Video]. *YouTube*.

Barlow, J. P. (1996, February 8). A Declaration of the Independence of Cyberspace. eff.org.

BBC. (2020, June 28). Princeton to Remove Woodrow Wilson's Name from Policy School. bbc.com.

Becker, J. (Writer). Polcino, D. (Director). (2017, July 30). Rickmancing the Stone (Season 3, Episode 2) [TV series episode]. In J. Roiland & D. Harmon (Executive Producers), *Rick and Morty*. Williams Street.

Big Think. (2023, March 23). The Ultimate Guide to Rationality, with Harvard's Steven Pinker [Video]. *YouTube*.

Boghossian, P. (2021, September 8). My University Sacrificed Ideas for Ideology. So Today I Quit. The More I Spoke Out Against the Illiberalism That Has Swallowed Portland State University, the More Retaliation I Faced. *The Free Press*. thefp.com.

Boyce, B. A. (2018, July 17). Bret Weinstein Reasons with Evergreen Protestors [Video]. *YouTube*.

Bret Weinstein. (2020, August 15). DarkHorse Podcast with Greg Ellis and Bret Weinstein [Video]. *YouTube*.

British GQ. (2018, October 30). Jordan Peterson: "There Was Plenty of Motivation to Take Me Out. It Just Didn't Work" | British GQ [Video]. *YouTube*.

Brooks, M. (2020). *Against the Web: A Cosmopolitan Answer to the New Right*. Zero Books.

Brown, E. N. (2018, May 14). The 'Intellectual Dark Web' Is Just Rehashing Old P.C. Controversies in New Media. *Reason*. reason.com.

Burke, S. M., Manzouri, A. H. & Savic, I. (2017). Structural connections in the brain in relation to gender identity and sexual orientation. *Sci Rep* 7. https://doi.org/10.1038/ s41598-017-17352-8.

Burns, N. (2018, August 5). I Am Looking Forward to Comedy's Future in the Woke World. *Chortle*. chortle.co.uk.

Burr, B. (Performer). (2022). Bill Burr Live at Red Rocks [Video]. *Netflix*.

*Bust*. (2023). About Bust. bust.com.

Chaliand, G., & Blin, A. (Eds.). (2007). *The History of Terrorism: From Antiquity to Al Qaeda*. University of California Press.

Chang, S. (2019, March 28). Economist's Ben Shapiro Smear Spotlights Trope of Conflating Conservatives with Alt-Right. *CCN*. ccn.com.

Channel 4 News. (2018, January 17). Jordan Peterson Debate on the Gender Pay Gap, Campus Protests and Postmodernism [Video]. *YouTube*.

Chappelle, D. (2021, October 5). The Closer [Video]. *Netflix*.

Chirico, K. [@KristinChirico]. (2020, June 7). I Actually Appreciate How Much You Are Honest About Being a Huge Fucking TERF So That No One Is Confused About Whether or Not You're Awful [Tweet]. *Twitter*.

Chomsky's Philosophy. (2015, September 13). Noam Chomsky - Postmodernism I [Video]. *YouTube*.

Christakis, E. (2015). Email From Erika Christakis: "Dressing Yourselves" [Document]. thefire.org.

Christakis, E. (2016, October 28). My Halloween Email Led to a Campus Firestorm - And a Troubling Lesson About Self-Censorship. *The Washington Post*. washingtonpost.com

Christopher, J. (September 13, 2001). How Was It for You? *The Times*.

CNBC. (2017, August 16). Fired Google Engineer James Damore: I Was Pointing Out Problems At Google | CNBC [Video]. *YouTube*.

Coetzee, J. M. (1999). *Disgrace*. Vintage.

The Comments Section with Brett Cooper. (2022, May 24). Bill Maher's ULTIMATE Red Pill Moment [Video]. *YouTube*.

Conger, K. (2017, August 5). Exclusive: Here's The Full 10-Page Anti-Diversity Screed Circulating Internally at Google [Updated]. Gizmodo. gizmodo.com.

Covert, B. (2017, August 10). The Viral Google Memo Is About the Stereotypes That Hold Women Back: James Damore Put Into Writing the Type of Thinking That Has Kept Women Out of the Workforce Throughout History. *Cosmopolitan*. cosmopolitan.com.

Daily Mail. (2023, January 31). Nicola Sturgeon Flounders on Trans Policy for Female Prisons [Video]. *YouTube*.

DailyWire+. (2018, October 6). Leftist Woman Asks Shapiro If He's Transphobic [Video]. *YouTube*.

DailyWire+. (2019, November 9). Student Challenges Ben Shapiro on Transgenderism: "If It Makes Them Happier, what's the Harm?" [Video]. *YouTube*.

Damore, J. (2017, July). Google's Ideological Echo Chamber: How Bias Clouds Our Thinking About Diversity and Inclusion. s3.documentcloud.org.

DarkHorse Podcast Clips. (2021, March 23). Personal Responsibility and Changing the System (Jordan Peterson & Bret Weinstein) [Video]. *YouTube*.

Decoding the Gurus. (2021, October 30). Special: Interview with Sam Harris on Gurus, Tribalism & the Culture War (No. 30) [Audio podcast episode]. player.captivate.fm.

Del Giudice, M. (2015). Gender Differences in Personality and Social Behavior. In J. D. Wright (Ed.), *International Encyclopedia of the Social & Behavioral Sciences* (2nd ed.), 750–756. Elsevier. https://doi.org/10.1016/B978-0-08-097086-8.25100-3.

Douthat, R. (2018, February 28). The Rise of Woke Capital. *The New York Times*. nytimes.com.

Doyle, A. (2022). *The New Puritans: How the Religion of Social Justice Captured the Western World*. Constable.

Dunbar, R. I. M. (1992). Neocortex Size as a Constraint on Group Size in Primates. *Journal of Human Evolution*, 22(6):469–493. https://doi.org/10.1016/0047-2484(92)90081-J.

Enlightainment. (2018, August 1). Steven Pinker Defends James Damore Against Dishonest Slanderer [Video]. *YouTube*.

Eric Weinstein. (2018, June 8). Why the "Intellectual Dark Web" has Such a Crazy Name [Video]. Retrieved from *YouTube*.

Eric Weinstein. (2019, July 20). Peter Thiel on "The Portal", Episode #001: "An Era of Stagnation & Universal Institutional Failure" [Video]. *YouTube*.

Evans, R. J. (2005). *The Coming of the Third Reich*. Penguin Books.

*The Evergreen State College*. (2017). Off-Campus Schedule PDF Document. evergreen.edu.

Fagin, B. (2000, May). Goin' Down to South Park: How Kids Can Learn from "vile trash." *Reason*. reason.com.

Fahad. (2013, March 17). Richard Dawkins – Science Works Bitches! [Video]. *YouTube*.

Farrell, H. (2018, May 10). The "Intellectual Dark Web," explained: What Jordan Peterson Has in Common with the Alt-right. *Vox*. vox.com.

Feinberg, A. (2023, April 18). Trump Lashes Out at Elon Musk After Tech Mogul Says He Voted for BIDEN. *Independent*. independent.co.uk.

Ferguson, N. (2021, November 9). I'm Helping to Start a New College Because Higher Ed Is Broken. Institutions Dedicated to the Search for Truth Have Ossified Into Havens for Liberal Intolerance and Administrative Overreach. *Bloomberg*. www.bloomberg.com.

Feynman, R. P. (1974). Cargo Cult Science [Speech]. Caltech's 1974 commencement address. calteches.library.caltech.edu.

Flard. (2021, November 28). Late Night with Jimmy - South Park Post Covid [Video]. *YouTube*.

Flood, A. (2017, July 24). Richard Dawkins Event Cancelled Over His 'Abusive Speech Against ISLAM'. *The Guardian*. theguardian.com.

Foucault, M. (1991 [1975]). *Discipline and Punish: The Birth of the Prison* (A. Sheridan, Trans.). Vintage Books.

Foundation for Individual Rights and Expression. (2015, November 7). Yale University Students Protest Halloween Costume Email (VIDEO 3) [Video]. *YouTube*.

Fox News. (2017, May 27). Professor Objects to No White People on Campus Demand [Video]. *YouTube*.

The Free Speech Club. (2018, November 16). Ben Shapiro SHREDS Pro-Choice Argument | UBCFSC Talk [Video]. *YouTube*.

Freethinkers of PSU. (2018, February 26). James Damore at Portland State (2/17/18) [Video]. *YouTube*.

French, D. (2018, May 11). Critics Miss the Point of the 'Intellectual Dark Web'. *National Review*. nationalreview.com.

Friedersdorf, C. (2015, November 9). The New Intolerance of Student Activism. *The Atlantic*. theatlantic.com.

Friedersdorf, C. (2016, May 26). The Perils of Writing a Provocative Email at Yale. *The Atlantic*. theatlantic.com.

Friedländer, S. (2009). *Nazi Germany and the Jews, 1933–1945*. HarperCollins.

Gad Saad. (2020, November 7). My Begging Plea to Sam Harris and Other Key IDW Members (THE SAAD TRUTH_1163) [Video]. *YouTube*.

GeenStijl. (2018, January 23). Jordan Peterson's Philosophy of "How to be in the World" Distilled Down to its 5 Strongest Points [Video]. *YouTube*.

Gervais, R. (2022). SuperNature [Video]. *Netflix*.

Gibbon, E. (2008 [1782 Written, 1845 Revised]). History of the Decline and Fall of the Roman Empire [Project Gutenberg eBook]. gutenberg.org.

The Glenn Show. (2021, April 27). John McWhorter: The Conversation on Race and Cops Is Fake [Video]. *YouTube*.

Goldberg, J. (2018, May 8). Evaluating the 'Intellectual Dark Web'. National

Review. nationalreview.com.

GOV.UK. (2022, March 18). GCSE English and Maths Results: Ethnicity Facts and Figures. service.gov.uk.

Graham, P. [@paulg]. (2019, June 7). Hypothesis: Although Some Newspapers Can Survive the Switch to Online Subscriptions, None Can Do It and Remain a Politically Neutral "Newspaper of Record." You Have to Pick a Side to Get People to Subscribe [Tweet]. *Twitter*.

Gravitahn. (2016, December 6). Universities Must Choose Between TRUTH or Social Justice, Not Both - Jonathan Haidt [Video]. *YouTube*.

Gravitahn. (2016, December 15). Lesson from History: Transgender Mania Is Sign of Cultural Collapse – Camille Paglia [Video]. *YouTube*.

Gravitahn. (2016, December 29). Political Correctness Is "Decadent Phase" of Once Legitimate Movement – Steven Pinker [Video]. *YouTube*.

Guterman, D. & Ridley, R. (Writers). Polcino, D. (Director). (2017, September 10). The Ricklantis Mixup (Season 3, Episode 7) [TV series episode]. In J. Roiland & D. Harmon (Executive Producers), *Rick and Morty*. Williams Street.

Haidt, J., & Lukianoff, G. (2018). *The Coddling of the American Mind: How Good Intentions and Bad Ideas Are Setting Up a Generation for Failure*. Penguin Press.

Hamati-Ataya, I. (2012). Reflectivity, Reflexivity, Reflexivism: IR's 'Reflexive Turn' and Beyond. *European Journal of International Relations*, 19(4): 669–694.

Hasan, M. [@mehdirhasan]. (2022, December 3). Imagine Volunteering to Do Online PR Work for the World's Richest Man on a Friday Night, in Service of Nakedly and Cynically Right-Wing Narratives, and then Pretending You're Speaking Truth to Power. [Tweet]. *Twitter*.

Hawkins, J. (2021). *A Thousand Brains: A New Theory of Intelligence*. Basic Books. HenryJacksonSoc. (2015, January 9). 8 January: Douglas Murray Debates Charlie Hebdo Attack on Al Jazeera [Video]. *YouTube*.

HLN. (2015, July 18). The Moment This Transgender Debate Got Heated [Video]. *YouTube*.

Ibsen, H. (1999 [1882]). *An Enemy of the People, The Wild Duck, Rosmersholm*. Oxford University Press. Innomind. (2013, December 4). The First Principles Method Explained by Elon Musk [Video]. *YouTube*.

The 'Intellectual Dark Web' – The Supposed Thinking Wing of the Alt-right. (2018, May 10). *The Guardian*. theguardian.com.

Jackson, D. (2023, February 16). Why Did Nicola Sturgeon Resign as First Minister? *BBC*. bbc.com.

Joe Rogan. (2018, July 3). Dinner Last Night with a Bunch of Smart People [Photograph]. *Instagram*.

The Joe Rogan Experience. (2013, March 13). #338 - Shane Smith [Audio podcast episode]. *Spotify.*

The Joe Rogan Experience. (2015, November 19). #724 - Christina Sommers [Audio podcast episode]. Spotify.

The Joe Rogan Experience. (2015, December 15). #735 - Peter Boghossian [Audio podcast episode]. *Spotify.*

The Joe Rogan Experience. (2016, November 28). #877 - Jordan Peterson [Audio podcast episode]. *Spotify.*

The Joe Rogan Experience. (2017, June 3). #970 - Bret Weinstein [Audio podcast episode]. *Spotify.*

The Joe Rogan Experience. (2017, September 1). "#1006 - Jordan Peterson and Bret Weinstein" [Audio podcast episode]. *Spotify.*

The Joe Rogan Experience. (2017, September 6). #1009 - James Damore [Audio podcast episode]. *Spotify.*

The Joe Rogan Experience. (2017, December 20). #1055 - Bret Weinstein [Audio podcast episode]. Retrieved from Spotify https://open.spotify.com/episode/7hN5BdKjNW7 QqkygJbPIjq?si=0AujL19zREO3IymsWVZSgw

The Joe Rogan Experience. (2018, July 26). #1147 - Dr. Debra Soh [Audio podcast episode]. *Spotify.*

The Joe Rogan Experience. (2018, October 31). #1191 - Peter Boghossian & James Lindsay [Audio podcast episode]. *Spotify.*

The Joe Rogan Experience. (2018, November 16). #1203 – Eric Weinstein [Audio podcast episode]. *Spotify.*

The Joe Rogan Experience. (2019, February 12). #1245 - Andrew Yang [Audio podcast episode]. *Spotify.*

The Joe Rogan Experience. (2019, March 28). #1274 - Nicholas Christakis [Audio podcast episode]. Spotify.

The Joe Rogan Experience. (2019, August 6). #1330 - Bernie Sanders [Audio podcast episode]. *Spotify.*

The Joe Rogan Experience. (2020, February 5). #1423 - Andrew Doyle [Audio podcast episode]. *Spotify.*

The Joe Rogan Experience. (2020, July 2). #1501 - James Lindsay [Audio podcast episode]. *Spotify.*

The Joe Rogan Experience. (2020, July 16). #1509 - Abigail Shrier [Audio podcast episode]. *Spotify.*

The Joe Rogan Experience. (2020, August 5). #1520 - Dr. Debra Soh [Audio podcast episode]. *Spotify.*

The Joe Rogan Experience. (2021, March 2). #1613 - Ayaan Hirsi Ali [Audio podcast episode]. *Spotify.*

The Joe Rogan Experience. (2021, June 29). #1675 - Quentin Tarantino [Audio podcast episode]. *Spotify.*

The Joe Rogan Experience. (2021, December 7). #1745 - Matt Taibbi [Audio podcast episode]. *Spotify.*

The Joe Rogan Experience. (2021, December 31). #1757 - Dr. Robert Malone, MD [Audio podcast episode]. *Spotify*.

The Joe Rogan Experience. (2022, May 26). #1824 - Lex Fridman [Audio podcast episode]. *Spotify*.

The Joe Rogan Experience. (2022, July 27). #1848 - Francis Foster & Konstantin Kisin [Audio podcast episode]. *Spotify*.

The Joe Rogan Experience. (2022, October 11). #1880 - Tulsi Gabbard [Audio podcast episode]. *Spotify*.

The Joe Rogan Experience. (2022, November 7). #1895 - Matt Walsh [Audio podcast episode]. *Spotify*.

The Joe Rogan Experience. (2023, January 28). #1933 - Jordan Peterson [Audio podcast episode]. *Spotify*.

The Joe Rogan Experience. (2023, February 13). #1940 - Matt Taibbi [Audio podcast episode]. *Spotify*.

The Joe Rogan Experience. (2023, February 22). #1945 - Eric Weinstein [Audio podcast episode]. *Spotify*.

The Joe Rogan Experience. (2023, March 8). #1952 - Michael Malice [Audio podcast episode].

Jon Mercano. (2017, December 17). Empire Strikes Back Yoda Training Luke Part 1 (HD) [Video]. *YouTube*.

Jordan B Peterson. (2016, September 27). 2016/09/27: Part 1: Fear and the Law. *YouTube*.

Jordan B Peterson. (2016, October 4). 2016/10/03: Part 2: Compulsory Political Education: A Real World Case Study at the U of Toronto. *YouTube*.

Jordan B Peterson. (2016, October 6). 2016/10/05: Part 3: The PC Game (and Some Counter-Tactics). *YouTube*.

Jordan B Peterson. (2017, May 19). 2017/05/17: Senate Hearing on Bill C16. *YouTube*.

Jordan B Peterson. (2017, October 3). Modern Times: Camille Paglia & Jordan B Peterson [Video]. *YouTube*.

Jordan B Peterson. (2019, August 11). Steven Pinker: Progress, Despite Everything [Video]. *YouTube*.

Jordan B Peterson. (2021, May 18). An Atheist in the Realm of Myth | Stephen Fry | EP 169 [Video]. *YouTube*.

Jordan B Peterson. (2021, October 26). Enlightenment and the Righteous Mind | Steven Pinker and Jonathan Haidt | EP 198 [Video]. YouTube.

Jordan B Peterson. (2022, July 2). Article: Twitter Ban [Video]. *YouTube*.

Jordan B Peterson. (2022, July 16). Article: Butchers and Liars Reprise [Video]. *YouTube*.

Jordan B Peterson. (2022, July 20). The Current Crisis of Masculinity [Video]. *YouTube*.

Jordan B Peterson. (2022, August 26). Mean Tweets: An Apologia | Pageau and

Hurwitz | EP 282 Jordan B Peterson [Video]. *YouTube*.

Jordan B Peterson. (2022, September 13). Trans: When Ideology Meets Reality | Helen Joyce | EP 287 [Video]. *YouTube*.

Jordan B Peterson. (2023, March 21). Jordan Peterson Interviews Presidential Candidate Vivek Ramaswamy | EP 341 [Video]. *YouTube*.

Jordan B Peterson. (2023, April 21). In the Name of Wokeness: Institutionalized Racism | Heather Mac Donald | EP 350. *YouTube*.

Kant, I. (2002). *Groundwork of the Metaphysics of Morals* (M. Gregor, Ed. & Trans.). Cambridge University Press.

Kelleher, P. (2021, November 8). Kathleen Stock Helps Launch New So-Called University with 'Forbidden Courses' But No Actual Degrees. *PinkNews*. thepinknews.com.

Laërtius, D. (2018 [3rd century CE]). *The Lives and Opinions of Eminent Philosophers* (C. D. Yonge, Trans.) [Project Gutenberg EBook]. gutenberg.org.

Larkin, P. (2012). Wires. In C. Ricks (Ed.), *The Complete Poems*. Faber and Faber.

Lex Fridman. (2021, February 23). Eric Weinstein: Difficult Conversations, Freedom of Speech, and Physics | Lex Fridman Podcast #163 [Video]. *YouTube*.

Lex Fridman. (2021, June 14). Daniel Schmachtenberger: Steering Civilization Away from Self-Destruction | Lex Fridman Podcast #191 [Video]. *YouTube*.

Lex Fridman. (2021, November 9). Niall Ferguson: History of Money, Power, War, and Truth | Lex Fridman Podcast #239 [Video]. *YouTube*.

Lex Fridman. (2021, December 19). Albert Bourla: Pfizer CEO | Lex Fridman Podcast #249 [Video]. *YouTube*.

Lex Fridman. (2022, April 25). Alien Debate: Sara Walker and Lee Cronin | Lex Fridman Podcast #279 [Video]. *YouTube*.

Lex Fridman. (2022, May 15). Glenn Loury: Race, Racism, Identity Politics, and Cancel Culture | Lex Fridman [Video]. *YouTube*.

Lex Fridman. (2022, June 5). Jonathan Haidt: The Case Against Social Media | Lex Fridman Podcast #291 [Video]. *YouTube*.

Lex Fridman. (2022, June 21). Douglas Murray: Racism, Marxism, and the War on the West | Lex Fridman Podcast #296 [Video]. *YouTube*.

Lex Fridman. (2022, July 4). Joe Rogan: Comedy, Controversy, Aliens, UFOs, Putin, CIA, and Freedom | Lex Fridman Podcast #300 [Video]. *YouTube*.

Lex Fridman. (2022, August 20). Jordan Peterson: Live, Death, Power, Fame, and Meaning | Lex Fridman Podcast #313 [Video]. *YouTube*.

Lex Fridman. (2022, October 21). Balaji Srinivasan: How to Fix Government, Twitter, Science and the FDA | Lex Fridman Podcast #331 [Video]. *YouTube*.

Lex Fridman. (2023, January 26). Jeremi Suri: Civil War, Slavery, Freedom, and Democracy | Lex Fridman Podcast #354 [Video]. *YouTube*.

Lex Fridman. (2023, March 15). Sam Harris: Trump, Pandemic, Twitter, Elon, Bret, IDW, Kanye, AI & UFOs | Lex Fridman Podcast #365 [Video]. *YouTube*.

Lorber, J. (2017). Gender and Sexuality as a Social Construct. In D. Grusky & J. Hill (Eds.), *Inequality in the 21st Century: A Reader* (pp. 347–352). Taylor & Francis Group.

McWhorter, J. (2021). *Woke Racism: How a New Religion Has Betrayed Black America*. Portfolio.

Machiavelli, N. (1996 [early 16th century]). *Discourses on the First Ten Books of Titus Livy* (H. C. Mansfield Jr. & N. Tarcov, Trans.). University of Chicago Press.

Making Sense with Sam Harris. (2024, June 14). What the Hell Is Happening?: A Conversation with Bill Maher. Episode 371.

Manufacturing Intellect. (2019, April 27). Slavoj Zizek debates Jordan Peterson [HD, Clean Audio, Full] [Video]. *YouTube*.

Marx, K. (1969 [1852]). *The Eighteenth Brumaire of Louis Bonaparte*. International Publishers.

Mearsheimer, J. J. (2005). EH Carr vs. Idealism: The Battle Rages On. *International Relations*, 19(2), 139–152.

Michael Nayna. (2018, October 3). The Grievance Studies Affair - REVEALED [Video]. *YouTube*.

Michael Nayna. (2019, January 18). Part One: The Evergreen Equity Council [Video]. *YouTube*.

Michael Nayna. (2019, March 7). Part Two: Teaching to Transgress [Video]. *YouTube*.

Michael Nayna. (2019, April 24). Part Three: The Hunted Individual [Video]. *YouTube*.

Miessler, D. (2019, March 31). Defining the Values of the Intellectual Dark Web: How the IDW Could Do So Much More Good by Defining and Preserving Its intellectual Identity. danielmiessler.com.

Mill, J. S. (2011 [1859]). *On Liberty*. Andrews UK Limited.

Monty Python. (2009, January 14). What Have The Romans... - Monty Python's Life of Brian [Video]. *YouTube*.

Movieclips. (2015, June 6). Alien 3 (3/5) Movie CLIP - Just Do What You Do (1992) HD [Video]. *YouTube*.

TheMunkDebates. (2018, June 2). Munk Debate on Political Correctness - Opening Statement Stephen Fry [Video]. *YouTube*.

Murray, D. (2019). *The Madness of Crowds: Gender, Race and Identity*. Bloomsbury Continuum.

Murray, D. (2022). *The War on the West: How to Prevail in the Age of Unreason*. HarperCollins.

Musk, E. [@elonmusk]. (2022, November 23). Found in closet at Twitter HQ fr [Tweet]. *Twitter*.

Nietzsche, F. (1998 [1887]). *On the Genealogy of Morality: A Polemic* (M. Clark & A. J. Swensen, Trans.). Hackett Publishing Company, Inc.

NM05. (2006, March 14). She's a witch! [Video]. *YouTube*.

Nonzero. (2021, February 24). Patreon Q&A: The Work and Impact of Thomas Sowell [Video]. *YouTube*.

Nonzero. (2021, April 22). The "Badass MF" Problem in the Black Community | Glenn Loury & John McWhorter | The Glenn Show [Video]. *YouTube*.

Only Love. (2017, August 24). Steven Pinker - The Left Pole [Video]. *YouTube*.

Overington, C. (2020, August 29). What the Hell Happened to Jordan Peterson? Jordan Peterson Has Turned Out to Be the Self-help Guru Unable to Help Himself. *The Weekend Australian*.

Pangburn. (2018, August 31). Sam Harris & Jordan Peterson in Vancouver – Part 1 – Presented by Pangburn (CC:Arabic & Spanish) [Video]. *YouTube*.

Pangburn. (2018, September 14). Sam Harris, Jordan Peterson & Douglas Murray in London – Part 4 – Presented by Pangburn (CC:Arabic). *YouTube*.

Pangburn. (2018, November 29). Richard Dawkins & Bret Weinstein - Evolution [Video]. *YouTube*.

Peterson, J. (2022, June 16). We Are Sacrificing Our Children on the Alter of a Brutal, Far-Left Ideology. The Telegraph. telegraph.co.uk.

PhilosophyInsights. (2019, November 30). Jonathan Haidt: What Intersectionality Is Really All About [Video]. *YouTube*.

Pinker, S. (2012). *The Better Angels of Our Nature: Why Violence Has Declined*. Penguin Books.

Pinker, S. (2018). *Rationality: What It Is, Why It Seems Scarce, Why It Matters*. Viking.

Pinker, S. [@sapinker]. (2018, December 18). Are You Frustrated with the Stale Ideologies and Mutual Demonization of the Left and Right? Here's a Manifesto for Radical Centrism, Liberal-Tarianism, Bold Moderation, an Open Society, Smart Regulation, and a Liberal Democratic Capitalist Welfare State. [Tweet]. *Twitter*.

Pinker, S. (2019 [2002]). *The Blank Slate: The Modern Denial of Human Nature*. Penguin.

Pinker, S. (2018). *Enlightenment Now: The Case for Reason, Science, Humanism and Progress*. Penguin Books.

PKLugia. (2007, April 21). Monty Python's The Life of Brian - I Want to Be a Woman [Video]. *YouTube*.

Plato. (2003). *The Republic* (D. Lee, Trans., 2nd ed.). Penguin Books.

Pluckrose, H., & Lindsay, J. (2021). *Cynical Theories: How Activist Scholarship Made Everything About Race, Gender, and Identity - And Why This Harms Everybody*. Swift.

The Portal. (2020, October 24). 41: Douglas Murray - Heroism 2020: Defense of Our Own Civilization [Audio podcast episode]. *Spotify.*

The Portal. (2020, December 2). 42: Cashing Out My Trump & IDW Positions [Audio podcast episode]. *Spotify.*

PowerfulJRE. (2020, May 8). Joe Rogan Experience #1470 – Elon Musk [Video]. *YouTube.*

Rage Against the Machine. (1992). Killing in the Name [Recorded by Rage Against the Machine]. On Rage Against the Machine [CD]. Epic.

Real Time with Bill Maher. (2014, October 7). Ben Affleck, Sam Harris and Bill Maher Debate Radical Islam | Real Time with Bill Maher (HBO) [Video]. *YouTube.*

Real Time with Bill Maher. (2018, October 27). Jonathan Haidt the Coddling of the American Mind [Video]. *YouTube.*

Real Time with Bill Maher. (2019, September 7). Christina Hoff Sommers | Real Time with Bill Maher (HBO) [Video]. *YouTube.*

Real Time with Bill Maher. (2022, May 21). New Rule: Along for the Pride | Real Time with Bill Maher (HBO) [Video]. *YouTube.*

Real Time with Bill Maher. (2023, March 4). Bernie Sanders on Student Debt Forgiveness | Real Time with Bill Maher (HBO) [Video]. *YouTube.*

Rebel Wisdom. (n.d.). Our Vision. rebelwisdom.co.uk.

Rebel Wisdom. (2020, June 24). What Happened to the Intellectual Dark Web? Bret Weinstein [Video]. *YouTube.*

Rebel Wisdom. (2021, June 30). Eric Weinstein: Vaccines, Ivermectin & Dark Horse [Video]. *YouTube.*

Roberts, J. (2022, April 20). Guide to the Classics: Shakespeare's Hamlet, the Everest of Literature. *The Conversation.* theconversation.com.

Robespierre, M. (1997 [1794, February 5]). Maximilien Robespierre: Justification of the Use of Terror. *Modern History Sourcebook.* sourcebooks

Rogan, J. (2016, October 21). *Triggered.* Netflix.

Rowling, J. K. [@jk_rowling]. (2019, December 19). Dress However You Please./ Call Yourself Whatever You Like./ Sleep with Any Consenting Adult Who'll Have You./ Live Your Best Life in Peace and Security./ But Force Women Out of Their Jobs for Stating That Sex Is Real?/ #IStandWithMaya #ThisIsNotADrill [Tweet]. *Twitter.*

Rowling, J. K. [@jk_rowling]. (2020, June 7). 'People Who Menstruate.' I'm Sure There Used to Be a Word for Those People. Someone Help Me Out. Wumben? Wimpund? Woomud?/ Opinion: Creating a More equal Post-COVID-19 World for People Who Menstruate. *Twitter.*

Rowling, J. K. (2020, June 10). J.K. Rowling Writes About Her Reasons for Speaking out on Sex and Gender Issues. jkrowling.com.

The Rubin Report. (2016, January 16). Conservatives, Black Lives Matter, Racism | Larry Elder | POLITICS | Rubin Report [Video]. *YouTube.*

The Rubin Report. (2017, August 9). We Need Reason Now More Than Ever

Before | Richard Dawkins | ACADEMIA | Rubin Report [Video]. *YouTube*.

The Rubin Report. (2018, June 30). Jordan Peterson, Ben Shapiro, Eric Weinstein, and Dave Rubin LIVE! | POLITICS | Rubin Report [Video]. *YouTube*.

The Rubin Report. (2021, October 2). Why Did the IDW Fall Apart? Gad Saad, Peter Boghossian, Michael Shermer | ROUNDTABLE | Rubin Report [Video]. *YouTube*.

Russell Brand. (2023, February 19). [PROOF] WE DID IT! | Seymour Hersh First Nord Stream Interview [Video]. *YouTube*.

Sam Harris. (2018, January 6). #112 - The Intellectual Dark Web: A Conversation with Eric Weinstein and Ben Shapiro [Audio podcast episode]. samharris.org.

Sam Harris. (2020, June 13). Can We Pull Back From The Brink? (Episode #207) [Video]. *YouTube*.

Sam Harris. (2020, June 19). Can We Pull Back From The Brink? [Podcast Transcript]. samharris.org.

Sam Harris. (2020, November 19). Republic of Lies (Episode #225) [Video]. *YouTube*.

Seton Hall University. (2018, November 2). Poetry-in-the-Round with Slavoj Žižek (October 24, 2018) [Video]. *YouTube*.

Shackel, N. (2005). The vacuity of Postmodernist methodology. *Metaphilosophy*, 36(3), 295–320.

Shakespeare, W. (1609). Sonnets. Retrieved from the *Folger Shakespeare Library*. folger.edu.

Sharp, D. J. (2020, September 15). David Hume Tower: A Tale of Quiet and Shameful Erasure. *Areo*. areomagazine.com.

Shellenberger, M. (2020). *Apocalypse Never: Why Environmental Alarmism Hurts Us All*. Harper.

Shermer, M., Saide, A., & McCaffree, K. (2019, October 20). Shedding Light on the Intellectual Dark Web: A Preliminary Empirical Study. *Skeptic*. skeptic.com.

Smith, K. (n.d.). Keri Smith. kerismith.net.

Solzhenitsyn, A. (1998). *The Gulag Archipelago 1918–1956: An Experiment in Literary Investigation - Volume Two*. Westview Press.

Sullivan, A. (2018, December 7). America's New Religions. *Intelligencer*. nymag.com

Taibbi, M. (2020, June 29). On "White Fragility": A Few Thoughts on America's Smash-Hit #1 Guide to Egghead Racialism. *Racket News*. racket.news.

Terracciano, A., Abdel-Khalek, A. M., Adam, N., Adamovova, L., Ahn, C. K., Ahn, H. N. … Zupancic, A. (2005). Gender Differences in Personality Traits Across Cultures: Robust and Surprising Findings. *Journal of Person-*

*ality and Social Psychology*, 89(4), 518–528. https://doi.org/10.1037/0022-3514.89.4.518.

ThinkingAtheist. (2018, March 22). Sam Harris 2018 - What is The Intellectual Dark Web (with Eric Weinstein & Ben Shapiro) [Video]. *YouTube*.

Tolstoy, L. (1999 [1899]). *Resurrection* (L. Maude, Trans). Project Gutenberg. gutenberg.org.

Triggernometry. (2019, November 18). Posie Parker: "Trans Women Aren't Women" [Video]. *YouTube*.

Triggernometry. (2021, January 14). Transgender Clinic Whistleblower Speaks Out [Video]. *YouTube*.

Triggernometry. (2021, April 1). Trans Women Are Men ... Including Me - Debbie Hayton [Video]. *YouTube*.

Triggernometry. (2021, November 22). Kathleen Stock - Hounded Out for Trans Views [Video]. *YouTube*.

Triggernometry. (2022, September 8). Andrew Doyle: "Vote Left or Right, You Still Get Woke Politics" [Video]. *YouTube*.

Triggernometry. (2022, December 26). Andrew Doyle & Triggernometry DESTROY 2022 [Video]. *YouTube*.

Triggernometry. (2023, January 9). What's Causing the Trans Explosion? - Helen Joyce [Video file]. *YouTube*.

Triggernometry. (2023, April 17). Trans Clinic Whistleblower Speaks Out [Video]. *YouTube*.

Vice News. (2017, June 17). Campus Argument Goes Viral As Evergreen State Is Caught In Racial Turmoil (HBO) [Video]. *YouTube*.

Volokh, E. (2017, May 26). Professor Told he's Not Safe on Campus After College Protests' at Evergreen State College (Washington) [Weblog post]. *The Washington Post*. washingtonpost.com.

Walters, S. D. (2018). In Defense of Identity Politics. *Signs: Journal of Women in Culture and Society*, 43(2), 473–488. https://doi.org/10.1086/693557

Weiss, B. (2018, May 8). Meet the Renegades of the Intellectual Dark Web. *The New York Times*. nytimes.com.

Weiss, B. (2020, July 14). Resignation Letter. bariweiss.com.

Weinstein, E. R. (2011). Kayfabe. *Edge*. edge.org.

Wright, C. (2022, May 2). Elon Musk Tweeted My Cartoon. *The Wall Street Journal*. wsj.com.

Young, C. (2018, May 20). Who's Afraid of the "Intellectual Dark Web". *Medium*. medium.com.

# Index

# About the Author

Dr Jamie Q Roberts is a lecturer in the Department of Government and International Relations at the University of Sydney. There he specialises in international relations with a focus on international security and popular culture. But more broadly, he is a 'first principles' philosopher who is interested in the true, the good and the beautiful. He thinks that the best insights into the human condition are found in literature: Shakespeare, Conrad, Larkin and Tolstoy, to name a few. The beautiful that has stood the test of time contains the true and the good. He also writes music, science fiction, and is building a vast, immersive art environment (seriously).

www.ingramcontent.com/pod-product-compliance
Lightning Source LLC
Chambersburg PA
CBHW020751310726
48969CB00002B/492